ACHIEVING
VALUE
FOR MONEY

The Management of Health Care

Series Editors
John J. Glynn and David A. Perkins

Published:

Managing Health Care

Edited by John J. Glynn and David A. Perkins

The Clinician's Management Handbook

Edited by David M. Hansell and Brian Salter

Managing Health Service Contracts

Edited by Kim Hodgson

Other titles in the series:

The GP's Management Handbook

Edited by Peter Orton and Claire Hill

ACHIEVING VALUE FOR MONEY

Edited by

John J. Glynn

Professor of Financial Management and founding Director,
Canterbury Business School, University of Kent

David A. Perkins

Lecturer in Strategic Management,
Canterbury Business School, University of Kent

and

Simon Stewart

Consultant in Clinical Oncology at Hammersmith Hospital NHS Trust, London
and Senior Lecturer at the Royal Postgraduate Medical School

WB Saunders Company Ltd

London   Philadelphia   Toronto   Sydney   Tokyo

W. B. Saunders Company Ltd   24-28 Oval Road
London NW1 7DX

The Curtis Center
Independence Square West
Philadelphia, PA 19106-3399, USA

Harcourt Brace & Company
55 Horner Avenue
Toronto, Ontario M8Z 4X6, Canada

Harcourt Brace & Company, Australia
30-52 Smidmore Street
Marrickville, NSW 2204, Australia

Harcourt Brace & Company, Japan
Ichibancho Central Building, 22-1 Ichibancho
Chiyoda-ku, Tokyo 102, Japan

A catalogue record of this book is available from the British Library

ISBN 0-7020-2033-8

Typeset by Paston Press Ltd, Loddon, Norfolk
Printed in Great Britain by WBC, Bridgend, Mid Glamorgan

CONTENTS

CONTRIBUTORS

Louis Bell RMN, BSc, Medical Audit Co-ordinator, Southend Health Care NHS Trust, Education Centre, Essex, UK.

Ian Carruthers MBA, BA, Dip HSM, Chief Executive, Dorset Health Authority, Dorset, UK.

Edward Colgan BA, MBA, MHSM, DipHSM, Dip M, Director of Corporate Development, Dorset Health Authority, Dorset, UK.

Alison Frater BSc, Cert HSM, Dip Health Econ, M Phil, MFPHM(hon), Public Health Specialist, (Associate Director Health Strategy), Hertfordshire Health Agency, Hertfordshire, UK.

John J. Glynn MA, M Phil, FCCA, Professor of Financial Management and founding Director of Canterbury Business School, Kent, UK.

John Mitchell MB, FRCP, Partner, Mitchell Damon, London, UK.

Barbara Morris PhD, BSc, MIM, Director of Graduate Studies, Canterbury Business School, University of Kent, UK.

Fiona Moss MD, FRCP, Associate Postgraduate Dean and Consultant Physician, Central Middlesex Hospital NHS Trust, London, UK. Editor, *Quality in Health Care.*

Michael P. Murphy BA, Lecturer in Accounting and Senior Tutor MBA (Strategic Health Services Management), Canterbury Business School, Kent, UK.

David A. Perkins BA, PhD, MHSM, Lecturer in Strategic Management, Canterbury Business School, Kent, UK.

Judy Renshaw PhD, Project Manager, Health and Social Services Studies, Audit Commission, London, UK.

Simon Stewart BSc, MD, FRCR, FRCP, Consultant in Clinical Oncology, St Mary's Hospital NHS Trust; Senior Lecturer, Royal Postgraduate Medical School; Honorary Consultant in Oncology at the Ealing Hospital NHS Trust and the West Middlesex NHS Trust, London, UK.

PUBLISHER'S ACKNOWLEDGEMENTS

Figure 4.1, adapted and reproduced with kind permission of Professor Martin Knapp, London School of Economics and Political Science.

Figures 4.3, 4.4, 4.5, 4.6, reproduced with kind permission of the Audit Commission, London.

Figure 5.2, reproduced with kind permission of South East Thames Regional Health Authority.

Figure 6.1, reproduced with kind permission of South-Western College Publishing, Cincinnati, USA.

FOREWORD

Professor C. R. Pinkerton

Changes in the structure of the National Health Service over the last decade have been accompanied by the adoption, or imposition, of a range of management and business strategies applied to health care. Whilst there remains widespread suspicion of this and a feeling that the introduction of an expanded tier of management has simply made patient care more bureaucratic and difficult, the need to be familiar with the nature of changes and the concepts behind them is indisputable.

Few consultants have escaped being sent, or perhaps volunteering, for a range of management courses and some have even found them useful. It is difficult to argue against the need for efficiency within any healthcare delivery system, be it private or public. The inappropriate application of competitive pressure between trusts as a means of improving the service to patients, does not detract from the importance of a consumer orientated attitude to service development.

One may feel that the catch phrase 'value for money' should have been left in the supermarket, but the need for optimal utilization of resources, however inadequate or limited, is self-evident. No one would attempt to justify waste, but a situation where clinical decisions are primarily driven by resources must be avoided. Using judgement based on experience and published data remains the main safeguard of patient welfare. The most appropriate treatment may be the most expensive, or the cheapest, and resources should be sought to provide this.

Methods for assessing value for money within the Health Service remain in their infancy and have yet to be widely applied in the UK. Such assessments should be welcomed, provided the primary motive is not simply to save money (unfortunately, with the present financial straits of many NHS Trusts this is inevitable). Whoever our political leaders may be, having to justify resource utilization more carefully is with us to stay and the profession must be involved in determining the methods used to do this. If not, the laws of the market place in its crudest forms may be applied by default. Any text which addresses these issues in an accessible manner is therefore to be welcomed.

C. R. Pinkerton, MD
Cancer Research Campaign Professor of Paediatric Oncology

INTRODUCTION: A BROAD OVERVIEW OF 'VALUE FOR MONEY'

John J. Glynn and David A. Perkins

OBJECTIVES

◆ To explain the rationale for a book that addresses issues of value for money in the National Health Service.

◆ To outline basic interpretations of the term 'value for money'.

◆ To outline the structure of the volume.

INTRODUCTION

If there is a catchphrase which has entered the vocabulary of public sector provision it is 'Does this service provide value for money?' Most readers would say that they understand both the emphasis on 'value for money' and what this term means. The emphasis arises out of political and public concerns in the late 1970s and early 1980s that public expenditure was out of control and that there was little publicly available evidence to show if public services were operating effectively and efficiently. One of the key conclusions which led to the development of this volume was that often there is a failure to agree on what is meant by the term value for money and a failure to appreciate how value for money might be measured and reported up.

In the opening chapter we address three key areas. Firstly, we discuss why such a volume is now timely in that it specifically focuses on the NHS. Secondly, we discuss the key concepts involved when we analyse the term value for money. Finally, we outline the rationale for the various contributions which comprise this volume.

At the outset it should be recognized that many of the issues discussed can be addressed from a number of different viewpoints. For example, some issues are addressed from a client or patient perspective. Others are addressed from the perspective of an external reviewer. All these approaches are valid in attempting to broaden our collective thinking on what is meant by the provision of public services which represent value for money. The provision of public services does and has always represented a trade-off between available resources and the quality of services provided. Our aim is therefore to provide balanced contributions to help the reader appreciate both the tensions involved in making these trade-offs and the way in which service providers account for the services they provide. It also assists those involved in audit (in all its various guises) to understand some of the tensions when reviewing whether a particular service or programme has provided value for money.

WHY WRITE A BOOK ON VALUE FOR MONEY (VFM)?

There has been widespread concern about the performance of public sector organizations since the financial crises of the 1970s and this has increased through the 1980s with a succession of attempts to introduce performance measurement and review to the public sector. The early 1980s saw the introduction of performance indicators and the beginnings of a shift in interest from the measurement of inputs such as money, beds, staff, and other resources to a concern with what was achieved with that money. Considerable variation was thought to exist between the practices of different doctors and hospitals and lengths of stay were known to be very different for what appeared to be similar conditions. Whether such variations were justified was not clear but the mere existence of such variation suggested that a question needed to be asked, since the costs of treating similar conditions appeared to be very different in different localities, raising the question of the scope for improvements in efficiency and value for money. The Audit Commission was set up to examine the performance of local government and health services and the National Audit Office was set up to examine the performance of government departments and the new executive agencies. These bodies developed a methodology for carrying out investigations and then began to issue reports assessing the performance of departments and activities and pointing to good practice and the best means of improving performance. More recently this concern with performance has taken the form of requiring public organizations to present their accounts in forms which mirror those used in the private sector. While such formats show the patterns and balance of income and expenditure, the use of assets, and the income generated by those assets, public utilities cannot usually be measured according to the tenets of profit and loss. It follows that their performance is hard to monitor either in absolute or comparative forms.

Public funds have been increasingly scarce and the competition for such funds increasingly strong and so there has been pressure to reduce public expenditure or at least to show that the tax payer's pound is well spent. Despite promises to reduce public expenditure during the 1980s and 1990s the experience has been that public expenditure is very difficult to cap, especially when accompanied by recession and high levels of unemployment.

Government has been keen to show that even if the cost of public services cannot be significantly reduced the quality and volume of services can be improved in ways which are meaningful to the consumer, hence the Citizen's Charter, the Waiting Lists Initiatives, developments in complaints systems throughout the public services, and more recently plans to put nursery education in the hands of parents through voucher schemes.

The results of organizational research and managerial intuition suggest that what gets measured gets attention whereas those areas of activity immune from measurement attract less attention.

***WHAT DO WE
MEAN BY VFM?***

♦ Common sense interpretation: at all levels of the NHS and other public services the question arises – are we getting the best value for money from this activity, department or service? Answers to this question are of interest to government, managers, professionals, and consumers although they might determine value in different ways.

♦ Technical interpretations: various groups within, and outside, the NHS attempt to determine measures of value for money for a variety of purposes. They may take the view of a purchaser interested in maximizing the value obtained from the money spent on health services in a particular locality. They may be more concerned with the effectiveness of services or their impact on a given target group. Different groups will be better or less well placed to assess parts of the value for money equation. For instance, an accountant may set up complex costing procedures but will be handicapped by a limited understanding of the clinical processes involved, the different complexity and severity of procedures which may appear to be identical. Such a costing system may be complex but may not match the complexity of the clinical activity to which it refers. In contrast, the medical staff may wish to concentrate on the value side of the equation as suggested by the recent interest in evidence based medicine.

♦ It has been suggested that value for money is composed of three interrelated elements of economy, effectiveness and efficiency. Others have suggested that issues such as equity, ethics and probity (see Glossary of terms) need to be included when we are talking about important public services funded by public money. While we may be able to agree definitions for these components, it is not clear that they can be measured without ambiguity or whether such calculation is worth the effort.

♦ We take the view that the measurement of VFM is only of use if it provides answers to the question how are we doing and how can we improve the quality and quantity of services provided with available resources. In the process some measures will be relatively unambiguous while others will simply point to issues which require further detailed investigation. The measurement of an immunization rate tells us that x% of the target population have been immunized and are thought to be covered against a particular disease. A difference in the number of treatments for glue ear between neighbouring districts may require detailed investigation of treatment practices and the needs of children in the two localities.

Value for money within healthcare systems   The systems perspective is commonly used throughout medicine and managerial contexts and provides a useful means of simplifying what is a complex and interdependent set of activities. Figure 1.1 provides a simple systems diagram which spells out some of the key components of a systems approach.

We identify the following components:

Inputs
Inputs are made up of resource inputs, non-resource inputs, and processes and policies.

Resource inputs consist of the classic economic factors of production: land, labour and capital. It is particularly important to be clear about inputs since questions about value for money are frequently answered at the level of resource inputs. Thus questions about VFM and the police force might be answered in terms of the number of constables on the beat. This begs the question as to whether those constables are achieving the purpose for which they have been recruited and deployed. Likewise an increase in revenue funds to the NHS does not necessarily imply that those funds are used to create additional benefits for the population served.

Non-resource inputs are of critical importance yet they are not necessarily subject to managerial control. For instance, the attitudes of staff and patients have a considerable impact on the quality and value of services but they are not primarily determined by management or even by government. The social, epidemiological and political environment influence the pattern of services and also the way in which services are valued.

Policies and processes can also be seen as forms of inputs. Thus with markets as the preferred form of resource allocation in the 1990s, the NHS was redesigned to operate within a quasi-market format. These policies are often the result of previous management activity and learning and may represent responses to problems or the implementation of learning and knowledge of what seems to represent best practice.

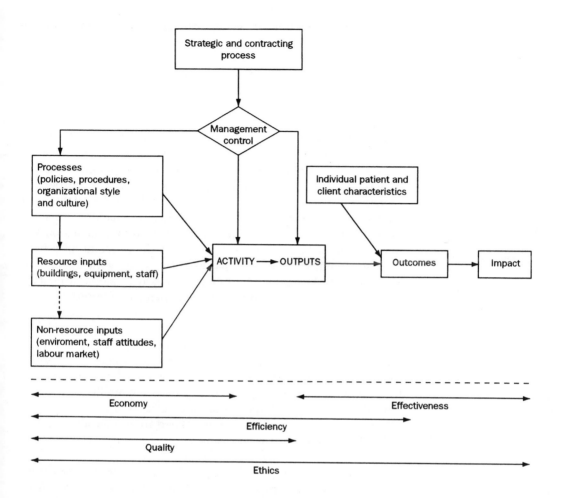

Figure 1.1
Managing for VFM

Activity
The activity refers to the combination of a wide variety of all categories of inputs designed to achieve the transformation process of inputs into outputs and outcomes. Much activity is open to observation and quantification but much activity is not self-evidently of value.

Outputs
Outputs are sometimes referred to as intermediate outputs by economists and refer to the treatments or services provided. Thus, 100 patients treated for varicose veins would be an output. As such it does not tell us if all those patients benefited from their treatment or whether their treatments went without unexpected side effects

such as cross-infection or healing problems. Outputs are the focus for counting in much discussion of performance and value for money since they appear to be relatively unambiguous. Many of the discussions later in this book wll show that this appearance is deceptive.

Outcomes

The term is used in the sense of the benefits for patients, clients and families. Thus the reduction of a fractured wrist should have the outcome that a child can, after an appropriate period, return to school and take up the full range of activities. The purpose of public services is to achieve outcomes for individuals and therefore this is a very important but complex level of evaluation. Outcomes may be affected by patient behaviour and circumstances outside the control of health professionals. Thus the outcome of a heart bypass operation may be jeopardized by continued smoking and the outcome of treatment for tuberculosis may be jeopardized if the individual is forced to continue living in damp conditions.

Impacts

Impacts are used to refer to the collective impact of services on populations and communities. The impact of a health promotion service might be measured by the changing levels of sexually transmitted diseases within a population. Rather like the police and the crime figures the question of causation is complex and claims about the impact of services need to be investigated carefully and not accepted at face value.

Clarity of definition is all very well but we are not measuring widgets. Healthcare procedures have an effect on people's lives, wellbeing and identity and so we must also consider the context for examining VFM (outside of a systems oriented framework) by including questions of wider social values and the ethics adopted by practitioners and those who dare to measure and interpret the performance of clinical services. The introduction of the NHS market with its purchases, providers and contracts means that VFM decisions are made at various levels and incorporated in various contracts or extracontractural referrals. The District Commissioning Agency may attempt to take account of the full range of needs among its population but the GP fundholder's interest will be restricted to the needs of his/her registered patients. The provider Trust will be concerned with its performance in meeting the demands of its contracts and balancing its income and expenditure. It may also have objectives which concern the development of particular services and the capabilities to provide those services in the future. Each of these stakeholders will examine VFM issues from a partial perspective determined by their position and aspirations within the market.

Box 1.1
An ethical framework
for the NHS

In a conference on rationing in the NHS Dr Kenneth Calman, currently Chief Medical Officer for England and Wales, produced his own summary of the guiding principles which underpin the provision of healthcare in the UK and should form a basis for decision-making. He identified an ethical framework and from it a decision-making framework for the NHS. This framework is not a description of the NHS but an attempt to identify the shared values which inform the expectations that various stakeholders have of the service.

The ethical framework rests on the following principles:

♦ Justice – the service should be fair and should be seen to be fair.

♦ Beneficence – it is assumed that healthcare services are provided to benefit the individual concerned.

♦ Non-maleficence – there is a particular requirement that health services should not harm individuals.

♦ Utility – health services should provide the greatest good to the greatest number.

♦ Autonomy – the needy individual should be entitled to all available resources.

He points out that these principles are frequently in conflict, causing the problems experienced by managers and clinicians.

From this ethical framework he proposes a framework for decision-making in the NHS

♦ A caring society – the NHS starts with the presupposition that society cares for its members.

♦ Public health matters – implies an integrated network of primary public and environmental health services.

♦ A primary care service – should be available to all.

♦ Hospital based services of proven value – should be available to all.

♦ Expensive/special services should be planned on a national basis.

♦ New procedures should be evaluated on a national basis.

Source: Tunbridge
(1993), Weale (1988)

The ethical principles are the subject of fierce debate. Is it the case that the service is thought to be fair? The accusations of a two tier service occasioned by the introduction of GP fundholding or the questions about the competing claims of different groups of patients immediately raise questions. How are we to compare the needs of a drug addict with those of a young child needing treatment for restricted growth?

Do healthcare services benefit the individual concerned or is there an element of social control in which society deals with people whom it perceives to be problems. The criticisms of medical technology include the accusations that it produces ill effects described by Illich (1977) as iatrogenesis. While there are many mechanisms such as ethics committees developed to protect the interests of patients, the proponents of evidence based medicine would suggest that it is hard to be clear about non-maleficence if we are not sure about the effects of particular remedies.

The question of utility implies that individual interests might have to be sacrificed to serve the interests of the community and instances such as the recent case of Child B highlight this problem. The development of QALYS (see Glossary of terms) and other mechanisms suggests that benefits can be compared using objective techniques although these are far from being widely accepted among professionals or public.

The autonomy of the individual informs much medical thinking yet it does not sit comfortably with the issue of utility in conditions of scarce resources and excess demand for health care.

The framework for decision-making includes some very important assumptions about the value of medical technology and its distribution. The importance placed upon public health is in line with evidence suggesting that key improvements in the nation's health have arisen from sanitation, housing, hygiene and the levels of individual incomes as well as from more reactive healthcare services. The importance of primary care is emphasized, recognizing that in many cases the GP will provide a service at a lower cost than hospital alternatives but questions remain about how the quality of GP services should be assessed.

Clear distinctions are made between proven and experimental services and between those services which should be available locally and those which should be planned on a national basis. This will raise questions about equity and autonomy, about balancing the needs of the individual with those of the population, and indeed those of the taxpayer.

We cannot assume that mere measurement will enable us to overcome the conflicts of the values or the practical dilemmas which result in everyday clinical practice. Why is it that services for drug addicts have low priority in resource terms when compared with services for children? If we were to appeal to public opinion would we find that some groups were effectively disenfranchised from the receipt of health services due to their status or behaviour? Are we happy that services are primarily provided for the individual rather than for the community which would prefer that some individuals be cared for, treated, or controlled out of the sight of the community?

STRUCTURE OF THE VOLUME   There are many interests with a stake in the questions of value for money and public health services. We have chosen to structure this volume in terms of *systems* based approaches which attempt to measure effectiveness and efficiency, *performance* based approaches which emphasize the questions of service performance and its measurement, *audit* approaches which adopt approaches from accounting and elsewhere focusing on the systems and operations of organization, and *management* approaches looking at the impact of strategic management and purchasing on VFM.

Systems based approaches   Systems approaches attempt a holistic view of organizations which places the detailed activities in the shade while placing questions of boundaries, inputs and outputs in sharp focus. It attempts to inform us about the transformation process in which an organization takes inputs from its environment and produces outputs which influence that environment. Organizations which manage this process in an effective way are more likely to survive in hostile or competitive environments. Subsequent sections focus on one or more parts of the healthcare system or on the views of particular interests within that system.

The heart of the value for money debate can be summed up in the two terms: effectiveness and efficiency. In the first section we address this issue from the three complementary perspectives of the academic, the health professional and the Audit Commission. Each of these approaches can be understood in terms of a systems perspective in which the concern is the relation between the inputs consumed by a service and the outputs or outcomes achieved.

David Perkins addresses some of the issues of effectiveness and efficiency at procedural and service levels, referring to ideas from the fields of health economics and health service evaluation. Alison Frater speaks from the perspective of a specialist in public health and focuses particularly on the measurement of clinical effectiveness and its impact on service management. Judy Renshaw introduces the approaches of the Audit Commission, which is statutorily responsible for assessing the efficiency of public services in the UK.

Performance based approaches   Where measurement is difficult or contentious other approaches have been adopted including performance indicators, quality management and control systems. These approaches have bases in other sectors and other disciplines yet they have been adopted in healthcare management bringing approaches which highlight issues given less attention in the systems approaches.

John Glynn and Michael Murphy examine the question of performance indicators: these have caused much debate about whether they get to the core of health service delivery or simply measure what is easy to measure. Barbara Morris and Louise Bell look at approaches to VFM based on a variety of approaches to quality many of which have clear assumptions about both parts of the VFM equation. David Perkins looks at performance from the perspective of control. How can services be controlled in such a way that optimal benefits are achieved and dysfunctional activities cease?

Audit based approaches   Most healthcare professions have adopted the practice of clinical audit which is increasingly seen as a sign of a responsible profession. Managers have been slower to adopt the idea of management audit and external audit has often been seen in a negative light, ignoring the value of objective review and concentrating on the question of error detection, fraud and assigning blame. Audit should be about the process of learning as systems and procedures are examined in the light of objectives and best practice.

John Mitchell and Fiona Moss focus on the practice of clinical audit and the ways in which clinicians can learn from their own practice allowing the possibility of continuous service improvement. Michael Murphy writes on management audit, which is somewhat underdeveloped in health care, pointing to the importance of service management in the achievement of desired impacts. John Glynn writes about external audit pointing to the value of this process and the learning opportunities which it affords if viewed positively.

Value for money and service impact   Recent developments in the NHS have enhanced the status of strategic management and implied a proactive and positive approach in comparison to older models of health service administration. New executive boards are charged with the task of managing to achieve maximum efficiency while purchasing authorities are expected to achieve identifiable impacts on the health of the populations for which they are responsible.

David Perkins asks whether strategic managers can influence value for money while Edward Colgan and Ian Carruthers focus on the impact of the newly developed purchasing function.

Future directions   The volume closes with informed speculation by the editors on the future of attempts to improve the value which is achieved by investment in public healthcare services.

REFERENCES   Illich, I. (1977), *Disabling Professions.* London: Marion Boyars.

Tunbridge, M. (Ed.) (1993), *Rationing of Health Care in Medicine.* London: Royal College of Physicians of London.

Weale, A. (1988), *Cost and Choice in Health Care.* London: Kings Fund.

SECTION I

ECONOMICS/ SYSTEMS BASED APPROACHES

SECTION INTRODUCTION Systems approaches are familiar to medical practitioners and to managers. The discipline of health economics has attempted to examine the ways in which resources are combined to create the maximum utility or value and to measure that value in ways which go beyond narrow or functional explanations. In this section we draw upon ideas from clinical and economic settings to describe what are commonly thought to be the major building blocks in the analysis of value for money. We focus in particular on the thorny question of measurement. As many managers would have us believe, it is difficult to improve performance if we are not able to measure current performance and be clear about the dimensions of improvement or deterioration. The development of evidence based medicine shows a similar trend in the clinical field. It is suggested that there should be an increased focus on the results of controlled clinical trials, consensus opinions, and guidelines agreed by the Royal Colleges and other competent authorities. The assessment of the efficiency of services raises similar problems in the generation and interpretation of data about the activity, outputs and perhaps impacts of those services.

Clinicians, economists, accountants and politicians have grappled with the application of value for money analysis at the level of the specialist service and at the level of the practice, hospital or health authority. It would be fatuous to suggest that there was a complete agreement about the terms used, their definition, or their application in practice. The three chapters which follow provide distinctive viewpoints from which to commence our examination of value for money. The building blocks of effectiveness and efficiency are tackled from a managerial or academic perspective, examining the issues in the light of research on the assessment of outputs and outcomes in health services. The issue of valuation is addressed as it highlights major difficulties in coming to decisions about the most appropriate course of action.

The measurement of effectiveness is addressed from a clinical perspective which focuses on the patterns of clinical measurement and the role of evidence and research in informing clinical practice. While there have been developments in this field for many years, there appears to be a concerted trend towards evidence based medicine in the 1990s and this raises fundamental questions of clinical choice and practice.

The Audit Commission has been appointed by government to address questions of efficiency in public services. Theirs is a distinctive approach and represents an established standard of practice in the assessment of value for money. Chapter 4 shows how their approach works in a variety of settings through the detailed exposition of case studies.

EFFECTIVENESS AND EFFICIENCY IN HEALTH CARE

David A. Perkins

OBJECTIVES

◆ To contrast the notions of the effectiveness and efficiency of healthcare provision.

◆ To discuss issues relating to the difficulties associated with the measurement of efficiency and effectiveness.

INTRODUCTION

The terms effectiveness and efficiency have lost much of their meaning in the political debate on health services. Frequently they are joined together to promote the merits of a department, service or Trust described as effective and efficient. In some cases this means no more than adequate or satisfactory. Used with care these concepts provide us with a groundwork with which to interrogate the qualities of healthcare procedures and services either as single entities or in comparison with similar providers or indeed with best practice identified through benchmarking or similar processes.

A variety of definitions have been identified for the terms effectiveness and efficiency and this discussion commences with

Box 2.1
Definitions

◆ *Effectiveness*
Defined as to how well a programme or activity is achieving its established goals or other intended benefits.

◆ *Efficiency*
Defined as the relationship between goods or services provided and the resources used to produce them. An efficient operation produces the maximum output for any given set of resource inputs; or, it has minimum inputs for any given quantity and quality of service provided.

Source: Audit
Commission (1983)

those developed by the Audit Commission in 1993 (Box 2.1). The Audit Commission is primarily concerned with the level of service provision and its remit does not extend to examining the efficacy of clinical procedures. Nonetheless its definitions are widely accepted and provide a useful starting point.

It follows from the definitions that a procedure requires clear, predetermined objectives if we are to assess its effectiveness. If a procedure is ineffective in that it seldom achieves its objectives then discussion of value for money is redundant. There may be other reasons why the procedure is performed or other objectives by which it is justified but the procedure cannot be called effective. An efficient procedure will achieve its objectives at minimum cost or will produce the maximum level of service with the available resources. Thus an efficient ophthalmology service will undertake cataract surgery at the lowest cost consistent with high quality outcomes, or put differently, will use its resources to treat the highest number of individuals minimizing waiting times.

A procedure may be effective but, because of its relative cost, it may be far from efficient. For instance, elective surgery accompanied with rest and relaxation may be highly effective but when compared with the day surgery alternative, it may prove relatively inefficient since it incurs higher costs. Questions of effectiveness and efficiency may be addressed at the level of the individual patient/procedure or at the level of a service, they may be concerned with achieving the desired outcome for a particular patient or they may be concerned with the impact of a service upon a particular population or group of patients.

The assessment of efficiency implies an appropriate calculation of the relevant costs of a particular procedure in a defined space at a particular time. It is not the case that a procedure thought to be relatively efficient will prove to be efficient if the necessary resources have been designed to support different patterns of care which do not suit the supposedly more efficient service. For instance, a switch to day care services will require considerable adjustments if the new pattern of services is to be efficient. This may include closing inpatient facilities, developing new facilities, redeploying and retraining staff and developing appropriate information systems to match the new services. Also it is important to be clear about which costs are included since a more efficient procedure may simply transfer costs previously borne by an institution or the state to a family or carer. Reducing inpatient stay may mean increasing costs to carers.

The effectiveness of clinical procedures is a controversial issue as demonstrated by the emergence of evidence based medicine and the continuing debates about the treatment of individuals with conditions or behaviours which doctors, or others, feel will not be substantially improved by existing treatments. It is therefore appropriate to examine the assumptions which underpin the assessment of effectiveness.

Clinical medicine claims to be based upon scientific foundations yet many clinical procedures have not been subject to what is now regarded as appropriate clinical and scientific evaluation. In some cases it is difficult to see how standard treatments can be withdrawn from subjects in the interests of scientific validation. Critics such as Cochrane (1972) and Illich (1977) make their points with varying degrees of venom yet they point to the shaky foundations of much of standard clinical practice. In recent years this critique has been recognized under increasing resource pressure and both Alison Frater (Chapter 3), Edward Colgan and Ian Carruthers (Chapter 12) point to the emergence and importance of evidence based medicine in the considerations of purchasing authorities.

As a minimum an effective procedure usually depends upon the following features:

♦ There will be an understanding of the disease process or injury from which the patient is suffering.
♦ The treatment procedure will have clear objectives which might differ according to the age and circumstances of the patient. For instance, treatment objectives for a professional footballer with damaged knee ligaments might differ from those for a senior citizen with the same complaint.
♦ Ideally there will be research evidence which supports the most effective pattern of treatment and deals with issues such as relative severity and complexity of the particular condition.
♦ The treatment will be undertaken in consistent fashion without unwarranted innovation or changes to the standard procedure.
♦ Selection for treatment will exclude those who cannot possibly benefit from treatment and include only those whose condition is capable of amelioration.
♦ Following treatment, patients will be observed or instructed to observe their own condition to ensure that the desired outcome is achieved.
♦ Unexpected outcomes or adverse symptoms will be investigated to further understand the treatment and to ensure desired outcomes.

In practice very few treatments or procedures are 100% effective due to the extent of variation in individual conditions, in the disease process, and in the consistency and quality of the treatment process. Many, if not most, drugs result in unintended or unwanted side effects which are inconvenient for most but serious for a few. Some treatments are effective in achieving limited objectives in clearly defined circumstances but those limited objectives may be worthwhile. Such considerations underpin the practice of palliative care in many hospices. Frequently the key presenting question concerns the relative effectiveness of alternative treatments for a particular condition and the question as to whether a novel treatment is significantly better than existing procedures.

MEASUREMENT   The measurement processes which enable consideration of effectiveness and efficiency are founded on the assumption that it is possible to identify and value the benefits and side effects of a particular treatment in a consistent and rigorous fashion. It is also assumed that it is possible to provide accurate costs for the procedure making appropriate decisions about the allocation of overheads and other shared costs. Economists insist that the full range of costs should be measured while managers and accountants are normally happy to address a more restricted range of costs. Cost-effectiveness (see Glossary of terms) analysis assumes that it is possible to accurately value or hold constant, the benefits of a treatment when examining the comparative costs of different treatment options. There is a long tradition of measuring the financial benefits of a successful treatment such as days lost from work or the number of days before return to work. Some measures are only useful for a minority of patients with a small range of complaints. It is much more difficult to measure the social benefits of treatment in soft currencies such as quality of life.

Measurement of the value of a particular treatment will depend on who is measuring and for what purpose. In a drug trial the clinician will record an agreed range of observations noting intended/unintended and unexpected phenomena but in normal practice the range of observations will be more limited. Consumers may have very different expectations of their treatment and may value intended and unintended effects differently. A referring GP will have his/her own expectations of treatment and will view the outcome from his/her own particular perspective.

A number of approaches have been adopted in the research field to develop objective measures of health status so that the effectiveness of a procedure can be assessed or compared with alternative treatments. The measurement of health status is designed to allow the determination of the effects of treatments by comparing health status before and after the intervention and seeing how this compares with what is known about the natural progress of the condition. Brooks (1995) provides a helpful introduction to these measurement approaches and the following paragraphs draw on his helpful review of the field.

Clinical measures are one of the simplest approaches in the sense that they are often single dimensional. For instance, the measurement of lung capacity before and after treatment might be thought to give evidence about the effectiveness of treatment for lung disease, while the measurement of cholesterol levels might be thought to demonstrate the effects of drug treatment or patient compliance following the advice from a GP. However, even these measures are not unambiguous and might indicate a variety of clinical processes; indeed, clinicians frequently require a range of measures of symptoms over an appropriate time period before coming to any conclusions in the diagnostic and treatment process.

Clinical measures require an understanding of single or multiple disease processes and frequently diagnoses will have the status of hypotheses with considerable levels of uncertainty which is matched by similar uncertainty about prognoses.

Functional measures can be described as multi-attribute measures and may include clinical indicators and other indicators related to activities of daily life or other capabilities which are regarded as important for the individuals or groups being measured. Some measures are specific to particular disease groups while others are generic and designed to be used across a wide range of conditions.

Wilkin *et al.* (1992) have pointed to the need for precision in the use of language. When we talk about human function they make an important and widely supported distinction between impairment, disability and handicap.

◆ *Impairment* is used to refer to any disturbance or interference with the normal structure and functioning of the body, including mental functions.
◆ *Disability* is the loss or reduction of functional ability and activity consequent on impairment.
◆ *Handicap* is the value attached to an individual's status when this departs from the norm – this must be related to some notion of social status or social function. (Brooks (1995), p. 18)

It follows that we cannot assume that a particular impairment in terms of the norms for an individual of a particular age and gender will result in either a significant disability or handicap. For instance, long sight is a clear impairment experienced by a large proportion of the middle aged population which is corrected by spectacles and for many does not result in significant disability or handicap.

Functional measures focus on disability and typically look at what are called activities of daily living (ADL). Basic ADL measures look at bathing, dressing, toileting, transfer, continence and feeding (Mahoney and Barthel, 1965). Instrumental ADL (IADL) measures look at activities in terms of shopping, cooking, housekeeping, laundry, use of transport, managing money, managing medication, use of telephone etc. While it can be seen that these indices do not apply universally, they do provide some means of assessing the impact of an impairment and of action to remedy the impairment. For instance, the IADL measure will not make much sense in looking at the impact of an impairment among young children without considerable modification.

These indices can be used in terms of yes/no answers or they can be graded according to severity.

Health profiles   The profile is an attempt to provide a consistent set of descriptors for a condition which can be used in the description of changes in health status.

One of the best known profiles is the Sickness Impact Profile (SIP) which has 12 dimensions and 136 items (Bergner *et al.* 1981). While this is thought to be a methodologically sound instrument it is so long that it takes considerable effort to deliver and has been less popular in research programmes than might otherwise have been the case.

The Nottingham Health Profile (Box 2.2) is a relatively simple instrument compared with the more complex SIP and is much easier to use (McEwen 1983, Kind and Carr-Hill 1987).

Box 2.2
Nottingham Health
Profile (McEwen 1983)

13 Dimensions 45 items

◆ Physical mobility

◆ Pain

◆ Sleep

◆ Energy

◆ Social isolation

◆ Emotional reactions

◆ Employment

◆ Social life

◆ Household work

◆ Sex life

◆ Home life

◆ Holidays

◆ Interests and hobbies

Such profiles are expensive to construct in a valid manner and can be attacked relatively easily on the basis of the samples used and the degree to which the sample is regarded as truly representative of the population in question.

Problems of   In the approaches described in this chapter rating has been under-
measures and their   taken by citizens, experts and clinicians, politicans and patients.
use   None of these groups can be regarded as disinterested but neither

can they be regarded as ignorant of the conditions or impact of treatments.

If their ratings differ, the researcher will want to account for the difference, to identify consistent bias in ratings and to assess the reliability of individual ratings; i.e. do they give consistent ratings to identical conditions.

A number of sources of bias are identified by Brooks (1995):

1. A doctor may carry forward an impression of a patient's function from one rating to the next to make the ratings consistent.
2. The rater may upgrade the score of a patient who is thought to be a complainer.
3. Imprecision may occur if different raters use different frames of reference.

Other sources of bias may occur where the process of judgement is inconsistent. For instance:

1. Two observers with the same information make different judgements (one only needs to look at the legal system to see how the courts come to different decisions about fact and severity of crimes).
2. A judge may be unable to explain how he used the information or how different bits of it were weighted in coming to a view.
3. Even if a judge is fully aware of all the information then he or she may use it inconsistently.

EFFECTIVENESS AND EFFICIENCY OF SERVICES

Health services are designed to meet the needs, and demands, of defined populations, bringing together different skills and coordinating their activity in complex patterns. Even elective surgery services imply a complex chain of activities provided by different individuals from different departments, specialties and professions. Emergency services imply a rapid response and the ability to combine skills in a sophisticated way with little or no notice.

It is quite conceivable that a service which provides effective procedures is ineffective in terms of service objectives. The experience of waiting lists and waiting times in the late 1980s and early 1990s might suggest that many services were failing to meet the needs of the local population. Alternatively a well-woman clinic might offer an excellent package of assessment and education, yet care may only be used by 20% of the target population. An immunization service may only be effective if more than 95% of the population are immunized even if the injection is nearly 100% effective for the individuals concerned. In this case the objective may be to eradicate a particular infectious disease from the population as was the case with smallpox.

A health economist will ask questions about distributional efficiency such as: Are the services distributed to those patients who will gain most benefit from them? Are we sure that the services are not provided for those who will not benefit from them? He/she will point to a theoretical state of affairs called allocative efficiency in which, given the available resources, it is not possible to reallocate resources to make one patient better off without making another patient relatively worse off. This might be applied to the use of resources within the NHS pointing to a position where it might be thought that there are no efficiency gains to be made, i.e. what is lost through reallocation will inevitably be greater than what is gained by using that resource in a different way.

If we examine diagnostic or pathology services we may wish to answer the question what is an acceptable or desirable standard of performance. Is it reasonable to assume that there will be no errors, no false positives or false negatives? Is it appropriate to adopt a benchmarking perspective in which a department aspires to the level of performance of the best in the field?

Box 2.3
Example

> One standard pattern of assessing the effectiveness of local pathology laboratories is that slides and other samples are sent from central to local laboratories to assess whether interpretation and reporting of samples is of consistently high standard.

Comparing the efficiency of services, practices and Trusts is fraught with difficulties since the objects of comparison are seldom identical. Is it reasonable to compare the efficiency of a metropolitan and a provincial accident and emergency service? While both may be fully accredited Accident and Emergency (A&E) centres they may operate in different environments with different levels and capabilities of staff, they may have a different workload and different resources to call upon in the adjoining hospital, they may also work alongside primary care services of different quality and capability. In short, a comparison of apples and pears must conclude that they are different.

However, this argument is often made by those who have no wish to expose the effectiveness or efficiency of their department to external scrutiny and so we should treat it with care. The comparison of the performance of a single department over successive time periods avoids some of the problems of inappropriate comparisons yet improvements may start off from a relatively low base. Even if we compare the same department over successive time periods we must be aware of cyclical patterns and seasonality which might influence our findings.

MEASURING
VALUES

Measuring the effects of a procedure or service on an individual in clinical or functional terms is one thing while assessing the value of that intervention is another. Two important and different approaches are those addressed below. One emanates from UK health economists (Box 2.4) and the other from a US state legislature attempting to deal with the problem of allocating scarce resources in ways which were clinically and democratically responsible (Box 2.5).

Box 2.4
Quality adjusted life years

Measuring the values which communities place upon various health and functional status is fraught with difficulties. For instance, the values which underpin perhaps the most popular compound measure – the QALY approach:

Rosser (Rosser and Kind 1978) asked various groups of doctors to describe the criteria by which they judged the severity of illness in patients. From their responses she identified two key components of severity, namely *observed disability* and *subjective distress*. From these components, following structured interviews with 70 raters (medical patients, psychiatric patients, medical nurses, psychiatric nurses, healthy volunteers and doctors), a two-dimensional classification of illness states were developed ranging from Disability: I No Disability to VIII Unconscious; and Distress: A No Distress to D Severe Distress.

As a decision aid this approach provides useful indications, and indeed the Department of Health holds information for interested parties on QALY studies of various conditions/treatments, but it is far from being recognized as a standard approach by practitioners and managers and part of this caution must stem from its research basis in the structured interviews.

These two approaches raise important questions about who should be involved in the assessment and valuation of health status. The approaches result from different situations and have different objectives. The QALY researchers were keen to create an objective measure which could be applied to a variety of conditions permitting a robust assessment of health status and permitting the assessment of the effects of specified treatments on health status. The Oregon Health Commission were attempting to increase the numbers of poor people qualified for the Medicaid health programme by reducing the range of treatments available to recipients from the full range of services to a selected list thought to be clinically effective and valuable. Both approaches go beyond the measurement of clinical effectiveness to address questions of social

Box 2.5
The Oregon
Programme

The State of Oregon was faced with a situation where half of those whose family income was below the US federal poverty level were not eligible for state health care. The 48% who were eligible were entitled to the full range of health-care services which would be provided through a private insurance scheme to a fully insured family. It followed that the 48% were entitled to some treatments of considerable expense and questionable effectiveness while 52% were not entitled to simple treatments of proven effectiveness which were thought to make a considerable contribution to an individual's quality of life.

A programme was proposed, revised and implemented which reduced the range of available treatments but raised the level of eligibility from 48% to 100% of those classified as below the federal poverty level.

The Oregon programme went through a complex series of activities to rank the full range of medical conditions and appropriate treatments according to clinically proven effectiveness, and a comparative evaluation of social value of procedures using a consensus methodology. A list of conditions and procedures were ranked and costs calculated on a procedural and cumulative basis. The state then matched the available funds with the ranked costed services and were able to determine on an annual basis what services would be available and which services would be excluded from the scheme on the bases of effectiveness, social value and cost.

The Oregon Health Commission assessed the clinical and social value of defined treatments for defined conditions (matched condition/treatment pairs). Clinical value was assessed by reference to technical evaluations in the clinical research literature. Social value was identified through research conducted by Oregon Health Decision, who conducted an extensive telephone survey and conducted 12 public meetings to ascertain the views and values of the Oregon public. While this methodology is open to a range of criticisms, the ranking of condition/treatment pairs does make some sense and the process of achieving the ranking created a measure of political and public support in Oregon not least because of the large numbers of poor people who were admitted to the public health care programme.

Source: (E. Paul Kirk, in
Tunbridge 1993)

valuation of different health status attempting to blend various opinions of practitioners, patients and members of the public. The QALY approach provides information as a decision aid while the Oregon approach has been implemented resulting in the enfranchisement of many poor people previously excluded from the healthcare scheme and the exclusion of a small number of procedures thought to be of little value or effect.

Attempts by purchasers in the UK to consult their constituencies have found that there are many pressure groups who have particular interests in local services and are ready to express them. It is not, however, clear that every group has a watchdog and some patients will find that their interests are not represented to great effect through public consultation.

MAKING DECISIONS ABOUT TREATMENT AND SERVICES

In an era of scarce resources hard decisions have to be made about the alternative uses of funds. In the past decisions were seen to be a matter for medical decision on clinical grounds and for consent by an informed patient. Increasing concern about the effectiveness and efficiency of clinical procedures has spawned concerns about the quality of life and the external factors, i.e. those outside the immediate concerns of doctor and patient. It is to these concerns of quality of life and external interests that we shall return throughout this volume. The efficiency of services is a vital concern if the fixed resources allocated to the NHS are to be used to best effect.

Box 2.6
Making decisions

> According to Brooks (1995) there are four aspects which should be considered in making decisions in the case of a particular individual or patient:
>
> ♦ *Medical indications* – principle of beneficence – avoiding harm. Clinicians should pay first attention to the needs and welfare of their patients.
>
> ♦ *Informed patient preferences* – patients have the right to accept or reject medical advice. Other considerations may apply where the patient is not competent, e.g. brain death, or where an adult agent is regarded as competent and acts on behalf of a child.
>
> ♦ *Quality of life considerations* – these should be primarily based on the informed judgement of the patient but may include the judgement of a doctor or clinical staff.
>
> ♦ *External factors* – these may include benefits or burdens on others, externalities, the safety of others, costs to society, the use of scarce medical resources, family wishes, and needs for medical research and teaching.

The pursuit of value for money will require clinicians and managers to pay attention to each of these factors. The challenge is to assess the correct balance of the four factors. It is clear that the pursuit of value for money will require attention to external factors which go beyond the direct interests of the individual patients and will result in conflicts of interest for patients, clinicians and communities.

SUMMARY

The clear definition of effectiveness and efficiency is a prerequisite to further progress in the understanding and achievement of value for money in healthcare services. While academic distinctions are helpful we are usually talking about relative effectiveness and relative efficiency although I would argue strongly that it cannot be efficient to do some thing that by virtue of its ineffectiveness is not worth doing. In many cases our knowledge of the effectiveness of procedures is deficient and clinicians have to rely on their best judgement in individual cases in the light of the balance of experience and research findings. Measurement of both effectiveness and efficiency is fraught with difficulties and the following two chapters look at these issues respectively.

Effectiveness must also be examined in terms of the impact on communities and this will be determined according to clinical and social valuations. There is no accepted common currency for these social valuations despite various attempts to measure social values of health status. Nonetheless, these attempts do highlight many of the issues concerned and so add to our understanding of value for money in health care.

FURTHER READING

♦ Cochrane, A.L. (1972), *Effectiveness and Efficiency*, Nuffield Provincial Hospitals Trust, London.

♦ Donabedian, A. (1966), Evaluating the quality of medical care, *Millbank, Memorial Fund Quarterly*, 44, 169.

♦ Brooks, R.G. (1995), *Health Status Measurement: A Perspective on Change*, Macmillan, Basingstoke and London.

REFERENCES

Audit Commission (1993), *Code of Practice*. London: HMSO.

Bergner, M., Bovvift, R.A., Carter, W.B. and Gilson, B.S. (1981), The Sickness Impact Profile. *Medical Care,* 19: 787–805.

Brooks, R.G. (1995), *Health Status Measurement: A Perspective on Change*. Basingstoke and London: Macmillan.

Cochrane, A.L. (1972), *Effectiveness and Efficiency*. London: Nuffield Provincial Hospitals Trust.

Illich, I. (1977), *Disabling Professions*. London: Marion Boyars.

Kind, P. and Carr-Hill, R. (1987), The Nottingham Health Profile: A useful tool for epidemiologist? *Social Science and Medicine.* 8: 905–910.

Mahoney, F.I. and Barthel, D.W. (1965), Functional evaluation: the Barthel index. *Maryland State Medical Journal*, 14: 61-65.

McEwen, J. (1983), The Nottingham Health Profile. In: Teeling Smith, G. (Ed.), *Measuring the Benefits of Medicines*, London: Office of Health Economics.

Rosser, R.M. and Kind, P. (1978), A scale of valuations of states of illness. Is there a social consensus? *International Journal of Epidemiology,* 7: 346-358.

Kirk, E. (1993), The Oregon Experience. In: Tunbridge, M. (Ed.), *Rationing of Healthcare in Medicine*, 2: 13-23. London: Royal College of Physicians.

Wilkin, D., Hallam, L. and Dogget, M.A. (1992), *Measures of Need and Outcome for Primary Care*. Oxford: Oxford University Press.

MEASURING CLINICAL EFFECTIVENESS

CHAPTER 3

Alison Frater

Alison Frater

OBJECTIVES

> ♦ To discuss the rationale behind the centrally driven clinical effectiveness initiative in the NHS.
>
> ♦ To describe the key sources of information and other resources arising from the initiative.
>
> ♦ To discuss the pros and cons of a number of practical means of measuring effectiveness.

INTRODUCTION

Improving the efficiency and effectiveness of health care was a central tenet of the NHS reforms. The challenge this provides is how to measure the efficiency of the health service in terms of resources invested in relation to the health gained by the population. Present measures of efficiency in the NHS are concerned only with the level of activity (e.g. numbers of procedures, bed numbers, drugs prescribed) rather than with the benefit to patients.

There has been increasing interest in measuring effectiveness both using the endpoint of mortality – most often employed in clinical trials – and in terms of health status and quality of life – measures which are of greatest importance to patients. Understanding the effectiveness of clinical care is the first step to reorientating health services towards one which places greatest value on the outcome of clinical care through appropriate use of tests, drugs and therapeutic interventions.

This chapter will discuss briefly the rationale behind the centrally driven clinical effectiveness initiative in the NHS and describe the key sources of information and other resources arising from it. It will discuss the pros and cons of a number of practical means of measuring effectiveness in a variety of clinical settings across primary and secondary care and assess the role of clinical effectiveness within a broader assessment of service effectiveness or quality of care.

WHAT IS CLINICAL
EFFECTIVENESS?

The notion of clinical effectiveness, hitherto a scientific concept comparing the local outcome or results from a particular intervention with the results of published trials conducted under so-called ideal conditions, now underpins the determination of quality in health care. Do healthcare technologies of any kind – initiatives to promote health by reducing risk factors such as smoking cessation clinics, treatments seeking to prevent premature mortality such as the use of chemotherapy in the management of breast and small cell lung cancer or rehabilitative services aimed at restoring function and quality of life – deliver the expected health benefits for patients?

The key measurement question being addressed is whether the health effect or outcome for the patient lies within an acceptable range compared with those obtained from clinical trials – the efficacy of the intervention (Box 3.1). For example, the extent to which successful control of blood sugar is achieved in diabetic patients, the dilation of vessels following angioplasty, relief of pain following cholesystectomy (removal of gall bladder) and improved joint function in knee or hip replacement.

Box 3.1
Definition of
effectiveness and
efficacy (Last 1988)

Effectiveness
The extent to which a specific intervention, procedure, regimen or service, when deployed in the field, does what it is intended to do for a defined population.

Efficacy
The extent to which a specific intervention, procedure, regimen or service produces a beneficial result under ideal conditions. Ideally, the determination of efficacy is based on the results of a randomized controlled trial.

Efficiency
1. The effects or end-results achieved in relation to the effort expended in terms of money, resources, and time. The extent to which the resources used to provide a specific intervention, procedure, regimen, or service of known efficacy and effectiveness are minimized. A measure of the economy (or cost in resources) with which a procedure of known efficacy and effectiveness is carried out.

THE THINKING BEHIND THE CLINICAL EFFECTIVENESS INITIATIVE

The rationale for scrutinizing health services to ascertain their effectiveness in relation to results based on research stems primarily from a body of evidence suggesting that there are variations in the judgements made by clinicians for which there appears to be little rational explanation (Wennberg 1993). These have been documented, for example, in thresholds for surgical interventions (McPherson *et al.* 1982), use of drugs (Ryan *et al.* 1992), or test ordering (Gulliford 1992) and do not appear to arise from differences in health, social or demographic characteristics of the patient populations involved. Although this view is now being challenged, it is widely assumed that these observations arise because of uncertainty in medical practice (Ellis *et al.* 1995). It is also widely believed that insufficient formal evaluation of healthcare interventions has led to a paucity in the knowledge base on which to identify gold standards or even a broad framework for judging the potential benefit of interventions for different patient populations. Where information on efficacy is available the endpoints measured may be limited in their scope for truly describing the impact of health care on people's quality of life, their social or role function. Mortality is a commonly used endpoint in intervention trials though relief of symptoms or enhancement of quality of life are the endpoints of value to patients.

Under these circumstances differences in referral or intervention thresholds may be accounted for by the differing views and opinions of clinicians in the light of the knowledge gap. A primary clinical reference source remains tradition or convention passed on through medical education and training or from the consensus existing among peers. This may in the light of rigorous information be open to wide interpretation even with similar patients in similar settings.

No doubt this situation can be substantially ameliorated by the improvements in the scientific basis for health care heralded by the recent research and development programme established by the NHS Executive. A closer look at the lack of congruency between patterns of care which might be achieved through adherence to information on clinical effectiveness and those seen in practice suggests, however, that this is unlikely to be sufficient. There is a danger of oversimplification in assuming that the acquisition of knowledge alone will improve care.

MEASURING EFFECTIVENESS

The measurement of effectiveness is not straightforward and there are relatively few areas of health care where clear and unequivocal results are available to guide the assessment of local effectiveness.

Even where good research evidence is available, such as in the use of thrombolytic therapy to reduce mortality after myocardial infarction (ISIS-2 Collaborative Group 1988) or in the use of prophylactic heparin for prevention of deep vein thrombosis

(DVT) (Imperiale and Sperof 1994) in patients undergoing hip replacement, results from trials may not be generalizable to local patient populations.

Differences between patients in care settings will always be greater than in those defined by the strict entry criteria of most research trials. Clinical trials are most likely to draw patients from white middle aged men in the population living close to specialist centres or large teaching hospitals. Patients from the general population presenting with the same conditions in routine clinical practice in smaller district general hospitals or indeed in primary or ambulatory care settings will have a broader age range and be more likely to have social and demographic characteristics or coexisting medical factors which will reduce their likelihood of achieving the best outcome. Clinicians will be unable to control for this level of variability or the random errors arising from the small numbers involved when comparing local results with those of large-scale randomized controlled trials.

Where the equipment and level of expertise available varies between centres setting limits for effectiveness will be difficult. Published results from studies of the management of the gastro-intestinal haemorrhage, for example, suggest that mortality rates of less than 4% can be achieved yet case fatality varies up to five-fold when measured in routine practice (Rockall *et al.* 1995). A recent review suggests that the best outcomes are obtained for patients in sites with dedicated gastroenterology suites with joint working between medical and surgical teams. Clearly certain characteristics of care likely to give rise to optimal outcomes for patients are potentially modifiable, others are not. The availability of dedicated endoscopy suites will depend on competing priorities for resources and judgements about the importance of health investment across the spectrum of prevention and treatment for particular diseases or conditions. Other characteristics – such as the quality of team working – can be improved and highlight the need for assessments of effectiveness to be set within an audit framework. The question is not what are the discrepancies between results obtained locally and those found in research studies but what are the most cost-effective means of improving care locally to ensure that health effects or outcomes for patients more closely approximate efficacy?

MONITORING PROCESS   As described above there are a number of important limitations to the measurement of effectiveness. In many areas of clinical care the use of proxy measures of process will be a far more efficient means of ensuring effective health care. Research evidence for the use of heparin in preventing deep vein thrombosis (DVT) following major surgery (Imperiale and Sperof 1994) or the cost-effectiveness of prophylactic antibiotic prior to caesarean section (c-section) is unequivocal (Enkin *et al.* 1994), yet it would be technically difficult and costly to attempt to monitor the incidence and prevalence of deep vein thrombosis following hip replacement or wound infection following c-section to assess local effectiveness. This would require more frequent monitoring intervals than are currently in place, the development of methods for accurate and validated diagnosis of symptoms and clinical events, closer working relationships between GPs and hospital based consultants, and sophisticated systems for collection and transfer of patient based information. Once the information has been collated, the potential for inferring cause and effect to the quality of care provided and the eventual outcome given the many potential confounding factors is low.

On the other hand, it could be argued that direct measurement of outcome is a quality priority for reassuring patients and ensuring that health investment achieves health benefits. Such an approach would identify the need for improved patient monitoring with longitudinal cohort studies and shared information systems across primary, ambulatory, acute and tertiary care settings. The problems of interpreting the information contained in such large databases is discussed below (See section on measuring mortality, below.)

More compelling is an approach which identifies the key characteristics of care in process terms drawing on research evidence to delineate the standards required for optimal patient management to achieve preferred outcomes. Audit mechanisms can be used to ensure implementation of research based practice and to address local issues of organization and management of care which may influence outcome. The direct assessment of health outcome in such a quality monitoring programme may be appropriate for some attributes of health alongside process and proxy outcome measures. The relative emphasis given to different kinds of data collection will depend on the level of interpretation possible and the likely impact of the information for improving the quality of care. The relative impact of finding that a high proportion of patients continue to suffer pain and immobility after hip replacement on the work of an orthopaedic team may be greater than a finding that heparin is administered in an unacceptably small proportion of patients. Both results should prompt a review of the care offered to patients; the former finding is open to wide interpretation but the latter is unacceptable and should be tackled urgently.

THE DH CLINICAL EFFECTIVENESS INITIATIVE (NHSE 1996)

The main thrust of the central initiative on effectiveness is to embed research evidence of efficacy into clinical practice and to ensure implementation through audit. To this end, the NHS Research and Development (R&D) programme has stimulated a great deal of new research to improve the knowledge base for clinical practice and to describe effective means of organizing and managing health care to ensure delivery of optimum care to patients. A number of information sources are emerging to guide the work of clinicians in pursuing effective and cost-effective practice. These include the Cochrane Collaboration and the Centre for Reviews and Dissemination in York (see Further Reading).

Publications such as *Effective Health Care Bulletin, Effectiveness Matters, Bandolier* (see Further Reading) also seek to present information on effectiveness in an interesting and readily amenable context with direct recommendations for purchasers as well as providers in ensuring healthcare delivery. Other publications geared towards this initiative include the new journal *Evidence Based Medicine*, a recently launched *BMJ* publication edited by D. Sackett. Guides for clinicians on efficient mechanisms for reviewing literature and linking research to practice are also available, the most comprehensive of these being by *Clinical Epidemiology* (see Further Reading).

Population Health Outcome Indicators

In its programme of health outcome assessment, the Department of Health (McColl and Gulliford 1993) recommends the measurement of health outcome under certain conditions. These are set out as a series of health outcome indicators and build on the work of Charlton and Holland (Charlton *et al*. 1983) in measuring avoidable mortality.

Measures such as standardized mortality ratios (SMRs) following hip fracture, SMRs for cervical cancer and diabetes are suggested using 5 year moving averages for people in defined age categories. It is acknowledged that such measures have value for long-term monitoring by purchasers but little relevance for routine monitoring of effective care in clinical practice.

COMPARATIVE APPROACHES TO MEASURING EFFECTIVENESS

A number of authors seek to define effectiveness by generating a comparison of the results of care achieved across a series of providers. In this case the standard used may or may not be based on the best evidence for the efficacy of the intervention under review. The standard set is arbitrarily based on the apparently best result achieved across a series of providers or on the median or middle value arising from a set of data comparing providers. Mortality league tables now frequently published in the USA take a similar approach though there is often more published information to inform the standard setting process. Attempts have been made in the USA and more recently in the UK to measure the effectiveness of health care by comparing changes in health status of patients following healthcare interventions for both acute and chronic conditions. The work of Ware (Stewart *et al*. 1988) and others in the USA has sought to develop this approach to enable standardized comparison of providers on the basis of improvements in general health for patients.

Comparing outcomes of care based on routine data involves the development of databases or reference groups which collect baseline information on the health of patients on admission or at first contact with the health service and then at subsequent visits usually immediately following an intervention in the case of acute care and then again at regular intervals to assess recovery, general health, any adverse events or changes in clinical symptoms and signs. For patients with chronic conditions a similar schedule might be followed but with modification to account for the longer-term nature of the condition and the changing expectation for the patient in terms of general health and wellbeing.

A number of studies have demonstrated the problems of inferring effectiveness from routine information where systematic bias and confounding factors can substantially influence the results of the study. A comparison of transurethral resection of the prostate (TURP) with open prostatectomy in the management of benign prostatic hypertrophy (BPH), based on information collected from routine patient information in a number of different hospitals in the USA, showed a higher mortality in TURP than in open prostatectomy. A subsequent detailed review (Concato *et al.* 1992), adjusting the data for severity of the condition and the general health of the men undergoing the operation, suggested that the adjusted relative risk of death was lower in those undergoing transurethral resection of the prostate.

MEASURING MORTALITY The question of whether comparing the mortality rates in different hospitals for common surgical and medical conditions can provide information on which to measure the effectiveness of clinical care has been explored by a number of authors, particularly in the lay press. Much of the debate on the value of this approach has been stimulated by the publication in the USA of outcome data comparing death rates in hospitals across the USA (Park *et al.* 1990). These are now frequently published in the news media and may have profound consequences for the future role of low ranking (i.e. those with apparently high death rates) hospitals in the healthcare market. Despite a trend towards the preparation of league tables for comparing aspects of care such as waiting lists for operations, the proportion of operations carried out in day case or numbers of cancelled operations, the application of mortality data in this way has been resisted by the Department of Health in England, although some limited information has been made available from the Scottish Home and Health Department (Scottish Office 1993).

The validity of this approach for elucidating quality or effectiveness of care in routine practice has been examined in a detailed study by McKee and Hunter (1994) reviewing data from hospitals in the North Thames Region. Using a means of adjusting the data from each hospital for the severity of illness of the patients involved they were able to calculate expected death rates for each hospital for eight conditions: aortic aneurysm, carcinoma of the colon, cervical cancer, cholesystectomy, fractured neck of femur, head injury, ischaemic heart disease and peptic ulcer. A detailed evaluation of the method of adjustment they used has been undertaken for UK data and shown to be valid and acceptable.

McKee and Hunter found unexpectedly high levels of mortality in some of the hospitals studied which were not explained by differences in the kind of patients treated. For example, two hospitals showed substantial differences in death rates for aortic aneurysm which seemed to be independent of severity or mode of admission with one hospital achieving consistently lower death rates. For both aortic aneurysm and cancer of the colon, hospitals with the highest volumes appear to achieve relatively better outcomes. The high death rate from head injury in some hospitals appeared to be related to selective transfer of the more severe cases from other hospitals. In other cases there may have been real differences in the quality of care. In fractured neck of femur, for example, more detailed enquiry from the poorest performing hospitals revealed very poor cooperation between orthopaedic and geriatric medicine departments.

The study highlights the many problems involved in making inferences about the quality of care in different hospitals using mortality data:

◆ Technical difficulties in obtaining a complete and accurate set of records for analysis are common in NHS hospitals. Hospital records are often missing or incorrectly coded. This probably applies particularly to those of patients who have died where records may lodge with the coroner for some time and be omitted from routine reports; such omissions will introduce substantial biases into the study.
◆ Mortality data is affected by confounding factors; some hospitals, for example, systematically treat less severely ill patients and indeed the instrument used in this study to make adjustments for severity relied on routine data collected from the case notes of patients, which may be inadequate in describing important differences in the patient mix.
◆ The numbers of deaths in hospital for specific conditions is very small. Differences between small numbers often arise as a result of random fluctuations in the data rather than any real effect of the kind of care delivered to the patients.
◆ Finally the data is subject to manipulation either from episode inflation which will affect the death rates obtained within a hospital or from issues such as the allocation of diagnostic and severity codes to patients at higher risk from operative mortality.

In making inferences about the effectiveness of care using this information McKee and Hunter identify the importance of not relying on a single year's data because of the problem of small sample sizes and the crucial importance of adjusting for case mix including severity of disease, age of patient and method of admission. They recommend the approach used in the American Disease Staging severity scale (McKee and Pettigrew 1993), though they point to the problems of transferring many of the weighting factors used in the data to UK data. The development of a scale based on UK data is needed before such an approach to measuring effectiveness could be adopted widely.

CONFIDENTIAL ENQUIRY

The development of the confidential enquiry (Campling *et al.* 1993) seeks to promote a method for examining unexpected deaths in routine practice which addresses the problems of measurement error in understanding the effectiveness of care in routine practice. Results of confidential enquiries are generally available only to those involved in the process of care. They focus on summarizing likely events leading to adverse events and make no attempt to infer attributability based on a series of results in routine practice.

MEASURING HEALTH STATUS AND QUALITY OF LIFE

There are compelling reasons why the direct measurement of health outcome for patients might be undertaken to understand the effectiveness of service delivery offered. Measures of health status and quality of life record experience of outcome from the patient perspective. They are feasible to obtain, and acceptable to patients, in contrast with the difficulty of routine assessment of more conventional measures. It is likely that an audit framework is the most suitable basis for applying such an approach. This would enable the local setting of standards for the outcome of care, based as far as possible on the optimal result expected for the intervention, and using a measurement instrument which is most likely to capture concerns of importance to the patient. Measures are:

- ◆ subjective based on patients' self-assessed health status;
- ◆ objective based on an independent assessment of the patients' function and quality of life; or
- ◆ monitoring the progress of a group of patients against a set of agreed criteria in a longitudinal follow-up study or within a cross-sectional study.

Such an approach is based on the view that measurement of health outcome can be a valid measure of the effectiveness of care irrespective of whether it is possible to identify precisely the contribution of care to the observed changes (Shanks and Frater 1993). In reality different health outcomes are attributable to health care to differing extents and the relative contribution of external factors may also vary. Success in reducing blood pressure using a particular kind of antihypertensive medication may be entirely due to the treatment in one patient but due to broader factors in another person if they are able to address lifestyle factors such as a stressful job. The success of an antismoking campaign will be different against a background of rising prices of cigarettes than in a situation where the price was falling steeply.

Patients and their carers may value a particular prognosis even though gaps remain in the knowledge of the forces which shape it. There are also situations where the patient may have received treatment of proven efficacy in the management of a particular condition with a positive outcome in terms of *physiological* symptoms and signs but where the patient is unhappy with the result.

The sequelae of healthcare interventions are unlikely to have a single effect on the lives of individuals. In assessing the impact of early intervention in the management of rheumatoid arthritis discrepancies were found between successful results showing reduced ESR (erythrocyte sedimentation rates) and the determination of HAQ (Health Assessment Questionnaire) scores which suggested that health status in terms of both the patients' functional ability and depression ratings had declined.

There is in addition evidence to suggest that the patient preferences have a direct effect on the outcome of health care. The extent to which a patient is satisfied with the outcome of care will be determined directly by their expectation of care and the ability of the clinical team to interpret the risks and benefits of all possible management plans in meeting that need. An active young woman with small children and a full-time job may feel highly motivated in her acceptance of a strong regime of oral steroids in the management of asthma. She may wish to achieve a high level of control within a busy lifestyle where some alternatives such as increasing leisure time or eliminating fully all potential allergens are not available to her because of lack of resources, lack of time or due to the inflexibility of her structural environment. This patient will measure satisfaction as the extent to which the therapeutic plan helps her to meet her commitments. Her outcome will depend on how convinced she is that a determined adherence to the management regime proposed will deliver the control she seeks and on the understanding developed of her particular needs among the clinical team involved in her care.

A second more sedentary individual whose anxieties centre more on the lasting consequences of long-term steroid use than on their potential benefits in terms of function or activity, and who in any case is unlikely to comply with a specific regime, would take a different view. He would be more likely to assess benefit in terms of offsetting more severe symptoms. His clinician would be unlikely to see an improvement that relied on long-term compliance to a regime the patient was not keen to accept.

Recognition of alternative outcomes sought by patients with similar conditions may provide a basis for limited routine assessment of outcome in clinical care. Such an approach would not seek to define attribution by ascribing causation to the intervention under review. It would not constitute research in the sense of using the information gained to test a hypothesis. Rather the approach would be based on the patient and clinician's focus on the intended outcome for the patient. Information collected from the assessment of health status using a validated instrument (such as the Health Assessment Questionnaire in rheumatology or the Oxford hip score in total hip replacement) would provide the basis of an audit of the quality of care in terms of the expectation of improvements in health.

There is a growing acceptance of the potential value of collecting information on health outcomes in routine clinical practice. Even where the contribution of health care is well understood there remains the problem of reconciling different perspectives on the same endpoint. The advantage of measurement is to make explicit the differences and to move towards achieving the preferred management regime which bridges the patient and clinical view of the optimal outcome. Studies of the health outcome of health care have focused on the value of this information for improving quality of care, its role in enhancing the communication between the individual patient and the clinician or in order to raise questions for research – as well as to assess the local effectiveness of care.

A number of studies provide practical experience of using information on the health outcome of health care. The CASPE/ Freeman study (Bardsley and Coles 1992) examined the practicalities and applications of agreeing suitable indicators of health outcome for patients with clinicians, the practicalities of data collection and the value of the information in improving patient care for two chronic and three acute conditions – diabetes, cholesystectomy, knee replacements, care of the elderly and percutaneous transluminal coronary angioplasty (PTCA). Using well described and validated health status instruments, including the Nottingham Health Profile (McColl and Gulliford, 1993), a modified version of the Sickness Impact Profile and the Barthel scale for the study of elderly people, the study aimed to assess the impact of interventions on five dimensions of health: physical health, mental health, social functioning, role functioning and general health perceptions. A baseline measure of patients' health status was made on admission with subsequent assessments on discharge and at 3 and 12 months after the intervention. The success of the intervention was determined as changes from baseline to follow-up.

The authors point out the value of using instruments which have been well validated on similar groups of patients in similar settings. The instrument should be capable of detecting change in relevant aspects of health status and responsive to change over time. Preferably the measure should also be quick and easy to use in routine practice and capable of application across a range of ages and abilities. The study demonstrated the practicality of collecting information on health status finding high patient compliance with completion of postal questionnaires; response rates were as high as 90%. Collecting information retrospectively from notes was feasible providing it is possible to ensure consistent data definitions. The authors recommend that the costs of data collection can be minimized by using information from existing data sources wherever possible.

CAN
EFFECTIVENESS
EXCEED EFFICACY?

Support for the recognition of the importance of considering a broad range of factors in understanding the derivation of clinical effectiveness comes from control groups receiving placebo in intervention trials. Such groups often achieve improvements in health beyond that expected from comparison with untreated individuals outside the remit of the trial. Notwithstanding the obvious bias introduced by patient selection in intervention trials – which restrict entry to the trial from individuals with particularly complex health or social care needs – such findings have been attributed to the higher quality of care found in units used to undertaking research because of features such as more frequent follow-up, increased attention paid to symptoms and progress, increased numbers of investigations and in general more effort made by the clinical team in assessment and review. In such circumstances it may be possible to hypothesize that effectiveness could exceed efficacy. A key priority in intervention trials is to ensure that the measures of efficacy are drawn from a relatively homogeneous patient group. In clinical practice patient selection is neither possible nor desirable yet similar or better results could potentially be obtained if emphasis is given to the features of care most likely to maximize the outcome for the patient.

MEASURING
SERVICE
EFFECTIVENESS

The continued practice of some common interventions despite evidence of their relative ineffectiveness, the slow rate of uptake of findings from research and the evidence of poor application of research findings through, for example, poor patient selection suggest that more complex behaviour underlies the relationship between research and practice or between innovation and application. Such factors which are probably unrelated to the scientific basis for medicine are likely to bear equally on the achievement of high quality health care as the knowledge base of the clinicians. Clues to the clarification of the factors underlying these trends is more likely to be found in the organization and management of healthcare systems, in the roles and relationships of clinical teams

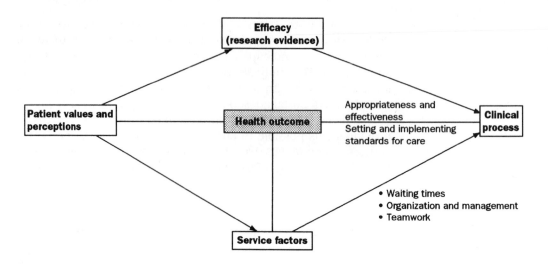

Figure 3.1
Influence and attributes of clinical effectiveness

in the delivery of health care and in the values and preferences of patients for alternative outcomes than in the ether of clinical science. Whatever the full story, it is clear that the achievement of high quality patient care will rely firmly on an understanding of attributes of the health service beyond its knowledge base.

Figure 3.1 describes a possible approach to defining the attributes which are likely to bear on the effectiveness of clinical care. They include factors affecting the staff, the organization and management of care including the teamwork of the staff involved in patient care, an understanding of the relationships involved, the level of mutual respect, and understanding of the skills base and the concerns and values of patients. These will include the timeliness of the intervention and the manner and style in which patients are assessed, but will also include importantly the values and choices patient use in assessing their preferred outcome. A possible scheme for assessing the effectiveness of care is given in Box 3.2.

SUMMARY

It is possible to devise methods for measuring effectiveness in routine clinical practice. Indirect methods are the most usual approach; they involve audit of process to ensure that practice is based on research evidence of effectiveness. Direct methods which compare health outcomes measuring either mortality or health status are often practically more difficult to do in routine practice. The information obtained is more difficult to interpret in the absence of detailed information on patient case mix. The benefit of direct measurement of health outcome can, however, be

Box 3.2
Schema for assessing
effectiveness in clinical
change

- Identify the health outcome required by the patients assessing all possible alternatives through discussion between clinician and patient.

- Process measures must be defined for patient management based on a review of research evidence for efficacy of proposed intervention.

- Assessment of quality of care should be sufficiently comprehensive to include the key features of care most likely to set the limits for effectiveness in clinical care. These attributes will include patient based subjective measures of outcome and cover the aspects of importance to all those involved in care: the roles and relationships of the clinical team, patient values and preferences for alternative outcome, safety of care for the patient and the organization and management underpinning care.

- Measures used should be defined by the clinical team. Ownership of the approach is vital since it is the key to change (Lomas and Haynes 1987).

- The features under review should as far as possible be precise and capable of objective measurement – data collection based on routine sources is most straightforward and capable of integration within the working pattern of the provider.

considerable since the information emerging carries a potentially greater influence on producing change in clinical practice and may as a consequence give rise to rapid improvements in clinical care.

Information on the effectiveness of care may have its greatest impact within an audit framework. Measures should be agreed by the clinical team; the instruments used should be well validated, be sensitive to the characteristics of care being assessed and be responsive to change. Once the information has been obtained it should be shared with and discussed by all those involved in the care of patients under review. A comprehensive approach to monitoring effectiveness will include measure of process and outcome *and* draw on the criteria identified by the clinicians as most likely to affect patient health outcomes. This will include organization and management of care as well as appropriate delivery of investigations and all therapeutic interventions.

FURTHER
READING

♦ **NHS Centre for Reviews and Dissemination**
University of York,
Heslington,
York, YO1 5DD

♦ **Database of published reviews**
The Centre holds an international register of good quality research reviews of the effectiveness of healthcare interventions and the management and organization of health services. The database is being built up prospectively, and concentrates on interventions relevant to Health of the Nation targets and other selected topics. Records will normally include a structured summary and a quality assessment of the reviews.

♦ **Database of economic evaluations**
A register of published economic evaluations of health interventions. Records will normally include a structured summary and a qualitative assessment together with details of any practical implications for the NHS.

♦ **Text database**
Including reviews undertaken by the NHS Centre for Reviews and Dissemination or by other agencies it has commissioned. This will include the full text of the *Effective Health Care Bulletins*. Topics covered to date include:

Effective Health Care Bulletins
- screening for osteoporosis to prevent fractures
- stroke rehabilitation
- management of subfertility
- treatment of persistent glue ear
- treatment of depression in primary care
- cholesterol screening and treatment
- brief interventions and alcohol use
- clinical guidelines
- menorrhagia
Planned future issues:
- benign prostatic hypertrophy
- pressure sores
- cataract
- hip replacement

♦ **UK Health Outcomes Clearing House**
The UK Clearing House on Health Outcomes
Nuffield Institute for Health
71–75 Clarendon Road
Leeds, LS2 9PL (Tel: 01532 333940)
Publishes 'Outcomes Briefing' and maintains database on health outcome assessment in the UK.

♦ **Health of the Nation Key Area Handbooks**
Published by the DOH
- CHD and stroke
- cancers

- mental illness
- accidents
- HIV/AIDS and sexual health

◆ **Health of the Nation Target Effectiveness Documents**
Target effectiveness and cost-effectiveness guide for CHD/stroke. Target effectiveness and cost-effectiveness guide for cervical cancer.

◆ **Epidemiologically Based Needs Assessments**
Available in book form
Stevens, A. and Raftery, J. (Eds) (1994), *Health Care Needs Assessment,* Radcliffe Medical Press, Oxford
- diabetes mellitus
- total hip replacement
- total knee replacement
- stroke
- renal disease
- dementia
- mental illness
- alcohol misuse
- prostatectomy for benign prostatic hyperplasia
- varicose vein treatments
- coronary heart disease
- cancer of the lung
- people with learning disabilities
- hernia repair
- cataract surgery
- colorectal cancer
- lower respiratory disease
- community child health services
- family planning, abortion and fertility services
- drug misuse

◆ **Guidance for Purchasers on Prescribing Issues**
An advice document for purchasers on prescribing is due to be distributed shortly. It outlines issues which purchasers will wish to tackle in order to maximize the quality and cost-effectiveness in prescribing and medicine usage across both primary and secondary healthcare sectors. Examples of good practice and of success criteria are also included.

◆ **Public Health Common Data Set**
Incorporates data on morbidity, mortality, trends and Health of the Nation Targets and is published annually by the Department of Health. The current data set incorporates the updated population Health Outcome Indicators as well as new indicators.

◆ **Cochrane Centre**
Somertown Pavilion
Middle Way
Oxford, OX2 7LG
Tel: 01865 516300
Fax: 01865 615311

The Cochrane Pregnancy and Childbirth Database is now available on disk by annual subscription. As well as the 600 systematic reviews of randomized trials, it also contains six tables which summarize the effectiveness, or not, of different forms of care. The next subject-specific database to become available will be on stroke, and other databases are planned.

◆ **Confidential Enquiry Reports**
DOH (1994) *The Report of the National Advisory Body on the Confidential Enquiry into Still Births and Death in Infancy.* Department of Health, March 1992 to July 1993, HMSO, London.
DOH (1994) *Report on the Confidential Enquiries into Maternal Deaths in the United Kingdom 1988 to 1990,* HMSO, London.
Campling, E.A., Devlin, H.B., Whorle, R.W. and Lunn, J.N. (1993) *The Report of the National Confidential Enquiry into Perioperative and Operative Deaths 1991/2.* Conference of Colleges, London.

◆ **Health Outcomes**
McColl, A.J. and Galliford, W.C. (1993) *Population Health Outcome Indicators for the NHS: a feasibility study,* available from the Faculty of Public Health Medicine, Royal College of Physicians, 4 St Andrews Place, London.

◆ **Bandolier** edited by Moore A., Muir Gray J.A. and McQuay H.
Available from Pain Relief Unit
The Churchill
Oxford, OX3 7LJ
Available on Internet at http://www.jr2.ox.ac.uk/Bandolier
Produces a readable synopsis of cost-effectiveness studies on topics of current interest in health care. Draws from national and international sources and covers drug use, test use and medical and surgical interventions. Also tackles methodological issues concerned with reviewing and interpreting research based information.

◆ **Effectiveness Matters**
Effectiveness Matters is an update on the effectiveness of important health interventions for practitioners and decision-makers in the NHS. It is produced by researchers at the NHS Centre for Reviews and Dissemination at the University of York, in collaboration with subject area experts. *Effectiveness Matters* is extensively peer reviewed.

◆ **Evidence Based Medicine Journal**
Available from:
Specialist Journals Department
BMJ Publishing Group
BMJ House
Tavistock Square
London, WC1H 9JR

◆ **Guidelines**
The examples given below have the support of the relevant professional bodies and also take account of research evidence of best clinically effective practice.

Making the Best Use of a Radiology Department
Royal College Radiologists

Management of Asthma
British Thoracic Society

Management of Diabetes in Primary Care
British Diabetic Association

Investigation and Management of Stable Angina
British Cardiac Society and Royal College of Physicians

Management of Leg Ulcers in the Community
Nursing R&D Unit, Liverpool University

Management of Neonatal Respiratory Distress Syndrome
British Association of Perinatal Medicine

Aspects of the Management of Head Injury
Royal College of Surgeons including:
- criteria for skull x-ray after head injury
- admission to hospital
- CT scanning in general hospitals
- consultation with the neurosurgical unit

Managing Cancer Pain
National Council for Hospice and Specialist Palliative Care Services

Control of Epidemic Methicillin-resistant Staphylococcus Aureus
Hospital Infection Society and British Society for Antimicrobial Chemotherapy

Management of Ovarian Cancer
Standing Medical Advisory Committee

Management of Lung Cancer
Standing Medical Advisory Committee

Back Pain
Clinical Standards Advisory Group

◆ **Health Technology Assessment Programme**
Examples of treatments currently being evaluated for effectiveness and cost-effectiveness through the Health Technology Assessment Programme:
- Trial of continuous hyperfractionated accelerated radiotherapy (CHART) versus conventional radiotherapy for
  - non-small cell carcinoma of the bronchus
  - head and neck cancer
- Trial of faecal occult blood screening for colorectal cancer

- UKCCCR trials of breast cancer screening
  - screening from age 40
  - yearly screening
  - two-view mammography for screening
- Trial of neonatal extracorporeal membrane oxygenation (ECMO)
- Trial of lithotripsy versus non-treatment for small asymptomatic renal calculi
- Evaluation of picture archiving and communication systems
- Evaluation trial of transmyocardial revascularisation (TMR) for intractable angina
- Laparoscopic surgery for colorectal cancer
- Interactive videos for informing patients on therapies

◆ **NHS Executive Letters**
Improving Clinical Effectiveness EL(93)115
Improving the Effectiveness of the NHS EL(94)74

REFERENCES   Bardsley, M.J. and Coles, J.M. (1992), Practical experience in auditing patient outcomes. *Quality in Health Care*, 1: 124–130.

Campling, E.A., Devlin, H.B., Whorle, R.W. and Lunn, J.N. (1993), *The Report of the National Confidential Enquiry into Perioperative Deaths 1991/2*. Conference of Colleges, London.

Charlton, J.R.H., Silver, R., Hartley, R.M. and Holland, W.W. (1983), Geographical variations in mortality from conditions amenable to medical intervention in England and Wales. *Lancet*, 25 March 1983.

Concato, J., Horwitz, R.I., Feinstein, A.R., Elmore, J.G. and Schiff, S.F. (1992), Problems of comorbidity in mortality after prostatectomy. *Journal of the American Medical Association*, 267: 1077–1082.

Ellis, J., Mulligan, I., Row, J. and Sackett, D.L. (1995), Inpatient general medicine is evidence based. *Lancet*, 346: 407–410.

Enkin, M., Keirse, J. and Chalmers, I. (1994), *A Guide to Effective Care in Pregnancy and Childbirth*. OUP.

Gulliford, M.C. (1992), Evaluating prognostic factor: implications for measurement of health care outcome. *Journal of Epidemiology and Public Health*, 46: 323–326.

Imperiale, T.F. and Sperof, F.T. (1994), A meta-analysis of methods to prevent venous thromboembolism following total hip replacement. *Journal of the American Medical Association*, 271: 1780–1785.

ISIS-2 Collaborative Group (1988), Randomised trial of intravenous streptokinase, oral aspirin, both or neither among 17,187 cases of suspected acute myocardial infarction. *Lancet*, ii:349–360.

Last, J.M. (1988), *A Dictionary of Epidemiology* (2nd Edn). Oxford University Press.

Lomas, J. and Haynes, R.B. (1987), A taxonomy and critical review of tested strategies for the application of clinical practice recommendations from 'official' to 'individual' clinical policy. *American Journal of Preventive Medicine*, 4: 77–94.

McColl, A.J. and Gulliford, M.C. (1993), *Population Health Outcome*

McKee, M. and Hunter, D. (1994), *Mortality League Tables. A comparison of hospital death rates in the North West Thames Region. Methodological considerations, possible explanations and scope for further action.* London School of Hygiene & Tropical Medicine.

McKee, M. and Pettigrew, M. (1993), Disease Staging: A case mix system for purchasers? *Journal of Public Health Medicine*, 15: 35–36.

McPherson, K., Wennberg, J.E., Hovind, O. *et al.* (1982), Small area variation in the use of common surgical procedures. An international comparison of New England, England and Norway, *New England Journal of Medicine*, 307: 1310–1314.

NHSE (1996), *Promoting Clinical Effectiveness. A framework for action in and through the NHS.* NHS Executive.

Park, R.E., Brook, R.H., Kosecott, J. *et al.* (1990), Explaining variations in hospital death rates: randomness, severity of illness, quality of care. *Journal of the American Medical Association*, 264: 484–490.

Rockall, T.A., Logan, R.F.A. and Devlin, H.B. and Northfield, T.C. for the National Audit of Acute Gastrointestinal Haemorrhage (1995). Variation in outcome after acute upper gastrointestinal haemorrhage. *Lancet*, 346: 346–350.

Ryan, M., Jule, B., Bond, C. and Taylor, R. (1992), Knowledge of drug costs: a comparison of general practitioners in Scotland and England. *British Journal of General Practice*, 42: 6–9.

Clinical Outcomes Working Group. (1993), *Clinical Outcome Measures Report*, June, Scottish Office.

Shanks, J. and Frater, A. (1993), Health status outcome and attributability: is a red rose red in the dark? *Quality in Health Care*, 2(4): 259–262.

Stewart, A.L., Hays, R.D. and Ware, J.E. (1988), The MOS short form general health survey. *Medical Care*, 26: 724–735.

Wennberg, J.A. (1993), Small area analysis and the medical care outcome problem. In: Research methodology: Strengthening causal interpretation of non-experimental data. *AHCPR Conference Proceedings*, 177–206.

MEASURING EFFICIENCY IN HEALTH CARE: THE ROLE OF THE AUDIT COMMISSION

Judy Renshaw

Judy Renshaw

OBJECTIVES

> ◆ To outline the role of the Audit Commission in seeking to ensure that healthcare services provide 'value for money'.
>
> ◆ To illustrate the nature of their investigations by analysing three of their studies.

INTRODUCTION

Providers, professionals and purchasers of health care are becoming increasingly interested in efficiency, in a world of limited resources and ever growing demand, brought about by advances in medical technology and the needs of an ageing population. The health service reforms of 1991 and the creation of an internal market aimed to introduce further incentives to improve efficiency. Commissioning authorities have to obtain the best value for money they can, using the knowledge available to them. The introduction of a degree of competition between providers is intended to stimulate improvement in performance and encourage local initiative.

This chapter will discuss the following issues:

◆ A theoretical view of the process of delivering health care and the components of that process.
◆ What is efficiency? The requirement to consider effectiveness and economy, since efficiency is best understood within a context of the 'three E's'. Economy is mainly concerned with the inputs to the process, while effectiveness is mainly concerned with the outcomes. Efficiency considerations span the whole of the care delivery process.
◆ How to measure effectiveness and efficiency.
◆ The role of the Audit Commission in 'value for money' work.

♦ An outline of three value for money studies carried out by the Audit Commission in day surgery, management of medical beds and mental health care, to illustrate some ways in which efficiency can be measured and performance assessed.

THE PRODUCTION
PROCESS

Efficiency is not just about minimizing cost. It requires a consideration of the links between costs, resources, processes and their outcomes. This relationship may be viewed as analogous to a production process, as in the 'Production of Welfare' framework (Figure 4.1) (Knapp 1984, Davies and Knapp 1981).

Resource inputs, such as staff, buildings, equipment and consumable supplies, each have an identifiable cost. These are not only the direct financial costs but include the 'opportunity costs' of alternative uses of a resource which have been lost. For example, the opportunity cost of attaching a community psychiatric nurse to a GP practice for two days a week is not just the monetary cost of two-fifths of his or her salary, national insurance and so on. It is the lost opportunity for work that could otherwise have been carried out, such as supporting 15 more people with severe illnesses like schizophrenia.

For this reason the 'savings' identified in value for money studies are not usually expected to be realized in monetary terms. They are more usefully translated into alternative uses of resources, such as the extra number of surgical procedures that could be carried out, or the additional number of supported housing places that could be made available for people in the community.

Non-resource inputs are factors which influence outputs, but are less tangible and do not have an associated cost. They include some environmental factors, the local labour market, the attitudes and

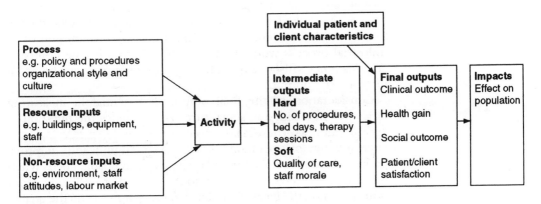

Figure 4.1
The production of health or social care, adapted from Knapp (1984)

personalities of staff and the caring or social environment which is created.

The processes of providing health or social care, such as policies and procedures, organizational style and culture, also influence the outputs. The dividing line between non-resource inputs and processes is far from distinct, but the latter can be more easily influenced by management. The importance of process has been emphasized in recent theories of quality, notably in Total Quality Management (TQM). In this theory, the achievement of quality is viewed as a continuing process, in a cycle of continuous improvement and ever-rising customer expectations, rather than an end feature of a product (Oakland 1989). One important feature is that it is considered to be independent of cost, which separates it clearly from the resource inputs. So efficiency, which should take into account the quality of the output, has a qualitative as well as a quantitative dimension.

Intermediate outputs are the most obvious products of the system and can be measured in both 'hard' and 'soft' ways. The 'hard' measures are (or should be) obtainable on a simple routine basis – the numbers of surgical procedures carried out, bed days occupied, therapy sessions provided or home visits paid. The 'soft' measures include the observable quality of care – which could be compared with that of similar facilities, perhaps using a standard rating scale. The morale and satisfaction of the staff might also be included, since it is of interest both for its own sake and as a likely concomitant of the quality of care.

Final outputs are the ultimate goals of the system, namely clinical outcome, health gain and social improvements. Effectiveness is the achievement of these goals. In health and social care they are usually multiple, and may include recovery, improved morale and self-esteem. Patient or client satisfaction is likely to be closely associated with these goals and is important anyway in its own right. Social outcomes – such as quality of life, independence, morale, social integration and reduction of family stress – will be inextricably linked with health outcomes, especially where community services are concerned. (The equivalent final outputs of an industrial process would be the profit achieved by the company and customer satisfaction, with the production of goods being an intermediate output.)

Consideration of the final outputs is essential in measuring efficiency in health and social care. This includes the question of appropriateness. There is little point, for example, in carrying out a large number of operations which do not significantly improve people's health, nor accommodating people in hospital beds when this produces little improvement to their health or wellbeing. More often than not, the level of efficiency directly impacts on the quality of service provided and hence the overall effectiveness of individual services.

The basic premise of the model is that final and intermediate outputs are determined by the level and modes of combination of resource inputs, non-resource inputs and processes.

The ultimate endpoint of the process might be considered to be the wider impact, or collective effect that it has on a given population. Performance measures could include the local morbidity figures for particular conditions. A drawback with these as measures of the performance of a healthcare system is that local morbidity is likely to be at least as affected by other factors – such as the quality of the housing stock, the level of air pollution or the employment market – as by the provision of health care.

EFFICIENCY AND EFFECTIVENESS

Effectiveness is an indicator of the latter parts of the process, the outputs of the system and their effect on individuals and communities. It is a prerequisite to efficiency; a service or activity cannot be efficient if it is not effective in producing intermediate, and more importantly final, outputs. The more complex the procedure and the more time an individual spends engaged in the service, the more important qualitative factors such as personal interaction and nature of the environment are likely to become.

Economy is a measure of the beginnings of the process. It is concerned with minimizing the resources used and their associated costs. A thorough examination of resources should consider where all of the costs fall, which may include several agencies and individuals. The cost of a voluntary helper, for example, will include the cost to the agency of some supervision, management and training, as well as the opportunity cost to the individual of other activities in which they could have otherwise engaged.

Efficiency measurement requires all parts of the process to be considered. It is a combined measure which depends on both economy and effectiveness.

Efficiency can be defined as the arrangement of a given level of inputs in a way which generates the maximum possible output. So carrying out more surgical procedures with the same level of staffing and overhead costs could distinguish an efficient from a less efficient unit. A firm or plant is said to be *technically efficient* when it produces the maximum set of outputs from a given amount of inputs. Alternatively, it could be considered to be the minimization of the cost of producing a given level of output (Knapp 1984). So achieving an equivalent number of procedures carried out, using fewer staff, would also indicate efficiency. *Price efficiency* is said to be attained when a firm or plant deploys its resources or inputs to produce a given level of output at minimum cost.

Target efficiency, although different in emphasis, is central to the provision of public services such as health and social care. It is a measure of the accuracy with which services reach those for whom they were intended (Bebbington and Davies 1983). *Vertical target efficiency* is the extent to which services go to those who need them rather than to those who do not. Establishing consistent criteria for eligibility for a service, such as home help, and screening procedures to assess individual needs against those criteria will enhance vertical target efficiency. *Horizontal target efficiency* is the extent to which services reach all of those who need them. Public awareness of the availability of a service and GPs' knowledge and referral practices will influence this. Campaigns to encourage older people to undergo free health checks and to encourage women to have regular cervical smears are examples of attempts to improve the horizontal target efficiency of these procedures.

MEASURING EFFICIENCY   Measuring efficiency depends on the measurement of both effectiveness and economy. The effectiveness of a service or an intervention is best assessed through the final outputs but these are usually the most difficult to measure. Some clinical outcomes are more easily measured than others. The reduction of pain and improved freedom of movement should be fairly easy to demonstrate, but others such as improved concentration and morale may be more difficult or may take more time to measure than is possible in a regular or routine manner.

It is often possible, however, to find reasonably reliable proxy measures for these where an association has been previously established. Activity levels or intermediate output indicators can provide useful ways to compare performance, provided that their relationship with final output has been demonstrated. For example, if a surgical procedure such as carpal tunnel decompression has been shown to improve the functioning of a limb and to reduce pain in the majority of cases, the proportion of operations for patients with similar characteristics carried out on a day case basis can provide a meaningful performance measure – once the outcome has been shown to be as satisfactory as for the same procedure carried out on an inpatient basis.

In a similar way, certain process and intermediate output measures can be used as proxies for each other. For example, the degree of continuity of nursing care might be a consequence of the methods of organizing care on the wards and allocating nurses to patients, and to the extent to which temporary nursing staff are employed on a ward. So regular monitoring of, for example, the use of temporary staff with a view to keeping it to a minimum, can provide a useful check on one aspect of the quality of care.

There are dangers, though, in too great a reliance on easily obtained measures. For example, the public emphasis on waiting lists and waiting times can lead to exaggeration of the importance of activities for which waiting lists develop, possibly at the expense of more important, but less visible, activities. This can influence the public perception of what is most important in the local health service and shift the priorities of key decision-makers. Such measures can also be misleading in themselves if not viewed in the context of different levels of local need and demand. The needs of different populations can vary considerably. For example, the need for mental health care varies by a factor of four or five and is closely related to the level of social deprivation (Glover *et al.* 1994).

Measures of effectiveness are most useful in a comparative context, which enables judgements to be made about the relative performance of different health providers, hospitals, community teams and so on. They may helpfully be compared with national averages or with a group which are similar in size, structure or population characteristics.

Measuring efficiency also depends on the measurement of the costs of the process. The costs to all those involved should be included in a comprehensive assessment, so social services, voluntary organizations and the opportunity costs to individuals should be considered.

THE ROLE OF THE AUDIT COMMISSION

The Audit Commission is responsible for the external audit of local authorities and NHS agencies in England and Wales (Figure 4.2). As well as reviewing the financial accounts, the auditors have a duty to undertake 'value for money' studies of selected topics each year. The objective is to ensure that the audited bodies make the best possible use of the resources available, to achieve maximum effectiveness.

To maximize the effectiveness of the 'value for money' work, a research study (usually two years) precedes the audits. The study leads to a published report, a training programme for the specialist auditors who will carry out the local work and an extensive audit guide to inform them of what to look for, what to expect and how

Figure 4.2
The work of the Audit Commission

to find it. The auditors are also provided with comparative data for England and Wales.

The three studies described below represent some of the topics which have been examined by the Health Studies directorate of the Commission. These are focused largely on providers and tend to emphasize improvements which could be made by managers and clinicians. Other studies have examined the work of purchasers in district health authorities, family health services authorities (FHSAs) and social services departments.

Day surgery (Audit Commission 1990)   There are many non-emergency surgical procedures, including a large number for which there are long waiting lists, which can be carried out on patients who enter and leave hospital on the same day instead of staying overnight. For properly selected patients, there is no difference in the clinical outcome of these procedures.

Day surgery is likely to be appropriate for patients who are medically fit; have someone to accompany them home from hospital and look after them while they recover; have a telephone and suitable accommodation at home; live near enough to the hospital and have transport to enable them to travel home on the same day.

The benefits of day surgery

The unit costs of the resource inputs are lower for day surgery – on average about 30% less per operation than for inpatient surgery. The difference reflects mainly the reduction in 'hotel' costs of nursing and catering, but may also arise from a more efficient use of resources, since day case units are often more compact and the work more routine than that of inpatient wards. Additional costs may sometimes be incurred, for community nursing and GP visits, but these have been found to be small, particularly since the development of improved surgical techniques and absorbable sutures. The extra costs to patients and their families for fuel, food, laundry and dressings are approximately offset by savings on hospital visiting and extra nightwear.

The use of dedicated day surgery units enhances some of the non-resource inputs such as staff morale (which are cost free). Nurse recruitment and retention are easier since the hours are regular, with no weekend work, and the working environment less stressful. Staff morale is frequently higher in these small units and staff turnover lower.

The final outputs either do not differ between the two types of procedure, or tend to favour day surgery. A recent review of clinical outcomes concluded that there were no differences in the incidence of complications and the rates of readmission to hospital. Patients often prefer to be treated on a day case basis since they benefit from shorter waiting times, less likelihood of their operation being cancelled and less time away from their home and family.

An Audit Commission survey of over 200 patients found that most of them preferred day treatment and 83% said they would recommend it to a friend in a similar situation. Their reasons included being home sooner and making a faster recovery at home. Almost all were able to go outdoors within three days and the majority were back to normal within a week. Both inpatients and day surgery patients were generally very satisfied with their care. None of the day case patients received community nursing or social services care after the operation and only 6% said they would have wanted this.

Measuring performance

For a 'basket' of 20 common procedures, the percentage per-formed under day surgery varies widely between hospitals (Figure 4.3). The 'basket' of procedures was selected as a basis for comparison of performance between authorities, since the existing local information was often inadequate. Many providers had previously included less complex procedures within their 'day case' records, such as colposcopy and gastroscopy, which could have been undertaken in an outpatient clinic.

There is a clear advantage in the main intermediate output – the number of procedures carried out – if more are done as day cases. In 1990, the Audit Commission calculated that, if all health authorities in England and Wales used day surgery to the same extent as the 25% that use it most, an additional 186 000 patients could be treated every year at no extra cost. Such an increase in activity would have a significant impact on waiting times for all types of surgery and existing waiting lists could be cut by 18%.

One measure of efficiency is the percentage of certain operations carried out on a day case basis. The Audit Commission has recommended a target percentage for each of the 20 procedures, based on the performance of the 'best' 25% of authorities.

In addition to improving performance on the basis of selected surgical procedures, efficiency could be improved in other ways. Many day surgery units could be used more efficiently. The use of such units for less complex surgical procedures takes up valuable capacity (an opportunity cost), and so should be reduced to around 25% or less of cases, as indicated by the best practice observed. The throughput in most units could be increased without any detri-mental effect on the quality of care.

The Audit Commission has provided benchmarks against which providers can assess their performance. If there are no physical constraints, such as the theatre and the ward being some distance apart, 346 cases could be treated per bed in a day surgery unit, assuming 90% of the maximum possible throughput to be an achievable target. Performance on these measures could be improved by better management and organization of the units. Higher efficiency is usually obtained by having self-contained units with their own ward and theatre, which can enhance the quality of service and lead to a reduction in running costs, although the initial capital costs may be higher.

Clinicians could be encouraged to make more extensive use of day surgery by providing them with better, up-to-date information. Training about current good practice is essential if clinicians are to maximize their efficiency. Previously, many mistakenly believed that the outcome of treatment was unlikely to be as good as that for inpatient treatment, that substantial community support might be necessary and that people preferred to be treated as inpatients. The evidence does not support these concerns; in fact the reverse appears to be true, provided that the suitability for day treatment of

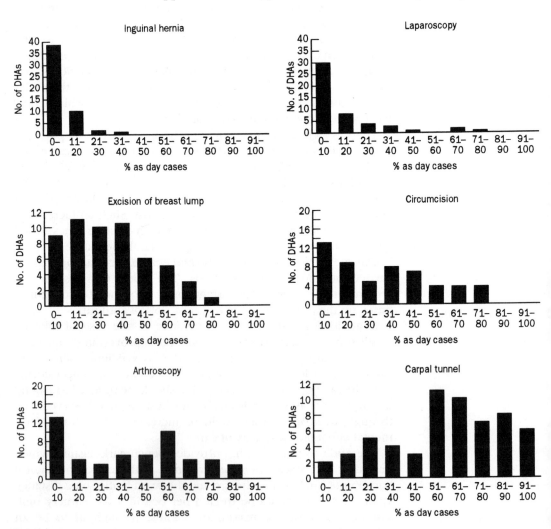

Figure 4.3
Comparison of the percentage of operations done as day cases by district health authority.
Source: The Audit Commission Analyses of Data from 54 DHAs in England (1988–89)

individuals and their circumstances are carefully considered. Only a small minority of patients tend to be unsuitable.

Other indicators of good practice include:

♦ the provision of clear operational policies which cover patient selection, the information given to patients, procedures for monitoring their satisfaction and standard systems for booking, admission and discharge;
♦ proper managerial control, ideally with a clinician involved in the day-to-day management of units; and
♦ better information available to managers – about current performance, costs, activities and patients' satisfaction with the treatment they receive.

The use of medical beds in acute hospitals (Audit Commission 1991)

The number of beds used by similar hospitals varies widely – and most of this variation is unrelated to the needs of the population they serve. The efficiency of their use seems to be dependent on the policies and practices of local clinicians. The Audit Commission has examined the use of medical beds in England and Wales and has found opportunities to improve efficiency at each step in the flow of patients through the hospital.

The main intermediate output is the number of patients treated, usually within a specified time period such as a year. This is known as throughput. A higher throughput for a similar level of resource inputs indicates greater technical efficiency. The main resource inputs are the number of beds and the associated staffing and equipment which is needed to service them. Although the final outputs, clinical outcome and patient satisfaction were not examined in detail here, research evidence has shown them to be associated with certain management processes.

Admission

The criteria for admission vary between clinicians and hospitals. Inevitably some admissions are inappropriate, especially when decisions are taken by junior doctors who tend to err on the side of caution. GPs may also refer inappropriately when they are unsure about what is needed.

Hospital screening procedures for admission could be improved by making an experienced doctor available at all times to assess patients on admission and enabling a consultant to see them as soon as possible, to sanction the use of any procedures. Inappropriate admissions should be discharged at an early stage. Providing a rapid second opinion to GPs would also reduce inappropriate referrals. This could be achieved by rescheduling urgent outpatient appointments and allowing direct telephone access to hospital consultants. Developing mutually agreed referral and treatment protocols has also been shown to reduce the variation.

These changes would have few cost implications but require considerable changes in hospital processes and professional style. Those which would entail a shift in resources, such as making an experienced doctor available at all times, should more than compensate for the cost elsewhere by reducing the workload due to inappropriate admissions.

The extent of inappropriate referrals for admission per GP practice could be monitored by logging the number of emergency referrals (per thousand population) for each practice and sampling them on a regular basis.

Placement

The procedures for placing and transferring acutely ill patients between wards could be improved in many hospitals. Some have a central office to coordinate all admissions, with a clear picture of the number and location of empty beds. Although this has resource implications, it can reduce the time that professional staff spend ringing wards to find empty beds, thus saving the opportunity costs of their time, and reduces the chances of placement on an inappropriate ward.

Transfer between wards should be minimized, although it is sometimes necessary, to provide the right kind of specialist care. Reducing the number of transfers should enhance the continuity and quality of care, thus improving some of the outputs without significantly increasing the costs. Appropriate placement also means the patients of individual medical firms not being spread too widely around the hospital; some were found to be placed on six or more different wards. Such scattering leads to a waste of doctors' time and a poorer overall quality of care.

Some hospitals provide an admissions ward for the first 24 or 48 hours of a patient's stay. This can allow staff more time to find the most suitable bed and can act as a filter to inappropriate admissions.

Useful monitoring indicators include:

- The time spent waiting in the A&E department before placement – an indicator of the efficiency of the placements procedure and the adequacy of the number of available beds.
- The average number of ward transfers per patient – an indicator of compliance with the policy on transfers.

Stay

The wide variation in length of stay for a particular condition and case mix reflects differences of medical opinion and practice. Consultants, who often practise in isolation, should be encouraged to participate in clinical audit and consensus conferences, which can provide guidance on the most effective treatment of common conditions. These should help to reduce the variation and can have a significant impact on the way in which scarce resources are used.

The data available for monitoring length of stay are frequently inaccurate or incomplete. Details of case mix are essential for adequate comparisons to be made between firms and hospitals. Their interpretation also needs to take account of local circumstances, such as whether there are beds attached to Accident and Emergency (A&E) departments. In this case the average length of stay appears to be longer as the medical specialties are not 'credited' with the short stay patients treated under the A&E consultant.

Administrative constraints such as the timing of ward rounds or the on-take rota can adversely affect the length of stay. Patients often have to wait until the next ward round before they can be discharged, even if their condition is straightforward and their hospital stay complete. Changing these procedures to allow the delegation of some decisions to the ward sister, or more frequent visits to selected patients, can speed up discharges and thus reduce costs and improve the quality of health care.

Patients' stays are often unnecessarily prolonged by waiting for the results of tests from laboratories, which only operate during office hours. At present, there is little incentive for laboratories to work more flexibly if their budgets are held separately. Laboratories should be encouraged to respond more flexibly which would lead to a reduction in the overall cost to the hospital, through a saving in bed days.

Discharge procedures

Administrative procedures, such as waiting for take-home medicines, transport or appointments to see specialists, can also delay the discharge of medically fit patients. Up to 20% of bed days in some wards could be saved by instituting a more systematic approach to the planning of patient care. Planning for discharge from the time of admission can lead to earlier discharge, fewer subsequent outpatient attendances, improved aftercare and fewer readmissions. Appointing a discharge coordinator has helped to smooth the process and has led to savings in some hospitals.

Sometimes discharge depends on the availability of resources provided by other agencies, such as residential or nursing home places. These are non-resource inputs since they are not under the control of the hospital. However, managers could encourage the involvement of social workers and gather evidence about the shortage of places, to bring to the attention of purchasers.

Useful indicators of performance include:

◆ the time of day patients leave hospital – an indicator of the appropriateness of the timing of ward rounds and discharge;
◆ the proportion of patients with a length of stay greater than

some benchmark – an indicator of the proper functioning of discharge procedures.

Bed availability and management

The throughput per bed for a particular condition – which is mainly a function of the length of stay – varies widely and is generally associated with fewer beds being available (Figure 4.4). It is clear that, within limits, the length of time which patients are kept in hospital can be altered to fit the resources available. The Commission has calculated that, if all districts could achieve lengths of stay as low as the lowest 25% of those sampled, the same level of activity could be provided nationally by 58 000 beds rather than the 85 000 currently in use. This would depend on both improvements in organizational processes and the development of some additional community resources. So it is not simply an increase in price efficiency that would be necessary – the same outputs for less money – but a change in the balance of the existing resource inputs. If such a shift were made, it could lead to an improvement in the quality of patient care – another important intermediate output – as well as an increase in efficiency.

An appropriate number of beds for each specialty can be determined jointly by clinicians and managers, taking into account the average length of stay and target turnover interval. From these, a planned level of bed emptiness and throughput can be worked out. This can be shown in a diagrammatic form, the 'Barber-Johnson diagram' (see Glossary) (Figure 4.5). If a specialty has an average length of stay of four days and a target turnover interval of one day, a level of bed emptiness of 20% would have to be planned.

Figure 4.4
The relationship between (age adjusted) throughput per bed, and bed provision in general medicine and geriatrics, England (1989–90). Bed availability and throughput per bed are inversely correlated.

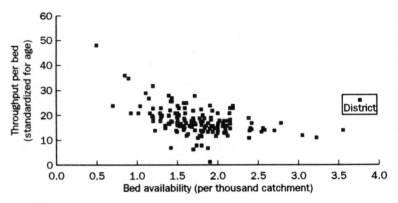

Source: the Audit Commission Analyses of the Department of Health Health Service Indicators (1991) and data from regional hospital episode statistics supplied via OPCS (1991)

Figure 4.5
The Barber–Johnson
diagram. The Barber–
Johnson diagram can
be used to inform
debate between
clinicians and
managers.

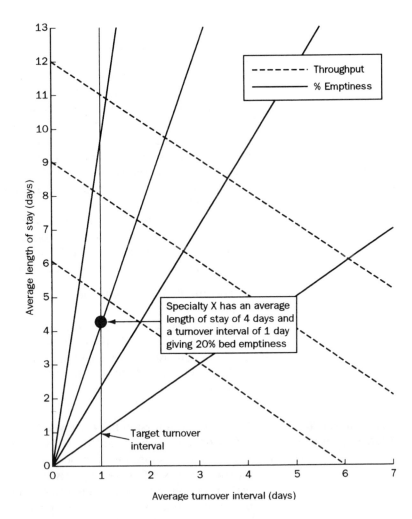

Source: The Audit
Commission (1992) and
Yates (1982)

An appropriate number of beds can be calculated if the number of expected admissions over a period and the proportion of these that are emergencies are estimated.

Typically there is considerable seasonal fluctuation in demand for beds; medical firms spill over into surgical beds in 90% of Trusts during the winter. The scope for interchange between specialties in a planned way, such as the reallocation for elective work during the summer, is rarely realized at present. If it were, the existing resources could be used in a more effective way.

The policies for gender pooling between wards, and between bays within wards, vary widely. It is usually more important for patients to be placed in the appropriate ward for their specialty than for the appropriate gender. There is considerable scope for greater pooling of beds provided that patients' views are sought – which occurs in only a few hospitals at present.

A number of structural innovations have been introduced in a few hospitals, which have resource implications but could lead to an increase in overall efficiency. Five-day wards would be cheaper to run and would suit the needs of many patients, since the average occupancy is always higher during the week than at weekends. These include many elective patients, whose stay is predictable and those admitted for planned investigations. Some hospitals provide Planned Investigation Units for this purpose. Patient hotels, as introduced in Sweden, could provide appropriate care for many patients who are recovering or undergoing prolonged treatment, do not need to be on an acute ward 24 hours a day, but are not yet able to go home.

Many of these recommendations require a substantial improvement in the information collected on a routine basis, in order to monitor the performance of the Trust.

Useful indicators for monitoring performance include:

◆ The number of empty beds each ward has each day – an indicator of the functioning of bed allocations.
◆ The reasons for refusal of admission and the subsequent history – an indicator of the effectiveness of screening arrangements.
◆ The readmission rates for particular conditions within a certain time – an indicator of whether patients are being discharged too soon.

Mental health care
(Audit Commission
1994)

The Audit Commission has reviewed the mental health services for adults which are provided by NHS and social services agencies. These include community based professional support, hospital inpatient care, staffed housing, day care and so on. The main focus was on people with acute and long-term problems in the community, rather than those who are or were long-stay residents of hospitals. Twelve districts were studied in depth and a further 90 surveyed via their local auditor. Users' views were elicited from an extensive trawl through existing reports and a survey of 10 local groups.

Most people with mental health problems suffer from short-term neurotic illness such as anxiety and depression from which they are likely to recover, either spontaneously or with limited professional help. People with long-term problems such as schizophrenia, however, may need help over many years. They often encounter difficulties in the practical necessities of everyday life, such as self-care, housing and finance. Final outputs for this group are unlikely to include complete recovery, but longer periods of stability in between relapses are important indicators of success, as are overall improvements in living standards, quality of life and users' satisfaction with their care.

Current policy for mental health care seems to be on the right track; it favours locally based services – a range of options to meet individual needs – and greater emphasis on care in community settings. But its implementation is struggling. The Commission's study identified four areas in which changes need to be made, if the effectiveness and efficiency of the service are to improve. These are: resource allocation between areas, resource distribution within areas, the targeting of services and the management and coordination of the service.

Resource allocation between areas

The need for mental health care varies widely between populations. The indicators of need include the number of compulsory admissions to hospital, the number of 'new long stay' patients accumulated on acute wards and bed occupancies of more than 100%. These all tend to be highly correlated with social deprivation, as measured by the Jarman index (see˜Glossary). The most deprived areas seem to need four or five times the amount of mental health care per head of population as the least deprived.

But the distribution of resources does not match. Many deprived inner city areas spend as little as £20 per head each year on mental health care while some of the more affluent surburban and rural areas spend over £80. The mismatch is partly historical in origin; districts which used to run the large psychiatric hospitals generally spend more, regardless of the needs of their population. A new weighted capitation formula may be needed to improve the allocation of funds. A 'needs for mental health care' index has been developed since the publication of this report, based on a composite of population characteristics which are closely associated with psychiatric admissions. It can be calculated for any combination of electoral ward areas.

Resource distribution within areas

Even if the level of funding is sufficient for the needs of the population, it is not necessarily spent on the most appropriate services, or 'resource inputs'. It is now widely recognized that people with severe mental health problems need a range of services in the community to help them to maintain steady and satisfactory lives and to avoid relapse and stay out of hospital. Service users and their carers are agreed that they want more and better community services, the opportunity to be listened to and to influence decisions about their care. Their priorities include alternatives to hospital in times of crisis, access to help during evenings and at weekends, and practical support with housing, finances and employment. No Trusts, however, were able to provide all of these things and only a few provided a reasonable mix of the types of facilities which are needed.

The main reason for this is that the money spent within districts needs to be better balanced. Although the number of hospital beds has declined sharply since the 1950s, two-thirds of the available resources are still tied up in hospital care in the 1990s. The development of community care is patchy, although some Trusts manage to make available a more extensive range of community services than others. A few have begun to move away from a traditional pattern of hospital based care to one which offers greater flexibility and supports more people in the community.

Better care can often be provided for the same or less money. For example, some Trusts have reviewed the use of their 24-hour staffed housing and found that many residents could be more appropriately accommodated in places with a less intensive level of staffing – which they also prefer. These Trusts have made the change to more flexible provision, based on individual needs, over about a four year period. If all providers revised their use of supported housing in this way, £40 million a year could be released to provide around 6000 extra places for people in the community.

Useful indicators for monitoring the performance of mental healthcare providers include:

♦ the balance of expenditure on hospital and community resources and tracing this balance over subsequent years;
♦ the availability of key community resources such as alternatives to hospital admission at times of crisis; professional support and services during evenings, nights and weekends; practical help with housing and benefits and employment services;
♦ the number and balance of supported housing places in the community (24 hour support and less intensive).

Targeting of services

Specialist mental health services should be targeted on those with the most severe problems to ensure that resources reach those who most need them. The Audit Commission study measured the 'vertical target efficiency' directly, by analysing the caseloads of community based professionals, most of whom were members of community mental health teams (CMHTs). The severity of individuals' problems was defined by their broad diagnostic group and previous admissions to hospital. The classification was unambiguous and simple to administer and was acceptable to the major professional bodies in mental health.

A wide variation was found in the caseloads of different professionals, although many spent most of their time with people who had less severe problems (Figure 4.6). This is worrying, since it implies that resources are not being used in the most effective way. The opportunity costs of staff spending time with those who have lesser problems could be the loss of a service to others with more severe problems (poor 'horizontal target efficiency'). In areas of high or moderate deprivation there are large numbers of people with severe mental illness even if they do not appear on the caseloads. This notion is backed up by research studies which

Figure 4.6
The composition of the caseload varies between providers. Many of those seen do not have severe mental illness.

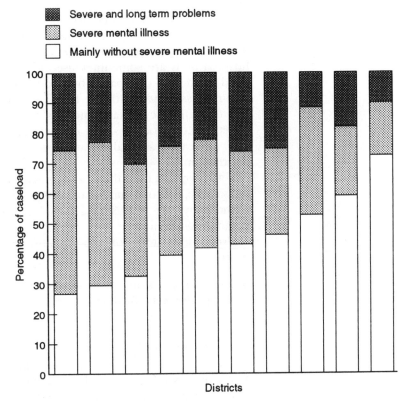

Source: Audit Commission (1994)

have shown that many people in the community with illnesses such as schizophrenia are not receiving specialist care.

The length of time on the caseload and frequency of contact were also recorded. People with severe and long-term problems were not necessarily seen more often than those with lesser needs, even though the nature of their needs implies that they would benefit from more frequent contact. Many of those with more minor problems remained on the caseload for over a year, even though most of them would have recovered within three to six months. This indicates a lack of clear plans for the management of care for such people.

If people with less severe mental health problems are not to be cared for by specialist teams they need to receive a good service from primary care. This is mainly a 'non-resource input' as far as the mental health services are concerned, but better training and back-up is needed from specialists to help the primary care team to intervene in the most appropriate way.

Hospitals, an essential part of the local service, could also improve the way they target people with severe mental illness. The use of beds in wards for people with acute illnesses was reviewed over a six month period. The percentage of bed days used by people with a psychotic diagnosis (a good indicator of targeting – about 40% seems to be appropriate) varied widely between districts; in some hospitals it was as low as 18%. This implies that hospital beds are sometimes used for people who do not really need them. The occupancy by people with a psychotic diagnosis was not associated with the level of social deprivation, implying that the efficiency of targeting was a consequence of clinical and management processes, not of local environmental factors. The rate of readmission also varied widely and was unrelated to deprivation.

If all hospitals used their beds as selectively as the 'best' two in the sample, the total number of beds in England and Wales could be reduced by 12%, releasing £100 million for the development of community services.

Useful indicators for the monitoring of performance could include:

♦ a regular 'caseload census' of all community based professionals, using the classification based on diagnostic categories and previous admissions to hospital which was employed in this study;
♦ regular monitoring of the frequency of contact and length of time on the caseload for those included in the census;
♦ regular assessment of the use of acute hospital beds, by diagnostic group, to monitor the use of bed days;
♦ monitoring of the readmissions of individuals and the time lapse between them.

Management and coordination
Professionals need clearer guidance and better management if they are to focus on those with the most serious problems. Too often they work almost completely independently, without regular monitoring of their caseload or open discussion of their activities. Too much of the work of many psychiatrists is based in hospitals, quite separately from community teams. The community mental health team should be the focus of the local service, through which referrals are taken, and access is obtained to other resources such as hospital or day care. This would enable consistent criteria for entry to all parts of the service, which would improve its overall target efficiency. Psychiatrists should work across all parts of the service, and ensure that the service functions as a coherent system.

One important development is the 'care programme approach' for coordinating the different elements of care for vulnerable individuals. Despite being a policy requirement since 1991, it has still not been established in many places.

Purchasing authorities must take a far more active role than they have done so far. They should specify very clearly the aims and priorities of the service, with explicit targets and timescales for their achievement. The information available to managers and purchasers for monitoring the activity and the achievements of mental health services has always been very limited. The kinds of information gathered in this study could, if collected routinely, provide a sound basis for assessing performance.

The balance of hospital and community services of different types is being examined in the audits which follow, to see whether a comprehensive network of care is available. This should include the things that local users want, such as out of hours access and practical help. The targeting of community and hospital services will be compared with that of other districts, to identify any opportunities for deploying the existing resources more effectively.

Useful indicators for the monitoring of performance could include:

- the numbers of people receiving care programmes and on supervision registers, in comparison with national figures and those for other local areas;
- the frequency of reviews for people on care programmes and supervision registers.

Box 4.1
Key issues

The 'Production of Welfare' framework

- Inputs
- Outputs
- Outcomes
- Effectiveness
- Efficiency
- Measuring efficiency
- Proxy measures
- The Audit Commission and value for money work
- Day surgery
- Management of medical beds
- Mental health care

CONCLUSIONS   Efficiency considerations run through the entire process of producing health care. Economy, or minimizing the costs of resource inputs, is essential at one end, while assessment of effectiveness in attaining the goals of the process is important at the other. The more that reliable evidence is available about the relationships between inputs, processes and final outputs, the easier the task of measuring efficiency becomes. If certain processes, such as developing care programmes for individuals with mental illness, coordinated by key workers, are known to be associated with better outcomes then their presence can be used as proxy measures for outcomes.

Specific performance indicators for the efficiency of different areas of health care have been developed from national studies, carried out by the Audit Commission. Examples in the areas of day surgery, medical bed management and mental health care have been described. Some of the measures developed in the study can continue to be applied locally, on a regular basis, to keep a check on the performance of the local service. Where comparisons with other providers are available, these are usually valuable as 'benchmarks' for the comparison of performance. Comparisons of the same service over time, using the same indicators, are also valuable.

SUMMARY

The combination of local, regular monitoring information and specific, large-scale data collections by an independent body is the best way to measure efficiency. There is a balance to be achieved between the development of ever better measures which use knowledge that might not previously have been available and the use of existing indicators which are more widely available, to allow comparison between areas and over time.

FURTHER READING

◆ Audit Commission (1990), *A Short Cut to Better Services:* Day Surgery in England and Wales, HMSO, London.

◆ Audit Commission (1991), *Measuring Quality: the Patient's View of Day Surgery*, HMSO, London.

◆ Audit Commission (1992), *Lying in Wait: the Use of Medical Beds in Acute Hospitals*, HMSO, London.

◆ Audit Commission (1994), *Finding a Place: a Review of Mental Health Services for Adults*, HMSO, London.

◆ Knapp, M. (1984), *The Economics of Social Care*. Basingstoke: Macmillan.

REFERENCES

Audit Commission (1990), *A Short Cut to Better Services: Day Surgery in England and Wales*. London: HMSO.

Audit Commission (1991), *Measuring Quality: the Patient's View of Day Surgery*. London: HMSO.

Audit Commission (1992), *Lying in Wait: the Use of Medical Beds in Acute Hospitals*. London: HMSO.

Audit Commission (1994), *Finding a Place: a Review of Mental Health Services for Adults.* London: HMSO.

Bebbington, A.C. and Davies, B.P. (1983), Equity and efficiency in the allocation of the personal social services. *Journal of Social Policy,* 1: 309–330.

Davies, B. and Knapp, M. (1981), *Old People's Homes and the Production of Welfare.* London: Routledge and Kegan Paul.

Department of Health (1991), *Health Service Indicators.* London: HMSO.

Glover, G., Robin, E., Emami, J. and Arabsheibani, R. (1994), *The Distribution of Need for Mental Health Services – A Study of the Socio-Demographic Predictors of Prevalence of Psychiatric Admission in a London Region.* Final Report to the Department of Health of a Project Commissioned Under the Research and Development Initiative.

Knapp, M. (1984), *The Economics of Social Care.* Basingstoke: Macmillan.

Oakland, J.S. (1989), *Total Quality Management.* London: Heinemann.

OPCS (1991), *Regional Hospital Statistics.* London: HMSO.

Yates, J.M. (1982), *Hospital Beds.* London: Heinemann.

SECTION II

PERFORMANCE BASED APPROACHES

SECTION INTRODUCTION In this section we focus on the different ways of viewing and studying performance. Most readers will be familiar with the pressure for clinicians and managers to develop Performance Indicators (PIs). To be of use PIs must be practical and the benchmark tests of their relevance is the degree to which they influence clinical practice and management control. As such PIs need to be tailored to specific needs and require multidisciplinary collaboration in their design and development. Often there is a tension between PIs developed locally and those imposed nationally. Sometimes PIs also develop because of benchmarking whereby one group of clinicians or managers examine systems already in place and seek to build upon this resource.

A key aspect to understanding the concept of performance is understanding the concept of 'quality' in relation to value for money. The rise of consumerism as typified by the Patient's Charter brings a broader perspective to the notion of performance than that perceived solely from a clinical point of view. Clinicians need to be aware of this perspective in order to appreciate that failure to meet broader quality standards cannot be compensated by clinical standards alone. For example, clinicians may not be too concerned about waiting times for certain patient groups but all patient groups are now covered by relevant contractual clauses and financial penalties may be imposed when these targets are not met.

Most clinical and management systems are process oriented. That is, they concern courses of action and sequences of observation, measurement, assessment, interpretation, decision and action over extended periods of time. Historically clinical control systems have been dominated by the exception case review which has meant little more than peer review based on an individual's assessment of a colleague's clinical judgement. Equally too, management control systems have tended to rely too much on the imperfect budgetary control model as the key mechanism for control. These approaches are no longer acceptable. There is a recognition that, in many respects, it is the non-financial reporting mechanisms that are relevant to ensuring patient care and satisfaction. Several experiments have taken place to revise this classic incremental budgetary model but these have so far failed.

While purchasers are indeed concerned to exercise control through the contractual arrangements which they agree with providers, this section chooses to focus at the provider level drawing illustrative examples from general practice and secondary care settings.

USING PERFORMANCE INDICATORS AS AN AID TO EVALUATING VALUE FOR MONEY

CHAPTER 5

John J. Glynn and Michael Murphy

OBJECTIVES

◆ To discuss the nature of performance indicators.

◆ To illustrate the use of performance indicators in measuring efficiency and effectiveness.

◆ To consider the managerial implementation of performance indicators.

INTRODUCTION This chapter provides contextual background to some of the discussion provided elsewhere in the book. Its focus is to discuss in a little more detail the importance of performance indicators (PIs) to the management of organizations, and in particular the achievement of value for money. It explicitly acknowledges the extent to which the quest for ensuring value for money from public services has led to great efforts being made to develop measures which can be used to assess whether it is in fact being achieved. Generically, these measures are normally referred to as PIs and they attempt to measure the performance of public sector organizations along the three core dimensions of value for money: economy, efficiency and effectiveness. In principle, it is relatively straightforward to develop measures of economy and efficiency, although there are cases where the measurement of efficiency can be problematic. Effectiveness, which is normally much less easy to measure, can be thought of as comprising three sub-elements: output, outcome and impact. As will be discussed later, the measurement of outcome and impact can pose real problems. One of these problems, and a very pointed one in the NHS, is exactly what it is whose effectiveness is being measured and who should have the responsibility of measuring this effectiveness. For example, at the service delivery level should it be the case that management have responsibility for administrative effectiveness and clinicians for treatment effectiveness, as measured in technical or epidemiological terms?

In the private sector much attention is focused on the existence of one 'catch all' PI – profit. Many commentators propound the rather simplistic view that profit is all that matters. Whilst this 'bottom line' figure is undoubtedly the most visible indicator of performance in the private sector, both internally and externally, no private sector enterprise can be managed successfully by only paying attention to profit. In fact, profit only comes from the successful achievement of a whole series of sub-objectives, both financial and non-financial. Each of these sub-objectives requires the development of PIs to enable the effectiveness with which it is being achieved to be assessed. Examples of such indicators include: sales per square metre of floor space and the percentage of repeat sales. Profit is a residual which results from the successful achievement of the sub-objectives. If profit at the anticipated level is not being achieved then it is to these sub-objectives and their PIs that management will turn to pinpoint the specific causes of the failure. The lesson here is that in the euphoria of their promotion of the new public sector management, claimed to be derived from the best private sector principles, some advocates over-promote the importance of a 'bottom line' indicator, particularly for management purposes. It must be remembered that health care faces various imperatives, e.g. an economic imperative which demands a balanced budget and a clinical imperative which demands quality health care. This inevitably means that multiple measures of effectiveness will be required and that these will be needed at different levels of aggregation. What is needed is a 'broad scorecard' of PIs. This 'scorecard' needs to incorporate PIs that are useful both *internally* to management and clinicians in helping them to achieve better and more cost-effective health care and *externally* to facilitate accountability by managers and clinicians to the government and public for their use of resources and achievement of healthcare objectives.

This notion of a 'broad scorecard' of potential PIs clearly brings to the fore of the debate about PIs the question of for whose benefit PIs are intended. As indicated above, they can be used as a means of demonstrating managerial and clinical achievements both internally, as part of an organization's internal control process, or externally in the annual reports of organizations or those produced by third party assessors such as the Audit Commission. It needs to be clearly recognized that public sector enterprises, and the differing groups of people involved with them, are involved in a multiplicity of different accountability processes, some financial, some clinical, and some political. These different accountability processes will require the development and use of different PIs. A danger which must be guarded against is that of producing PIs for cathartic reasons. As with all data, the utility of PIs rests with their capacity to provide meaningful and useful information, specifically information that can be acted upon to improve the achievement healthcare objectives. It is also important to recognize that this type of information is needed for all aspects of healthcare organizations – not just high profile direct patient care aspects. Ultimately, the overall quality of the achievement of the health service requires well managed support services (medical records, cleaning, catering, computer systems, building maintenance) as well as more purely clinical services. Badly managed support services can be a drain on scarce resources and cause inefficiencies and ineffectiveness in the provision of patient care. PIs need to be cooperatively developed and accepted by senior management teams, including but not limited to the finance function, line management and clinicians. This obvious and basic point is often overlooked by senior management who impose poorly thought out performance measurement systems. This is likely to alienate those responsible for carrying out activities as they perceive the imposed PIs as being irrelevant and/or unachievable.

There are four parts to this chapter. The first concentrates on the general principles involved in establishing useful PIs. The next two parts discuss issues germane to the development of PIs that focus on efficiency and effectiveness. The final part builds on this base by providing an overview of the extent to which PIs become an integral part of overall clinical and management control.

WHAT ARE PERFORMANCE INDICATORS?

Performance indicators have been defined as expressions, in measurable terms, of programme objectives, or the relative achievement of an objective(s). In essence they are financially or non-financially based measures that 'indicate' the standard (target) or actual results for identified contributory elements of a particular activity or programme. They are not abstract concepts and they have no meaningful existence independently of a defined programme, or activity, and the associated objectives. Failure to specify programme objectives and anticipated effects will have adverse implications for accountability, planning and control. Indeed, without clearly stated objectives and measurable indicators it is difficult for purchasers and providers to determine if particular programmes or services are in fact achieving intended results. As a Canadian *Guide* has stated:

> Without a clear understanding of what is to be accomplished, it will be difficult to plan and direct operations to ensure accomplishment. Unless there is clarity and specificity of programme objectives and effects, programme evaluation studies or performance information systems focusing on measuring programme objectives and effects will have limited use as either an accountability tool or a feedback

mechanism for making ongoing management decisions. (Auditor General of Canada 1981, p. 7.)

A potential problem here is that people may not want to define objectives and resourcing clearly as by doing so they are defining their own accountabilities much more precisely. Thus there is a natural tendency to avoid doing so and this is reinforced by the fact that not all programme objectives may be readily amenable to rigorous management. There are also a variety of constraints: ethical, state-of-the art, legal, financial, administrative and so on which may affect the types of measures that can be implemented. However, the continuance of these constraints should not simply be assumed. Where constraints are currently perceived as existing, they should be periodically reviewed to determine whether or not they do in fact continue to exist. Whilst the authors would concur with the view that indicators should be developed and measured at the lowest practicable level within an organization they also believe that it is an inescapable senior management (and audit) function to determine that they are adequate and reflect best current practice. Accordingly, agreement must be reached as to the validity and reliability of each indicator, the accuracy of underlying data and records, the appropriateness of performance standards or targets and the nature of the reporting mechanism, both internal and external.

Used appropriately, PIs can make four key contributions to improving organizational performance:

1. They can be used to demonstrate the achievement of results in relation to predetermined standards, targets or goals. This is useful for both contract management and staff motivational purposes. Contracts typically specify key control and quality PIs and clearly specified goals and measures also make it clear to staff what is expected of them and how they are doing.
2. They can assist in the planning and monitoring of budgets. The annual budgetary process in most organizations, public and private sector, tends to be both incrementalist and biased towards resource inputs. In this context, incrementalist means that the budget for the previous financial period and the actual results for that financial period tend to be the base for the next period's budget with attention being focused primarily on changes from that base. This is fraught with all sorts of inequities since such a budgetary process is heavily influenced by what can be collectively termed 'organizational politics'. Over the years a number of alternative budgetary models have been experimented with. For example, the Planning, Programming Budgeting System (PPBS) and Zero-Based Budgeting (ZBB), see Glossary for definitions of these terms, both had a number of conceptual advantages but unfortunately these were outweighed by their not inconsiderable administrative disadvan-

tages. Approaches such as PPBS and ZBB place a heavy emphasis on quantitative measures of output which are then translated into financial consequences. The traditional input oriented approach to budgeting is typically geared to the functional design of an organization and provides little or no information about the activities undertaken within the various departments and other functional centres (see Glynn (1993) and Glynn *et al.* (1994)).

3. They can help in bridging the gap in meeting the deficiencies inherent in the traditional budgetary process by providing concrete evidence to support the allocation and, where necessary, the redistribution of scarce resources. The use of PIs emphasizes a more process, rather than 'politically', orientated approach to budgeting which makes it less easy to avoid the difficult 'value' questions that are inevitable in health care. If greater use is made of PIs in determining budget priorities then such indicators can also provide useful information when it comes to assessing alternative approaches to service delivery.

4. They can assist in the difficult discussions that always take place in the trade-off between the efficiency and effectiveness of service delivery.

To achieve these gains PIs need to be carefully designed and appropriately implemented. Likierman (1993) reports on a research project involving 500 public sector managers over a three year period. This research indicates four groups of concerns that need to be taken into account in the managerial use of PIs. These are:

1. *Concept*: this concentrates on a clarity of understanding of what it is that the use of PIs is intended to achieve. Thus, it is important to ensure that indicators include all elements integral to what is being measured; to have sufficient indicators to avoid unnecessary distortion but not so many as to lead to a loss of focus; to incorporate qualitative as well as quantitative indicators; and to acknowledge explicitly the political imperatives inherent in public sector organizations.

2. *Preparation*: the focus here is on preparing the way for the implementation of the indicators. The evidence suggests that they are likely to be more useful when they are 'owned' by management as a result of their participation in the development of the indicators; that they need to avoid an overly simplistic short-term orientation; that they fairly reflect the efforts of managers (e.g. by the exclusion of non-controllable elements); that they have greater acceptability the more they are similar with those used in comparable organizations; and that the levels of any standards or targets inherent in the indicators need to be realistic and accepted by line management. The authors are struck by the classic military dictum

about time spent in reconnaissance never being wasted. However, their experience suggests that all too often such reconnaissance is not carried out.

3. *Implementation*: the core issue here is summarized in the cliché that 'if a thing is worth doing it is worth doing properly'. Unfortunately, all too often PI systems are implemented almost as an afterthought. Thus: they are not allowed time to develop – they are regarded as definitive from Day 1; they are implemented as macro-policing systems superimposed on existing systems rather than being integrated with such systems; they are designed for the accountees rather than the accountors – i.e. they may help to measure achievement, or the lack of it, rather than the factors leading to particular levels of achievement; the pressure, particularly external political pressure, to implement a system of performance indicators can all too easily lead to the use of inappropriate proxy measures; and there is often a lack of clarity in the accountability relationships upon which the indicators are intended to provide information.

4. *Use*: this is perhaps the darkest area of all. By their very nature and no matter how carefully designed and implemented PIs, particularly in the complex world of the public sector, are inevitably simplifications. This is not by any means to deny their importance and value. Rather it is to emphasize that they must be used with caution and understanding. Unfortunately, they all too often provoke a knee-jerk reaction when they are produced. They are used as definitive information on which value judgements are based rather than as indicators. They are regarded as providing answers rather than as identifying areas which warrant further questions. Questions such as: is the underlying data to be trusted; what are the managerial or clinical implications; what further investigation is needed; to what extent have there been trade-offs in policy/programme implementation; and most importantly, are standards/targets still appropriate in the current environment, are all too often ignored.

Likierman's research, which is supported by a growing body of similar work, does not provide a recipe for the implementation of PI based management systems. In many respects it is a case of 'new wine in old bottles' as it is strongly redolent of much of the earlier work on the implementation of budgetary management systems. Like this earlier work its value is in its attempt to promote a questioning approach to the implementation of PIs and its particular value is doing this using the vocabulary of, and examples drawn from, the changing management context of the public sector.

MONITORING
EFFICIENCY   It is a basic management responsibility to ensure that methods of operation and work practices are the most efficient, given prevail-

ing conditions and available technology. All too often, as the volume of activity increases, there is a disproportionate growth in resources used in comparison to the growth in workload. Efficiency is not simply productivity, i.e. the ratio of inputs to outputs. Rather it is the relationship of productivity to a performance standard or target. Usually, efficiency is measured in terms of a rate of production, the work content in time or the unit cost of an output. Based on Glynn (1993), consider the example of the Barchester Hospital Pharmacy shown in Box 5.1.

Box 5.1
Example: Barchester Hospital Pharmacy

A hospital employs two pharmacists who each work a 35 hour week. The standard *rate of production* is 6 prescriptions per hour; which in terms of *work content in time* is 10 minutes per prescription. Each pharmacist is paid £8.40 per hour so that the *unit cost per prescription* is £1.40. Statistics show that on average 924 prescriptions are dispensed each month.

Efficiency can be measured as follows:

$$1. \quad \frac{\text{Actual rate per hour}}{\text{Standard rate per hour}} = \frac{6.60 \text{ prescriptions}}{6 \text{ prescriptions}} \times 100$$

$$= 110\%$$

$$2. \quad \frac{\text{Standard time/prescription}}{\text{Actual time/prescription}} = \frac{10 \text{ minutes}}{9.09 \text{ minutes}} \times 100$$

$$= 110\%$$

$$3. \quad \frac{\text{Standard cost/prescription}}{\text{Actual time/prescription}} = \frac{£1.40}{£1.27} \times 100 = 110\%$$

Various points arise from this simple example. In comparing actual costs with standard costs management should first consider the economy of operations. Efficiency measures are only possible when outputs can be separated from each other and possess uniform characteristics. A straightforward repetitive process, as in our example, meets these criteria. There are instances where efficiency measures are neither practicable nor possible. An example of this might be a hospital's Accident and Emergency (A&E) department. Typically, such a department is staffed to function at some predetermined (perhaps contracted) level of activity but in practice caseload will follow a random pattern that at best approximates to anticipated peaks, troughs and caseload mix of activity. In addition, the very nature of the service offered is likely to involve regular bouts of frenzied activity. Hospitals, and indeed purchasers, are required to at least contemplate if not worst then severe case scenarios in planning and resourcing A&E departments. The high variability of the volume and type of work of such departments means that the type of routine efficiency performance indicator that might be helpful for a pharmacy is quite irrelevant. Instead, use is likely to be made of different approaches such as crisis management models and other scenario techniques. This said, the majority of patient treatment activity and support services do lend themselves to being monitored by efficiency indicators and by the comparison of such indicators with appropriate standards. Such standards might be derived from (budgetary) targets, time series (e.g. previous days/weeks/months), similar units (local, regional, national, international), private sector competitors or policy objectives.

When an internally agreed standard of performance does not exist, it can be useful to compare present performance with some previous base period (e.g. the corresponding month last year). Such a base period output/input ratio is termed an historical standard or target. The use of such a standard assumes that past performance should be indicative of required future performance – this may be inappropriate. For example, if a new service is building up a base of clientele then one would expect efficiency to improve over time. Nevertheless, in the absence of any other information, such an approach does at least enable some insight to be gained into the pattern of activity and output. Geographical comparisons are likely to be even more problematic, e.g. because of differing underlying epidemiology. Also the development of differing organizations in the internal market which hitherto might have shared/pooled statistical information but which now fear that to do so might reduce their 'competitiveness' makes such comparisons less likely to be truly informative. External agencies such as the Audit Commission do produce some data based on geographical areas and this can be used as a benchmark for organizations against which to assess their own service delivery, but this must be done with some caution. Standards and targets can often be imported or agreed internally by consultation. Frequently the various professional groups involved in health care will develop guidance on best practice, thereby providing a means for the development of suitable PIs. Required levels of activity can be gauged from contracts which, as indicated earlier, will often stipulate expected service efficiency criteria. Private sector comparisons may be useful, particularly when seeking to set efficiency measures for support activities such as those related to accommodation and catering services. Inter-authority comparators may, again because of the internal market, be less easy to obtain but, again, external agencies such as the Audit Commission can provide benchmarking information. Their reports cover a range of clinical and support services such as ones dealing with the maintenance of medical records, the level of management costs, the work of hospital doctors and the management of radiology services. Many organizations often fail to make sufficient use of available intra-departmental, intra-unit and intra-authority performance information. Patient management in, for example, the various outpatient clinics of an acute hospital Trust has many similar characteristics and these should be monitored and compared.

To summarize, the key elements that arise in implementing efficiency oriented performance indicators are:

1. An awareness of, and the determination to accomplish, programme goals in the most economical and efficient manner;
2. the need to plan activities in the most efficient way for the given level of resourcing;
3. the need to have a structured organization whose administration should follow prescribed work measures and procedures in order to avoid duplication of effort, unnecessary tasks, idle time etc; and
4. the provision of work instructions, in sufficient detail, to staff who are suitably qualified and trained for the duties they are required to perform.

Efficiency levels clearly impact on the quality and level of service provision. The efficiency of an operation is influenced by the quantity and quality of available resources. Changes in any of these aspects are difficult to interpret without monitoring all of them. Given a satisfactory rate of efficiency, further improvements might be made only at the expense of level or quality of service. Conversely, significant improvements in quality or level of service might only be possible with a significant increase in unit cost. For example, varying the delivery frequency of internal mail, that is the level of service, would have an effect on the cost of delivery. As another example, apparent savings resulting from an increase in the efficiency with which day patients are processed might be offset by the re-referrals due to a reduction in the quality of service offered.

MONITORING EFFECTIVENESS   As stated above, effectiveness embraces the notions of output, outcome and impact. Whilst outputs may well be measured fairly readily, in themselves they provide little information. Outcome, crudely as the patient recovered, is far more important. The problem is that outcomes are not necessarily immediate and may only be identifiable months, or even years, after an intervention. Some patient activity outcomes may be relatively easy to monitor, e.g. minor surgery, but some are far less easy to monitor, e.g. community based psychiatric care. The general view is that there should be an increasing emphasis on outcome monitoring. However, with the development of the internal market has come 'contract accountability' (Glynn 1996) which means that service providers have to 'account' according to contractual obligations.

Depending on the precise contractual terms, the emphasis is normally in terms of specified procedures, inputs and outputs. Who then monitors outcomes? Sometimes this is the service provider, sometimes the purchaser (such as a fundholding GP practice) but all too often it is not done on a coherent and consistent basis. Little or no attention is paid to impact since it is a far less tangible concept, related more to overall policy questions, and is frequently the result of a combination of different policy initiatives/programmes. For example, the policy objective of reducing the incidence of drug abuse is reflected in a variety of different programmes involving the NHS, Social Services, the Department of Education and Employment and police forces.

Within healthcare organizations two aspects of effectiveness are important: administrative effectiveness which is concerned with how efficiently activities are undertaken, budgeted output levels achieved and overall operational effectiveness monitored; and clinical effectiveness which relates in part to output but is more specifically focused on outcome. In Donabedian's (1966) terms outcome is 'a change in a patient's current or future health status that can be attributed to antecedent health care'.

A helpful approach here is to think of the provision of health care in terms of the model shown in Figure 5.1.

Administrative effectiveness will concentrate largely on the process (activity) dimension and will be concerned with issues such as whether or not immunization targets are being achieved; whether or not ambulance response times are being achieved and whether or not Patient's Charter standards (e.g. as regards waiting lists or the use of named nurses) are being met. In many ways administrative effectiveness is concerned with whether or not the antecedent conditions necessary for desired clinical outcomes are being achieved. It relates to the sub-objectives, achievement of which is regarded as contributing to the 'bottom line'. That 'bottom line' is clinical effectiveness which is more concerned with outcomes in Donabedian's terms. However, administrative effectiveness is not restricted to non-clinical activities. There are numerous well-established clinically related measures of administrative effec-

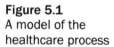

Figure 5.1
A model of the healthcare process

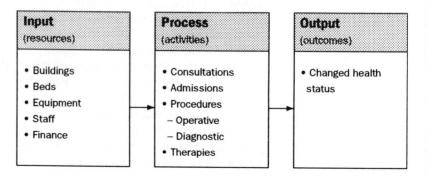

Input (resources)	Process (activities)	Output (outcomes)

• Buildings
• Beds
• Equipment
• Staff
• Finance
	• Consultations
	• Admissions
	• Procedures
	  – Operative
	  – Diagnostic
	• Therapies
		• Changed health
		  status

tiveness. In large part these are proxy clinical outcome measures and include ones such as: reinfection rates, readmission rates, adverse drug reactions, usage of inappropriate medication, and unplanned readmissions to theatre. Most indicators of this type are negative ones – they are measures of failure rather than success. There are two main reasons for this. Firstly, it is difficult to design measures of success for clinical interventions and secondly clinicians have not always been willing to cooperate fully in the development of such measures, which has meant that measures have all too often been developed by managers, and even politicians. Fortunately, with the emphasis on quality promoted by the White Paper *Working for Patients* (Department of Health 1989) and increasingly reflected in the internal market's contracting processes, this is changing and clinicians are more and more willing to get involved in the development of outcome measures.

The difficulty remains, however, that any meaningful assessment of outcome can only be made if there is a clear statement of objectives. As we indicated at the start of this chapter, individuals for a variety of reasons are not always willing participants in the preparation of such statements. There is also the problem of different actors in the healthcare process perhaps having different objectives and expectations. Thus, there is the individual clinician's therapeutic objective/expectation in treating a patient; there is the individual patient's expectation of the outcome of the treatment; and there is the health authority's expectation of the treatment of groups of patients by the clinicians in a provider unit. The full support of clinicians is essential if objectives are to be clearly stated for clinical interventions. Fortunately there is evidence that this is increasingly forthcoming and that we are moving towards a primacy of role for outcome measurement with the objective set out in the Green Paper *The Health of the Nation* (Department of Health 1991).

> Outcome measurement – that is measurement of the success of particular actions or sets of actions in improving health – shows not only change, but relates that change to identifiable actions, resources or events. It enables specification and quantification of objectives increasingly to be not in terms of process, but of improvements to health. It allows the effectiveness of policies to be evaluated.

This move towards an increasing primacy for outcome measurement in the use of PIs is evidenced by the growing use, on a regular basis, of mechanisms which explicitly incorporate outcome oriented PIs. Clear examples of this are the incorporation of such PIs as a standard part of the contracts agreed between purchaser and providers and the development of such PIs by medical professionals through the clinical and medical audit processes. Increasingly clinicians are working in a world where PIs are incorporated into contracts and protocols. As outlined above, these will relate to both processes and the anticipated outcomes for the patient. Also, internal review (via, for example, clinical and medical audit) is facilitated by the increasing adoption of explicit PIs.

MANAGERIAL IMPLEMENTATION OF PERFORMANCE INDICATORS

Earlier in this chapter we discussed the desirable characteristics of PIs and then proceeded to look at some issues regarding the design of indicators of efficiency and effectiveness. In this concluding section we want to turn to the use of PIs by management. In doing so we will move away from the macro issues of their being used to enhance control over public sector organizations – our focus will be on their use within such organizations. This is not to suggest that indicators designed for external accountability have no influence on the use of indicators for internal managerial processes. Far from it. As Smith (1995) clearly points out, the history of PIs in the NHS is one of a meld of internal and external accountability. Initially promoted as a means of helping managers they rapidly became a means of increasing government control with this feedback not just reinforcing their initial role as an aid to management but also developing a new role as a rationale for management action – 'we will be appraised on this basis so we must pay attention to it'. The hospital league tables of the last couple of years are merely a heightened, and more public, example of this process – one which is not unknown in the private sector with the emphasis on measures such as earnings per share. This 'internalization' process can lead to a number of potentially dysfunctional effects which management need to guard against. Smith identifies the principal ones as being:

1. *Tunnel vision*: a common, and understandable, human reaction is that if something is not being measured (i.e. it is not included in the PIs) then it is not regarded as being important. Conversely, those things for which there are PIs are by definition important. The consequence is that the former get ignored, and all too often as we have suggested earlier, these may be the really important things – the desired outcomes, simply because they are difficult to measure or because people prefer to justify strategy on broad policy grounds. Instead the emphasis is placed on what is more easily measured (managed?), e.g. inputs and procedures. This can easily lead to an emphasis on technical quality, i.e. doing something in a technically optimal way, rather than a questioning of whether it needs to be done at all.

2. *Suboptimization*: this is a common failing in devolved management systems, including those in the private sector, and derives from the 'looking after my own patch' phenomenon. In the public sector it is more prevalent because of the multidimen-

sional nature of organizational objectives and the lack of a common dimension with which to integrate differing organizational activities. The consequences are that interdependencies are all too often not recognized; that focus is placed on sub-objectives and that overall corporate outcomes are ignored. It goes with a rather egocentric 'my part of the organization is highly efficient' and fits well with an incrementalist approach to budgeting.

3. *Myopia*: this may be myopia in the sense discussed in the previous section but equally dysfunctional, and very common, is myopia in terms of time frame. Most performance indicators have a short-term focus (accounting profit being a classic example). This can be reinforced by the short-term tenure of most public sector managers. The combined effect is an emphasis on today rather than tomorrow, on cure rather than prevention.

4. *Convergence*: or 'running with the pack'. The issue here is that in public services, and in health care particularly, there is a lack of objective scientific benchmarks. Instead there is 'accepted/best practice' with great emphasis being placed on comparison with other units/organizations. This can all too often lead to managers seeking to 'keep their heads down' and avoid pressure and adverse comment.

5. *Gaming*: this is the well-known phenomenon in the public sector of managers seeking to maintain some slack in their resourcing and outputs. It largely derives from historic performance being used as a prime comparator for future performance and the determinant of future resourcing. Managers have an incentive not to perform too well – if they do perform at a high standard then this will become the benchmark for future performance.

6. *Ossification*: this is a synthesis of some of the earlier points. A rigid system of performance measurement will tend to discourage innovation because it is unlikely that the system (and particularly existing PIs) will reflect the value added derived from the innovation. The benefits may well be longer term rather than short term; they may not be captured at all by the current measurement system; the manager will be seen as doing something different and come under more intense scrutiny and even if the success is reflected by the system the manager may simply be making life more difficult for himself in the future.

7. *Misrepresentation*: this is a different form of gaming. A rigid system of PIs may be such as to differentially value activities and processes. Thus, managers will have an incentive to report their activities in the higher valued categories, e.g. a DRG with a higher workload rating rather than the one actually involved.

Many of these problems stem from regarding PIs as neutral reporting mechanisms and ignoring the contexts in which they will be used. This is exactly the same debate as that relating to the use of budgets and in fact PIs are really little more than an attempt to bridge the gap between financial and operational budgets. This is not to denigrate the importance of bridging that gap – this is in fact crucial if proper multidimensional measures of performance are to be achieved. Rather it is to say that the lessons that have been, sometimes painfully, learned in the implementation of improved budgetary procedures must not be forgotten in the development and use of PIs.

Fortunately, there is evidence that purchasers and providers of health care are increasingly systematizing their understanding and analysis of patient flows. By doing so it becomes much easier to determine what are relevant PIs, and what levels performance standards should be set, both in terms of processes and outputs/outcomes. Figure 5.2 presents a simplified form of the standard patient flows within an acute surgical specialty based on work

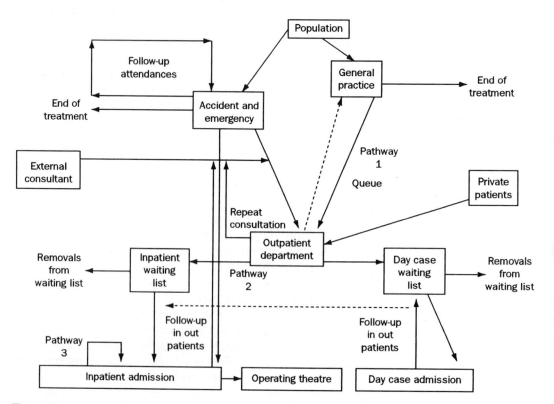

Figure 5.2
Patient flows within an acute surgical specialty.

carried out by South East Thames Regional Health Authority as reported in its *Annual Public Health Report* (SETRHA 1991).

The three patient flows identified in this model, prepared from the point of view of a purchaser of health care, are:

1. referrals from a general practitioner to an outpatient clinic for consultation, perhaps followed by an elective admission to either inpatient care or day case care;
2. entries to inpatient care via an A&E department;
3. referral via an external consultant, e.g. a tertiary referral.

Identifying these flows enables a purchaser, and by counterpart a provider unit, to focus PIs on critical elements of these pathways. These might include at a simplistic level: proportion of general practitioner referrals resulting in day case surgery; waiting times for day case surgery; waiting times for outpatient referrals; number of patients seen in A&E department and waiting time for follow-up visits by inpatients to outpatient clinics. At a more sophisticated level, PIs might be set which take into account the socio-economic and demographic characteristics of the population for which health care is being purchased and break the analysis (PIs) down into different diagnosis related group (DRGs). Similarly, they might be extended via a more detailed model to local performance within the provider unit. Similar pathway analysis might be used taking into account the movement of patients between wards and radiography, occupational therapy and physiotherapy. Using this type of analysis enables clinicians and managers to focus on the linkages between different elements of the healthcare process, thereby obtaining an integrated view, rather than concentrating simply on the effectiveness (or even technical efficiency) of part of the whole process. This approach is much more compatible with the new approaches to healthcare audit that are now being developed (Morris *et al.* 1995) and facilitates the development of *relevant* PIs.

SUMMARY

PIs are increasingly becoming a valuable tool for managers and clinicians alike. Their development to date has been evolutionary and this process is likely to continue, reflecting that as and when our understanding of processes and outcomes improves so should the way in which we develop PIs. It is also important to recognize that PIs, in one form or another, are a fact of life. They are not going to go away. Therefore it is important that clinicians and managers participate fully in the development of PIs which both properly reflect their performance for the purposes of external accountability and help them in their search for better healthcare provision.

***FURTHER
READING***

◆ Readers should periodically review the relevant publications of the Audit Commission (Accounts Commission in Scotland) and the National Audit Office. These reports tend to highlight best practice, including discussions on the appropriateness of relevant performance indicators. If they are to be effective, performance indicators need to be tailored to specific circumstances.

◆ It is particularly useful to make enquiries of the relevant faculties and Royal Colleges to review latest practice on the development and implementation of performance indicators for specialist services.

REFERENCES

Auditor General of Canada (1981), *Audit Guide: Auditing Efficiency.* Canada: Ottawa.

Department of Health (1989), *Working for Patients.* London: HMSO.

Department of Health (1991), *The Health of the Nation: A Consultative Document for Health in England.* London: HMSO.

Donabedian, A. (1966), Evaluating the quality of medical care. *Millbank Memorial Fund Quarterly*, 44: 169.

Glynn, J.J. (1993), *Public Sector Financial Control and Accounting* (2nd ed). Oxford: Blackwell.

Glynn, J.J. (1996), *Proceedings of a Conference on Performance Auditing.* Paris: OECD (in press).

Glynn, J.J., Perrin, J. and Murphy, M.P. (1994), *Accounting for Managers.* London: Chapman and Hall.

Likierman, A. (1993), Performance indicators: 20 early lessons from managerial use. *Public Money and Management*, October.

Morris, B., Bell, L. and Solieri, A. (1995), The use of blueprinting in auditing healthcare processes. *International Conference EUROMA*, University of Twente, Netherlands.

Smith, P. (1995), Outcome-related performance indicators and organisational control in the public sector. In Holloway, J., Lewis, J. and Mallory, G. (Eds), *Measurement and Evaluation*. London: Sage.

South East Thames Regional Health Authority (1991), *Annual Public Health Report.* Bexhill: South East Thames Regional Health Authority.

QUALITY AND VALUE FOR MONEY

CHAPTER 6

Barbara Morris and Louise Bell

Barbara Morris and Louise Bell

OBJECTIVES

> ◆ To explore the significance of different views of quality.
>
> ◆ To discuss the part quality plays in considering value for money.
>
> ◆ To examine ways of measuring quality, and their impact on service management.
>
> ◆ To examine current ways of dealing with quality in the NHS, and the implications of these for patients, providers and purchasers.
>
> ◆ To consider the limitations of current approaches to quality, and suggest ways in which these can be overcome, so as to provide better value for money.

INTRODUCTION   The primary purpose of this chapter is to consider how an understanding of quality colours or influences our understanding of what constitutes value for money. We describe different views of what quality is, and the impact of these views on the way in which quality is managed, and on value for money, are assessed. Current approaches to managing quality are discussed, and we conclude that limited views of the nature of quality impact significantly on the overall value for money achieved in health services because current methods of measuring and subsequently 'improving the quality' are too narrowly focused. We also discuss the way the main professional and managerial stakeholders are influencing the development of the quality agenda, and conclude that the current approaches to value for money led by those providing and purchasing health care could be improved by incorporating explicitly a broader view of quality.

BACKGROUND   In 1989 the government White Paper *Working for Patients* (Department of Health 1989) introduced significant structural and philosophical change into health services; with a focal theme of the paper referring to the requirement to achieve greater value for money in health services. The paper referred to the purchaser/ provider split, the creation of the GP fundholder role, and for hospital clinicians the introduction of wide-scale medical audit amongst medical staff. The paper states:

> To ensure that all concerned with delivering services to the patient make the best use of the resources available to them, quality of service and value for money will be more rigorously audited. (Department of Health 1989, p. 5)

and

> Hospital services must be funded in such a way which encourages more choice and more value for money. (Department of Health 1989, p. 30)

Since this paper the aim of achieving greater value for money in health services has been heavily emphasized. Measuring health outcomes for resources expended and measurement of health service activities more generally have become wider themes throughout health services, and healthcare purchasers are increasingly concerned with gaining the highest level and quality of services for their expenditure. GPs are asking for good value for funds they expend, and the more general requirements for the Patient's Charter (Department of Health 1991) have also been heavily emphasized throughout the NHS. The service is changing, with greater emphasis being placed on value for money issues, and central resources have been allocated for the specific purpose of looking at various aspects associated with the quality of health services.

This new emergent NHS is thus a service which is beginning to seriously evaluate its activities at all levels and associate the costs with the eventual outcomes. This represents a total change of philosophy organization wide; the service has moved from providing services within a budget apportionment to one that has to sell its services, and that is starting to evaluate pay-offs when determining its service portfolio.

General trends throughout the NHS reflect wider concerns relating to the costs of delivering health services and highlight the need for resources to be well used. Various factors have influenced these changes, such as: the increasing numbers of elderly people requiring health services; the decreasing numbers of young working people paying taxes; increasing medical technology which is prolonging life; the increasing costs associated with delivering health care; and concerns about the quality of health services generally.

However, although this change of emphasis has occurred, and certainly considerable improvements have been achieved in many areas, current approaches do not seem to be delivering an overall improvement in publicly funded health care. The contention of this chapter is that this is the result of a fragmented approach to quality and value for money. The two have been separated, initially by the White Paper; subsequently by government targeted activities which encouraged a split between the two that has been supported by activities at purchaser and provider level. Quality and value for money have been seen as separate issues. This has resulted in a piecemeal approach that has often delivered 'quality' in one area at the expense of quality in another, and has often reduced costs by reducing services.

THE MEANING OF QUALITY

Quality is almost a buzz word in today's healthcare services, yet it clearly means different things to different people. This in itself would be of academic interest only, were it not for the fact that the management of quality is inextricably related to the way in which it is defined. This has important implications for the use of resources, and value for money.

David Garvin (1988) has described five different views of quality: transcendent, product-based, user-based, manufacturing-based, and value-based.

The *transcendent* view is a perspective of quality as innate excellence; it seems to be related to the underlying philosophy that 'we know it when we see it' – although perhaps cannot define it at the outset. This notion of quality is most obviously seen in the creative arts: Dickens' books are of higher quality than romantic fiction; an Oscar-winning film is of higher quality than other films; a Rembrandt is 'quality', whilst my latest daub is not. Implicit in this approach is the idea that people learn to recognize quality only through experience and exposure to 'quality' and 'non-quality'. Somehow, there is 'quality' that is recognized when it is produced, but it can only be produced by the gifted few. This kind of view is not helpful. Suggesting that managers or customers will recognize quality when they see it provides little practical help for managing it. There is also an underlying notion that only experienced customers will recognize it, which is not helpful for services such as health care, where many users are inexperienced. Nevertheless, the notion of excellence embodied in this approach does encourage aspiration to higher standards.

The *product-based* view represents a view of quality as a variable. Just as one piece of glass can be thicker than another, so one product may be of higher quality than another. This perception of quality is reflected in the view that considers a Rolls-Royce car to be of higher quality than a Mini. Often, this view is allied to an assumption that higher quality costs more, and so a more expensive product or service must be of better quality than a cheaper one. This notion is clearly embodied in the perception of those who believe that 'quality' necessarily costs more than what is currently provided. Viewing quality as a variable in this way fails to account for differences in individual needs, tastes and preferences. Clearly, with this view of quality, a designer-label pair of shoes is better quality than a pair of gumboots – but a farmhand cleaning out a pigsty is unlikely to agree! The benefit, however, of the approach is that it focuses attention on the design of the product or service.

The *user-based* view tends to equate quality with customer satisfaction. With this type of definition, quality is judged by the user. This is a demand-oriented view that recognizes that different customers have different wants and needs, and for determining what to provide in a service or product it is a useful perspective. Less helpfully, though, it implies that quality is in the eye of the beholder, and that management of quality can only be done by trying to assess the customer's perception. Hence, managing quality is a reactive, rather than proactive, activity.

The user-based view is customer-oriented, while the *manufacturing-based* view is provider-oriented. This kind of definition is concerned with the determination of specifications (or standards, as they tend to be called in healthcare services), and conformance to such specifications. This type of view leads to consistency and reliability – which certainly many customers value – but since the specifications are normally determined by the provider, they reflect provider views of what is important, rather than user views, and the two do not always coincide.

Value-based definitions of quality encompass value and price, often through the notion of customer purpose. This usually implies a trade-off between price, design and conformance to design, and quality takes on the idea of affordable excellence. With this kind of view a Mini can be as much a quality product as a Rolls-Royce, and a two star hotel can be high quality, whilst a five star hotel can be low quality. Its benefit is that it clearly integrates quality with what customers are prepared to pay, which in turn reflects what they value.

Garvin's argument is that these different views of quality help to explain conflicts that can arise between managers in different functional areas, and we would expand this further to say that they also help to explain conflicts between managers and professionals in health care. This is helpful in understanding any conflict, but perhaps more helpful is Garvin's view that no single view of quality is adequate, because each has its own blind spots. The transcendent view, for example, focuses on the design, with price or cost being a very low priority. Both this view and the product-based view implicitly regard quality as some kind of objective characteristic that is independent of individual preferences, and hence both underemphasize the customer's view. By contrast, the user-based view focuses on customer satisfaction, but the easiest way to satisfy users is to customize everything, which means heavy use of resources. Hence, if taken to the extreme, this view may be highly effective, but very inefficient, and uneconomic. The manufacturing-based approach, with its emphasis on conformance certainly leads to efficiency and economy, but can result in ineffectiveness because of its lack of emphasis on the user. The product may be perfect, but if it is not what customers want, it will not satisfy them. The value-based view is the most comprehensive view, but because of its implicit perspective of a trade-off between value and price, can often lead to a satisficing approach that may eventually result in stagnation and lack of improvement. (Satisficing is a term used by the Carnegie school of organization theory (Simon, March, Cyert etc.) meaning a tendency to pick the first available alternative that meets one's often vaguely thought out criteria for picking a solution: i.e. an acceptable, or satisfactory solution; it contrasts with 'optimization', which is the thorough, systematic search for the *best* solution (Khandwalla 1977)).

Garvin argues that all these multiple perspectives are needed to understand and manage quality, shifting the approach as the product moves through its lifecycle from design into the marketplace, from development into maturity. Evidence from the commercial arena shows that this use of multiple perspectives is happening in successful companies. To a large extent this has happened because of competition from Japan, which has shown that consideration of consumer wishes is important for survival, and because of growing consumer pressure. Many companies have found that they cannot continue to rely solely on product or manufacturing based views of quality, which were the norm in the West until the late 1970s, but neither can they rely solely on user-based views. Customer views and customer satisfaction are important, but the other views are needed if customer needs are to be met efficiently. .

Garvin's analysis is primarily of product quality management, and although his views are generally applicable to the service sector, there are nevertheless significant differences to be taken into account when considering services. Fundamentally, three issues need to be recognized (Wilderhom 1991):

1. Services are produced and consumed simultaneously.
2. Services are dependent on client interaction.
3. Service industries involve deeds (intangible).

When considering quality in services such as health care, therefore, we are forced to recognize that the quality of the service product is not enough; the way in which it is delivered or supported is equally important. A doctor's primary product is the treatment or advice given to patients, but keeping to appointment times, understandable communication, helpful attitude and so on are a fundamental part of what is perceived by the patient as a total service package. This idea has been expressed by many writers on services, but two suffice to illustrate the argument:

> From the customer's perspective, product quality and service quality are virtually inseparable. Delivering high service quality is now absolutely essential to creating good customer value. (Naumann 1995)

> [Quality service] can be as cheap as instilling more responsive attitudes in professional staff, and it tends to be infinitely more visible to clients. (Maister 1993)

Maister argues that quality work is not the same thing as quality service, and this is an important issue to recognize. Just as with manufacturing, quality of the core service product is not sufficient. The core service may be excellent, but if it is let down by the way in which it is provided, customers will perceive it as being poor quality. Gronroos (1990) identifies the quality of the core service activity as the technical quality, and the quality of the way in which it is delivered as the functional quality; both of these have to be achieved in order to satisfy the customer. If this is the case, then efforts to improve the technical quality – the clinical intervention or the quality of the food served in hospitals, for example – will not produce a perceived improvement unless they are matched by similar improvements in the functional quality, for example, the attitudes of staff or good communication with the patient. Resources addressed to only the technical quality, therefore, may not have the desired impact on what patients perceive as quality, and hence involve waste.

VALUE FOR MONEY AND QUALITY

Hence we believe that quality and value for money are not separate issues; they are integrally linked wherever there is a price to be paid. This is demonstrated graphically by Naumann (1995).

The customer value triad consists of product quality, service quality, and value-based prices. In healthcare terms, we can translate this as technical quality, functional quality, and value-based prices as shown in Figure 6.1. The three need to be in harmony to maximize the value perceived by the customer. Prices set too high for a given level of technical and delivery quality will not be perceived as good value. Excellent technical quality allied to poor functional quality will not be perceived as good value. Customer value is created when customer expectations in each of the three areas are met or exceeded.

Poor technical and functional quality not only reduce value, and hence what is perceived as the value-based price, but also increase costs, because they incur waste. The price set has to match what the customer perceives as value. However, the price set must also recover the cost of providing the service. Often costs are inflated by poor quality. Poor quality in either the technical core or the

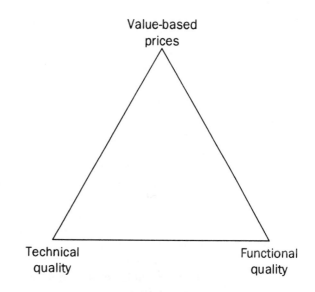

Technical quality and functional quality are the pillars
that support value-based prices

service delivery will almost certainly increase costs, because resources are wasted in doing the job incorrectly or in delays between stages in the process. Often this results in inflated costs to the organization: extra stocks of materials have to be held to cover for misuse or waste incurred in not doing the job correctly in the first place and then having to recover it, or in poor planning that results in work being duplicated; space and resource has to be provided for patients to wait; patients have to be kept in hospital longer than necessary; expensive drugs have to be provided because resources are not available to provide the inpatient treatment that will alleviate or remove the need for drugs; resources are wasted in providing things that are not valued by patients or purchasers. All of these increase the cost of providing the service, and result in inflated prices. The patient also bears the cost of poor quality: psychological costs are incurred in delays, appointments not kept on time, and repeat visits that have to be scheduled because tests, x-rays etc. cannot be planned as an integral part of a single outpatient appointment; extra financial costs are incurred in lost wages and transport costs when repeat appointments are needed, or when associated costs of getting the service, such as babysitters, have to be extended. These reduce the value perceived by the patient.

Thus a vicious cycle can be created by poor quality: poor quality both reduces value and increases costs; in turn, prices have to be inflated to recover the costs, and the resultant higher prices have a negative impact on perceived value for money.

In publicly funded health care, as in many other services, there are several different customers, and this can be problematic when considering quality and value for money. The immediate customer, because of the role played in specifying services and deciding which to buy, is the purchaser. However, purchasers, in principle, represent the users, the patients, and as such, should be concerned about what patients consider to be important, and ought to be accountable to them. Government also plays a customer role, in that it allocates the money, on behalf of the population at large, to pay for the services. As with purchasers therefore, Government should be concerned with what patients and potential patients want, and be accountable to them. Unfortunately, the accountability link between users and purchasers, and users and Government, is extremely tenuous, and there are no mechanisms for individual users to hold purchasers or government to account for the purchasing. Collectively, dissatisfied users can make life uncomfortable for both parties, and individuals can certainly become a thorn in their flesh, but dissatisfied users, in general, cannot take their business elsewhere. GP fundholding, amongst other things, is intended to provide an opportunity for users to have more choice and better service, and as yet it is too early to state categorically whether or not it has been successful. However, a recent study (Brown 1995) provides some evidence that users have less say in what is provided in fundholding practices than previously – although Community Health Councils, arguably representing users, do seem to have some influence.

The term 'value for money' in the context of healthcare services generally refers to ensuring that for each pound spent, most is used to provide effective and efficient health services, rather than wasted or misused. In practice in the health service the term actually refers to ensuring that medications, laboratory tests, lengths of stay in hospital, treatment regimes and other costs associated with delivering health care are well used. One problem with the approach is that users are rarely consulted, and the judgement about whether or not what is done represents value for money tends to be made by managers on the provider side, and purchasers and government agencies, such as the Audit Commission and the Department of Health on the customer side, whilst technical quality is judged by the professional staff who provide it. A further problem is that it tends to focus on direct costs to the provider; hidden costs, such as waste, are rarely included. In part this is because many hidden costs, such as extended bed occupancy, administrative costs in making multiple appointments, provision of extended waiting areas etc., are subsumed in a general overhead, and in part it is because such costs are often not explicitly recognized.

Box 6.1
Value for money in
acute services

The following example highlights the meaning of the term value for money in a situation which considers emergency admissions for fractured neck or femur (Morris *et al*. 1995). This is a commonly provided service, that consumes heavy amounts of NHS resource.

On admission to Accident and Emergency, individuals with a suspected fractured neck or femur are all seen by a junior medical member of casualty staff who orders x-rays, blood tests, a bed, an operation etc; subsequently a nurse may administer pain relief and a bed will be found for the individual patient. An operation is then carried out to deal with the fracture, normally involving the fitment of a prosthesis.

Value for money issues raise questions regarding the effectiveness and efficiency in such instances, as well as perceived value to the patient and the purchaser. We do not intend to discuss the particular issues arising from the audit, but to comment generally on issues affecting cost, value and quality.

A significant area for consideration is waiting time and delay. The longer an individual patient waits for his or her operation, the more costs are associated with the treatment episode because of the increased length of stay pre-operatively. Other more indirect costs relate to the health outcome for the patient in that if patients wait immobile for an operation they are at risk of complications associated with prolonged bed rest such as chest infections, pressure sores etc. These all impact on costs by increasing requirements for medication such as antibiotics or chest physiotherapy. These infections may further unnecessarily delay the operation because the individual may then be unsuitable for anaesthetic, thus again increasing the number of bed days used and hence increasing the associated costs. Common sense dictates that waiting and delay be eliminated if good value for money is to be achieved, costs are to be kept at minimal levels, and smooth flow of patients through the service is to be maintained. Concern for quality also dictates that delays be eliminated because they adversely affect the functional quality. The technical quality of the various interventions may be excellent, but many of them are unnecessary, and unnecessary pain, discomfort and possible direct cost are incurred by the patient.

Another important issue is variation in treatment. At the individual patient level a plethora of different actions are undertaken for different patients, for example, some having blood tests which differ from those given to others, despite individual patients having an identical diagnosis, the same gender and being of similar age.

A further issue is variation in the process flows and the time taken for treatment and tests to be ordered and carried out. Much depends on whether the patient is admitted to an orthopaedic ward under the care of an orthopaedic specialist, or a ward for care of the elderly under the care of a geriatric specialist. If this were related to the nature of the condition, one might consider it to be related to the type of service required. However, it seems more often to be the result of where beds are available, and reflects lack of standardization of processes. Lack of system and managed flow within the health process generally can result in poorer technical and functional quality for some patients, and in widely differing costs.

Box 6.2
Value for money in community health services

Community services are also involved in achieving value for money, although this may be more complex than achieving value for money in the acute hospital sector. In contrast with acute services, community services are generally not involved in the provision of hospital care, although respite or small-scale hospital services may be available in crisis situations. The community services are subject to the same statutory requirements, however, and are required to adhere, for example, to the Patient's Charter standards. Value for money in such services may be more difficult to define because the requirement for laboratory tests, x-rays etc., is less, and the technical core is often more diffuse than acute service interventions. There are, however, many ways in which one can look at value for money in this sector and examples are given below:

A patient with psychiatric problems is being cared for in the community. The patient attempts suicide by slitting his wrists, and is referred to the local hospital. The patient arrives at the A&E Department of the local hospital for emergency treatment of the wounds, and is then referred to a psychiatrist. The psychiatrist decides to admit the patient to the local psychiatric unit for assessment and treatment; after this period the individual is discharged apparently well. Four days late he returns with the same problem. Concern for value for money and quality would lead to investigation of readmission rates and the reasons for re-entry into the inpatient sector, and the establishment of what had caused the re-emergence of the problem.

A further example is of a patient who tries to arrange an appointment to consult her GP about a back problem. The surgery is fully booked for the next ten days. On the eleventh day, she sees the GP and is referred for physiotherapy. Three weeks elapse before she receives an acknowledgement, offering an appointment in five weeks time. In pain, the patient refers herself to an osteopath.

In the community sector one would thus need to consider the need for seamless patterns of care which provide a smooth transition for individuals after discharge and offer adequate levels of support to the individual, and which can provide all the elements of treatment without intervening delays. Methods taken from the quality field would enable one to look at all such issues and suggest areas where improvements could be made to improve quality and thus increase value for money.

In real life, however, this is more complicated than one may first assume with the mixture of NHS, voluntary, social and private groups providing health services. The GP practice may, for example, be fundholding and thus may provide its own district nurses, rather than those based in the local community Trust, which complicates the hospital/community/social services provision yet further. Certainly establishing whether community services are providing value for money is a complex issue that is further complicated by the increasing numbers of providers offering services which represent services that are 'locally defined', and are not standardized throughout the country. Generally, when referring to value for money initiatives, one considers them in the context of the acute sector which traditionally has consumed the majority of the resources expended on health services, but with the increasing focus of the community as the provider of services previously provided in the acute sector, and increasing devolvement of fundholding to GPs, value for money is just as important in the community sector.

Value for money in health services thus becomes complicated because not only does it need to consider actual costs, it also becomes involved significantly in the pursuit of quality. A simple study focusing solely on the costs of delivering health care to individuals with fractured neck of femur may fail to address some of the more complex details involved in the provision of care throughout the episode, and thus fundamental issues closely associated with achieving value for money may be missed. Similarly, a simple evaluation of the costs of providing treatment in the community may miss considerable hidden costs borne by the patient.

INITIATIVES
ASSOCIATED WITH
VALUE FOR MONEY
AND QUALITY

Given our view that quality and value are integrally related, we now need to consider the way in which current initiatives tackle these issues. A wide variety of both national and local initiatives has begun, but we argue that these are fragmented, and treat value for money and quality as separate issues.

The Patient's
Charter and
quality

The Citizen's Charter, setting standards for all public services and containing various sub-charters such as the Post Office Charter, the Patient's Charter etc., was largely intended to specify to the general public the standards they could expect public services to deliver. These Charters have been widely introduced throughout the public sector and health services are all required to adhere to the national standards. *A National Guide to Monitoring the Patient's Charter*, produced by the National Health Service Management Executive (1994a), highlights the high level of importance placed on achieving charter standards, and certain acute health providers have been fined for failing to adhere to the waiting times for operations.

The Patient's Charter, unfortunately, was not based on the systematic study of what matters to patients; rather it focused on areas identified by a working party of individuals. One may say therefore that while the Charter was well-intentioned it did not actually represent any dimension of quality for patients, except insofar as those individuals (in common with the remaining population) on the working party were probably all funding or using health services at some level.

In fact research into what patients consider quality to be (for example, Morris and Bell 1993, Bell *et al.* 1995, Tomes and Ng 1995) has shown that while the Charter represents some issues that patients value, there are some that they clearly do not. The lack of systematic appraisal of what quality really is for individuals, or specific groups of the population, means that the Charter directs attention to some issues that patients do not perceive as important, or as representing quality. Given this, we can only question the extent to which the direction of resources to these issues represents value for money.

Systematic appraisal of patients' views prior to the introduction of the Charter, then, might have reflected the nature of quality and its meaning to patients more than is currently the case. This would in turn have allowed resources to be directed more towards things that patients do value, than to those which they do not.

Monitoring of charter standards throughout the UK occurs at regular intervals and we consider such activities to be costly and not necessarily reflective of good value for monies expended. If the things being monitored are not actually of value to patients, monitoring them may well provide useful information for managerial control purposes, but will not improve quality. Thus the money is not well spent for service provision and improvement. In contrast the systematic appraisal of service users at a local level and the generation of local relevant standards set by service users may prove more appropriate than the current centrally imposed series of standards.

Complaints and quality   The Patient's Charter makes much of the issue of complaints and suggests that all complaints will be answered within a specified time frame (Department of Health 1991, p. 21). In a situation where quality is defined in a user-based way, complaints have a key part to play in improving quality. However, where the view of quality is product or manufacturing based, complaints can only be perceived as a criticism. What happens, therefore, is that instead of seeing complaints positively, complaints are perceived to be problems, and often the health service concerned with addressing the complaint directs its attention to exoneration or the attribution of blame. Complaints are about what went wrong, and often a complainant making criticisms of health services does so under extreme duress when problems are great. Patients are often loath to utter negative statements about health services for fear of retribution either on themselves, or on staff they generally perceive as hard-working, and this leads to a failure to make complaints that might lead to service improvement. When patients are sufficiently upset to make complaints, they are often past the stage of wanting improvement, and are looking for recompense or atonement. The hostile attitudes resulting from this kind of confrontation are hardly likely to lead to improvement. Defences are set up, and the object becomes containment of the situation, rather than wider improvement. Complaints, and the way in which they are generally handled, have placed great emphasis on what is wrong and they are perceived negatively, focusing on problems and significantly associated in the minds of many health service staff with the medico-legal minefield.

Most healthcare providers have attempted to elicit complaints or suggestions for improvement, but the way in which this is done often does not lead to success. A common way of doing it is to put up notices or add such requests to printed information about services. In a situation where there are no other cues about commitment to quality, or where, as is commonly the case, the request is phrased in formal language with the emphasis on complaints rather than suggestions for improvement, patients do not normally feel encouraged to do so.

The pursuit of quality relates to doing things right, to improvement, and to learning from mistakes. Complaints are therefore extremely important if used within a general framework associated with establishing their relevance in the general and specific context of the complaint, but they should not be the purpose for a witch hunt or blame-allocating investigation. In a quality context, complaints should be dealt with systemically, by looking to see how the information they provide can be used in services more generally, rather than dealing with each as a stand-alone incident. Further, in a situation where customers (patients) are in a dependent position, considerable effort needs to be put into creating the kind of environment where they feel comfortable with making complaints or suggestions.

The standard setting approach The nature of the standards contained in the Patient's Charter and their questionable appropriateness highlight a general trend toward standard-setting occurring throughout the health service in the attempt to improve the quality of health services. There is, however, some confusion in the way the term is used. It is applied to both the specification or design of the service (design quality), for example, 'patients in hospital will have a named nurse', and to standards of conformance (quality of conformance), such as '90% of patients will be seen within 20 minutes of their appointment time', i.e. 90% will meet or conform to the specification of being seen within 20 minutes.

The setting of standards represents a product or manufacturing based approach to managing quality, depending on whether the standards are related to the service design or to conformance to the specification. As such, they have an important part to play in ensuring quality. However, in common with all such approaches, they may neglect the views of the user. They are mainly set by various stakeholder groups providing, managing or financing health services, and the nature of these various groups is that the standards fit with their agendas. This has led to a situation of a quality monopoly in which purchasers, managers and the various professional groups all contribute their understanding of what quality is and patients are passive recipients.

When considering the advent of the new profession of management in the NHS subsequent to Griffiths (1983), we need to recognize that this actually added another group of stakeholders to the NHS equation. In addition to the clinical stakeholder agendas of promotion, merit awards, clinical autonomy, status etc., were added the managerial agenda relating to achievement of specified targets, achieving effectiveness and efficiency and gaining promotion, thus creating additional complications regarding quality and quality initiatives. Instead of one group of clinical professionals as stakeholders, from this point on there were two, who were both significantly more powerful than the user group (Brown *et al*. 1994). In considering the influence of these two main professional stakeholder groups involved in the provision of health, the managers (non-clinical professionals) and clinicians (clinical professionals), several key points (McCartney *et al.* 1993, p. 49) need to be borne in mind.

1. Managers in the NHS are not the same kind of professionals as are traditionally found in law, medicine or the clergy.
2. Managers' specialist professionalism is based on specialist knowledge of management and organizations which they believe clinical professionals do not possess.
3. The clinical professions tend to view themselves as traditional professions.
4. There is some resistance, and even hostility, to NHS managers on the part of clinicians which is seen as resulting from the different views of the nature of professionalism.

Traditional thinking about professionalism stresses that the professions are carriers of a higher form of rationality and morality than other groups.

> A profession is a largely autonomous, self-regulating and self-perpetuating institution, the altruistic members of which are filled with the desire to work for the common good in the most effective way. (Brante 1988, p. 122)

In contrast some current thinking about professionalism discounts ideas which stress universal (and altruistic) qualities in favour of views considering professions as arenas where self-interest, demarcation and closure apply. Alvesson (1993) suggests that the professional ethical code is best seen as a symbolic vehicle, which supports the political interests of the profession, rather than as a set of norms that safeguards the morally superior behaviour of its members. Witz (1990) in a similar vein suggested the status of a profession as essentially a labour market strategy which aims to achieve an occupational monopoly over the provision of certain skills and competencies in the market for services. A debate about the extent to which these views represent objective fact is outside the scope of this chapter, but each of them has significant implications for standard setting.

The traditional view puts patients into a position of benign dependency, with the professional deciding what is best for them in terms of technical quality, and managers determining what represents value for money. The modern view represents professionals as more self-seeking, with clinical professionals safeguarding technical quality, and managers often in conflict with them in an attempt to overcome the self-interest, and pursue their own objectives. Again, the patient is in a dependent position, but the dependency is not so benign.

Certainly, health service clinical professions are all powerful groups with their interests, both collective and individual, often presiding over those of their patients. Professionals are well-established monopoly groups who preside over specific aspects of caring for patients under the guidance of the most powerful professional of all, the doctor. Patients are always under the care of the doctor and often other health professionals may communicate nothing of significance without the prior consent of the doctor.

We thus have a situation where technical quality of medical or clinical interventions is the prerogative of clinical professionals, and the technical quality of support services is the prerogative of management. This is reflected in the way in which standards are set. For example, considerable initiative has been taken by the nursing profession, both in the development of standards, and the development of a methodology for writing standards. These standards relate to the quality of nursing care, and the approach is well established and fairly sophisticated. However, it does tend to exclude the views of the patient, and is clearly focused on nursing, separate from other aspects of health care.

Another area where the clinical professions have been heavily involved is the development of guidelines in order to encourage clinicians to manage their patients in the same way. One problem

Box 6.3
Guidelines for the management of fractured neck of femur

In 1989 the guidelines were developed subsequent to the identification of a major health problem associated with the increasing incidence of fractured neck of femur and the high risk of mortality this condition was causing among elderly Caucasian women. The document was lengthy and described the epidemiology of this health problem, the incidence and the costs associated with managing the condition.

Royal College guidelines for the management of fractured neck of femur specify the level of surgeon who may best perform this operation (in this case that a senior level surgeon perform this operation), which highlights the nature of the profession and the way this collegiate structure itself determines the maintenance of the professional role in health services.

These particular guidelines also make suggestions regarding the way the operation be performed and the time period associated with the best health outcome for the patient; but the current literature regarding this condition is diverse and often conflicting (Lu Yao et al. 1994). Lu Yao et al. carried out a meta-analysis relating to fractured neck of femur which suggested that there were problems regarding the validity of the current body of medical knowledge relating to this medical condition, much of which was contradictory.

with guidelines is that they focus solely on clinical issues, reflecting current professional knowledge, which is sometimes conflicting or uncertain. We illustrate the nature of the problem with reference to one particular early set developed by the Royal College of Physicians (1989).

We therefore question an approach based on guidelines, where there is conflict about the nature of treatment. The lack of certainty highlights the kind of problem associated with the science of the clinical professions, which tend to focus on the empirical model. To this is added the lack of consideration of functional quality.

Managerial approaches focus rather more on value for money and, in dealing with quality, tend to rely on managerial judgement about what patients perceive as quality. Given the need to satisfy purchasers and broader issues of resource utilization, quality is often left to the discretion of managers responsible for particular functions, such as hotel services, or maintenance. Such approaches tend to be rather broader than the primarily clinical (technical quality) focus of clinical professions, and often incorporate both technical and functional quality. However, given the nature of the clinical professions, and the perceived separation of clinical from other issues, managerial approaches tend not to impinge on what is perceived as the prerogative of clinicians.

We therefore have a situation where quality is specified along clinical and departmental lines allied to the organization structure. Technical quality of clinical interventions is the responsibility of clinical professionals, technical quality of support services and functional quality is the prerogative of management, and the purchaser attempts to link the two elements through contract specification. These standards are useful, but inherently limited, because they are not necessarily grounded in knowledge of the total phenomenon and focus on isolated parts.

Medical and clinical audit   The standard setting approach, as with the Patient's Charter series of standards, is widely used to audit the quality of various aspects of health services including medical and professional practice. The audit model used is seen as closely linked to a model described by Shaw (1986) in a King's Fund paper *Introducing Quality Assurance*, which describes the audit cycle as consisting of setting standards, measuring actual activity against practice, changing practice where needed and then re-auditing to establish whether the changes have created any impact on the topic studied. This model has been given particular emphasis within the context of medical audit activity.

Medical audit

Medical audit was explicitly introduced in the White Paper *Working for Patients* (Department of Health 1989) which stated that medical audit would become a requirement for all clinicians practising medicine in the health service. Almost £220 million over the last four years has been allocated to medical audit, but there is little evidence to suggest the financial scale of any saving resulting from this activity. In a recent report commissioned by CASPE (Buttery *et al.* 1994) the structure of medical audit throughout the UK was discussed, addressing most provider units, but it did not mention the cost savings resulting from medical audit. The authors suggest in fact that a more qualitative approach may have proved more useful, particularly had this dealt with the depth of activity and the nature of changes to the provision of health care resulting from audit activities.

The view of the medical profession on audit and quality is that this is largely an internal professional issue, with the Confidential Enquiry into Perioperative Deaths (CEPOD: Campling *et al.* 1990) serving as a good example of this. Following the CEPOD model the Royal College of Surgeons undertakes to perform confidential audit of surgeons' practice using the allocation of pin numbers to ensure clinician confidentiality. This type of approach has proved very useful as a means of tackling technical quality, but it deals with professional, rather than user concerns, and is not integrated with other mechanisms for improving quality. The activity is isolationist in nature, and does not represent an integrated study of all facets of quality associated with anaesthetic or surgical procedures.

Clinical audit

The medical audit model formed the basis for audit in other clinical professions, but the most recent development has been the advent of a much wider and more multiprofessional audit. A recent publication from the National Health Service Management Executive (1994b) suggested that multiprofessional clinical audit is a natural evolution of programmes already underway, and it emphasized the importance associated with auditing clinical care collectively, i.e. multiprofessionally and across the primary/secondary interface. Prior to this point, activities began with medical audit in hospitals, followed the next year by medical audit in primary care, and clinical audit amongst all other professions allied to medicine.

The clinical audit model currently being introduced, however, suffers from similar flaws to the medical audit paradigm, and what is generally happening in practice is individual professions auditing their practices in almost splendid isolation regardless of the service processes and interactions encountered by the patient. This is very similar to the way in which medical audit has been practised.

Clinical and medical audit are both deeply grounded in the perspectives of professionals, and focus on clinical and medical interventions. However, whilst clearly the technical quality of professional interventions is important, it is not the only consideration.

Individual   The issues discussed so far are practised throughout the NHS, and
initiatives   insofar as one can identify anything approaching a national strategy
for quality, they are its main constituents. Accompanying these
approaches, however, are thousands of initiatives at unit or department level. These include formal quality assurance systems, such as
BS 5750, the British Standard for quality assurance systems, targeted
activities such as reduction in waiting times, and the specification
of quality elements in contracts. A very welcome recent development has been the 'one stop shop' approach to the redesign of
specific services. These approaches are used particularly in outpatient clinics, where they attempt to eliminate separate visits for
tests, consultations etc, by planning all the necessary activities into
one longer visit. These are the currently very few quality related
approaches that try to integrate a variety of patient-related interventions into one coherent, planned service.

Many of these have had significant effects on quality, but the
main problem with them is that they are idiosyncratic, reflecting
the commitment of individuals, and there is little evidence of
learning from others' experiences. Many repetitions of similar
improvements can be found throughout the health service, but
most of them have been developed *ab initio* in house. The NHS is a
huge organization, and it is clearly difficult for staff to keep abreast
of developments elsewhere, but considerable resource seems to be
wasted in reinventing the wheel. Some mechanisms exist to help
with this, such as a national database of quality initiatives, a national
initiative on benchmarking, and the Association for Quality in
Healthcare, but they are not well known.

EVALUATION OF   All health services are complex service industries, involving face-to-
CURRENT   face contact between customers (patients) and contact staff; these
INITIATIVES   latter are split between clinical and medical professionals, who
provide the technical core interventions, and non-clinical staff,
who provide the support activities. The work of other non-clinical
professional groups (managers) takes place at a level removed from
direct face-to-face contact with patients, but involves contact with
clinical professional groups and other non-clinical professionals
such as health purchasers.

The vast majority of quality activities are directed towards
particular activities, rather than towards the whole service package
experienced by patients. Clinicians are concerned with the quality
of clinical interventions; support staff are concerned with the
quality of support activities; management is concerned with
resource utilization, but is prevented by the nature of clinical audit
from being involved in judgements about the quality of clinical
interventions. In effect, quality is managed along organizational
function lines, as shown in Figure 6.2.

Figure 6.2
Management of quality
through organizational
function lines

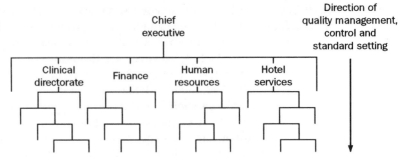

There is no doubt that improvements in quality have been achieved by these approaches, but each element of the service package, such as clinical intervention, administration, hotel services, laundry, sterile supplies etc., is dealt with separately. Sometimes the separate initiatives fit together, but sometimes they do not. A common problem is that improvements in one area are not matched by improvements in another. For example, the quality of a clinical intervention may be good, but the patient service is let down by poor appointment administration, or loss of medical records. Improvement of the clinical quality in this situation will not improve the service, and arguably, it is better value to focus attention on appointments or medical records.

The nub of the problem is that the service, for the patient, is not solely the clinical intervention, or the quality of the food; it is an integrated package that includes everything involved in getting the service – from referral to discharge – as shown in Figure 6.3.

For the patient, the service is not a collection of isolated activities; the clinical intervention, the handling of the appointment, the food, the availability of medical records, when required, the attitudes of staff and so on, are all part of the service package. Good value is represented by integration of all the elements, and

Figure 6.3
Patient perception of
service

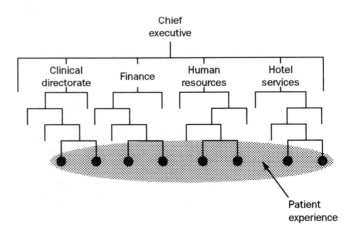

equal quality in all of them. The piecemeal approach improves individual elements of the package, but quality of the whole is limited by whichever element has the poorest quality. Further, quality improvements directed by what the provider thinks is important may also not represent good value if the patient or the purchaser does not share that perception.

Professionals have developed knowledge about what quality is for them but they have not focused on the place for the patients' views within this framework and unfortunately neither did the Patient's Charter. The focus on specific activities fails to recognize the multi-faceted nature of the total service package experienced by the patient. It also fails to recognize adequately all the dimensions of quality that are important to patients. Maxwell (1984, 1992), for example, has identified accessibility, acceptability, appropriateness, equity, effectiveness and efficiency as key dimensions of quality. These correspond, in part, to five dimensions of service quality, tangibles, reliability, responsiveness, empathy and assurance, identified by Parasuraman *et al.* (1985, 1988) in the commercial sector. Both of these are supported by research carried out in Southend Community Care Services NHS Trust (Bell *et al.* 1993), but with an added dimension of privacy. Most of these dimensions are concerned with the way in which the service is delivered, functional quality, and by their very nature, most of them concern the total package of health care. Current initiatives in the NHS, whilst achieving much in terms of improving technical quality, do not deal with these more holistic aspects.

The nature of the current approaches to quality becomes more questionable when one further considers the confidential nature of auditing and thus quality activity which focuses on the professional arena. The nature of the purchaser/provider split has failed to improve this problem because while the purchasers can buy specific audit activity, they cannot enforce changes to clinical management other than by removing contracts to another provider unit, and in many parts of the country, such a shift is not possible, or considerably inconveniences patients. Most providers and clinicians act with the interests of their patients placed firmly at the centre of all their activities, but unfortunately the very nature of their professionalism and knowledge influences all their thoughts and activities. Hence their efforts, whilst well-intentioned and certainly often improving technical quality, do not offer an integrated structure with which to evaluate quality and increase value for money.

FUTURE DIRECTIONS

Of the major stakeholder groups, professionals, managers, purchasers and patients, certain stakeholders are more powerful than others, with patients being the least powerful group of all. The stakeholder groups in the NHS have vastly different concerns, with the user group being the most dependent and traditionally power-less. Members of this group are generally unwell and suffering and they are often unaware of the kinds of help available. The most general aims of service users reflect their need to gain easy access to services and to get required health care to facilitate a speedy recovery to health; generally the concerns of patients are very different from the concerns of health service professions.

Patients assume the NHS exists for them, and its fundamental purpose is to be achieved restoring them to health or keeping them healthy (Brown *et al.* 1994). Recent changes in the NHS, fuelled by much publicity about controversial decisions on closures, and rising interest in consumerism and consumer issues, have created considerable interest in the NHS, and often created concern about what is sometimes seen as a deterioration in service. The NHS is a service delivering health care to the majority of the population in the UK, and it is also the largest employer in this country. The customers (patients) are those same taxpayers financing the service, and as such the entire population is a patient or potential patient of the service. As taxpayers who are financing the service, together with their role as customers using these services, this interest is considered right and proper; and health services are subjected to constant scrutiny. Value for money associated with the expenditure of large amounts of public money has been a major factor influencing the value for money debate. Not only are those purchasing health services directly for patients concerned about these issues, but general practitioners, Community Health Councils, financial auditors, and the Audit Commission are also involved in the continual quest to achieve value for money. However, whilst current approaches to value for money and quality are certainly delivering improvements as viewed by these major stakeholders, we consider that their impact on users is more limited than it need be, primarily because their views are not expressly considered. Decisions are taken on their behalf, using criteria considered important by those making the decisions. As reflected in this chapter, these do not always adequately reflect user concerns.

SUMMARY

A much more integrated, holistic approach is needed, which deals with both technical and functional quality by treating the complete service package as a whole, rather than as separate activities, and focuses on what users want, rather than what providers think they want, and recognizes that user needs go beyond the purely technical quality of clinical or other interventions. This requires the following:

♦ The separate strands of auditing, and clinical and support function activities, need to be brought together into an integrated framework that considers in an holistic way the total service package. Fundamentally, this means switching from a focus on the separate functions to a multidisciplinary approach that involves both clinical and non-clinical staff.

♦ User interests need to be identified and addressed. Primarily this requires marketing and customer research, but this is made problematic by the intervening role of purchasers. Currently, providers are closer to patients than purchasers and, in terms of resource availability, access to patients and knowledge, are better placed than purchasers to carry out this activity. However, unless purchasers recognize the importance and validity of patient views, they may not necessarily recognize user-based issues in contract specifications. Ideally, then, purchasers should carry out such research and task providers with meeting the needs. Where this is not done, purchasers need to accept provider recommendations where they are based on reliable customer research. Attention to patient wishes will allow resources to be directed where they are valued.

♦ There needs to be wider recognition of the impact of conformance on reliability and cost. Currently, most activity is directed towards the setting and auditing of standards or the redesign of services. Much is to be gained, particularly in cost reduction, from attention to conformance. There is little to be gained from standard-setting if activity is not directed towards ensuring that standards are met consistently, and little to be gained from redesign unless it incorporates mechanisms for ensuring consistency. Higher specifications, where there are already inconsistencies in delivery, are of questionable value. Thus, we advocate the incorporation of a more manufacturing-based view of quality that focuses on conformity; this would in our view reduce waste.

♦ Efforts need to be made to calculate the costs of quality. Some very limited attempts have been made to do this, but quality costing is currently in its infancy. It is salutary to recognize that in the commercial sector, the costs of poor quality (largely in the areas of resource wasted by not doing things right first time, and having to carry excess resource to cater for such problems) typically amount to 25–35% of operating costs. This in health service terms represents a huge amount of money that is spent unnecessarily.

Much has been achieved over the past few years, but the fragmentation of quality initiatives imposes limitations on what can be achieved. Equally, failure to recognize explicitly the cost of poor quality, and the cost of treating the wide variety of clinical and support activities separately, rather than as an integrated whole, leads to excessive costs. Finally, lack of incorporation of patients' views can lead to resources being misdirected. Tackling all of these, as outlined above, will ultimately deliver both quality and value for money.

FURTHER
READING

♦ Seddon, J. (1992), *I WANT YOU TO CHEAT!: The unreasonable guide to service and quality in organisations*, Vanguard Press.

♦ Koch, H. (1991), *Total Quality Management in Health Care*, Longman.

♦ Koch, H. (1992), *Implementing and Sustaining Total Quality Management in Health Care*, Longman.

REFERENCES

Alvesson, M. (1993), *Organisation as Rhetoric: knowledge-intensive firms and the struggle with ambiguity*. Paper presented at the 11th EGO Colloquium, Paris.

Bell, L, Brown, R. B. and Morris, B. (1995), Involving patients in the provision of community care: a change in philosophy. *International Journal of Health Care Quality Assurance*, 8 (2).

Bell, L., Morris, B. and Brown, R. (1993). Devising a multi-disciplinary audit tool. *International Journal of Health Care Quality Assurance*, 6 (4): 16–21.

Brante, J. (1988), Sociological approaches to the professions. *Acta Sociologica*, 31 (2).

Brown, L. (1995), *Patient Participation in Contracting for Health Care*, unpublished MBA dissertation, Canterbury Business School, University of Kent.

Brown, R.B., McCartney, S., Bell, L. and Scaggs, S. (1994), Who is the NHS for? *Journal of Management in Medicine*, 8 (4).

Buttery, Y., Walsh, K., Coles, J. and Bennet, J. (1994), *Evaluating Medical Audit: the development of audit, findings of a national survey of healthcare provider units in England*. CASPE: London.

Campling, E., Devlin, H., Hale, R. and Lunn, J. (1990), *The Report of the National Enquiry into Perioperative Deaths*. NCEPOD.

Department of Health (1989), *Working for Patients: Medical Audit, Working Paper No. 6,* Command 555. London: HMSO.

Department of Health (1991), *The Patients' Charter.* London: HMSO.

Garvin, D.A. (1988), *Managing Quality*. Free Press.

Griffiths Report (1983), *NHS Management Inquiry.* London: DHSS.

Gronroos, C. (1990), *Service Management and Marketing*. Lexington Books/D C Heath & Co.

Khandwalla, P.N. (1977), *Design of Organizations*. Harcourt Brace Jovanovich.

Lu Yao, G., Keller, R., Littenberg, B. and Wennberg, J. (1994), Outcomes after displacement of the femoral neck. *Journal of Bone and Joint Surgery*, 76a (1): 15–25.

Maister, D.H. (1993), *Managing the Professional Service Firm*. Free Press.

McCartney, S., Berman-Brown, R. and Bell, L. (1993), Professionals in health care: perceptions of managers. *Journal of Management in Medicine*, 7 (5): 48–55.

Maxwell, R. (1984), Quality assessment in health. *British Medical Journal*, 288: 1470-1472.

Maxwell, R. (1992), Dimensions of quality revisited: from thought to action. *Quality in Healthcare*, 1.

Morris, B., Bell, L. and Solieri, A. (1995), *The Use of Blueprinting in Auditing Healthcare Processes*. In Draaijer, D., Boer, H. and Krabbendam, K. (Eds), *Management and New Production Systems*. University of Twente on behalf of the European Operations Management Association.

Morris, B. and Bell, L. (1993), Patient-defined audit. In Johnston, R. and Slack, N. (Eds), *Service Superiority - the Design and Delivery of Effective Service Operations*. Operations Management Association UK.

National Health Service Management Executive (1994a), *A National Guide to Monitoring the Patient's Charter*. London: HMSO.

National Health Service Management Executive (1994b), *Clinical Audit: 1994-95 and beyond*, Executive Letter (94) 20, Health Publications Unit, Heywood.

Naumann, E. (1995), *Creating Customer Value*. Thompson Executive Press.

Parasuraman, A., Zeithaml, V. and Berry, L. (1985), A conceptual model of service quality and its implications for future research. *Journal of Marketing*, 49.

Parasuraman, A., Zeithaml, V. and Berry, L. (1988), SERVQUAL: A multiple-item scale for measuring consumer perception of service quality. *Journal of Retailing*, 64 (1).

Royal College of Physicians in London (1989), *Fractured Neck of Femur: Prevention and Management*. London: The Royal College of Physicians of London.

Shaw, C. (1986), *Introducing Quality Assurance*. London: King's Fund.

Tomes, A.E. and Ng, S.C.P. (1995), Service quality in hospital care: the development of an in-patient questionnaire. *International Journal of Health Care Quality Assurance*, 8 (3).

Wilderhom, C. (1991), Service management/Leadership: different from management in industrial organizations. *International Journal of Service Industry Management*, 2 (1): 6-14.

Witz, A. (1990), Patriarchy and professions: the gendered politics of occupational closure. *Sociology*, 24 (4).

CONTROL AND VALUE FOR MONEY

David A. Perkins

OBJECTIVES

- ◆ To discuss the basic assumptions underpinning a control system.
- ◆ To recognize that control systems in health care have to deal with complexity.

INTRODUCTION

The mere mention of the word control in relation to the delivery of health services will cause disquiet in some constituencies. To control the quality, or indeed availability, of public services is one thing but to control the quality or quantity of health services is something else. Yet who should control health services? At the time of writing a health authority has announced that it is not to fund a variety of services in the coming year ranging from the insertion of grommets to treatment for infertility. Doctors are to have no discretion in the treatment of cases of particular severity who present for these treatments as has happened in the past. Furthermore providers will be expected to meet existing levels of service at a price 3% lower than that in existing contracts. It appears that the powers of doctors are being eroded by the actions of the purchaser. He who pays the piper calls the tune, or defines the treatment protocol. Is this an appropriate, or even an effective, form of control yet without action much of what has been discussed in this volume is an empty exercise. Control implies that we go beyond the collection and interpretation of data and take some form of management action but how should we do this?

Controlling is part of management, it is part of operational/ clinical activity and we all do it every day as managers and professionals. Who should be responsible for control and how should that responsibility be exercised? What are the essential elements of the control process and how might they be applied within health services?

This question can be addressed in relation to three important strands of thought which have influenced our understanding of organizations. The scientific management school and their descendants indicate that control is a function of management or of specialist inspectors. The behaviouralists argue that individuals need to be motivated and empowered in their work; they further argue that inspectors do not add value directly to the productive process, they should be seen as a cost and where possible individuals and work teams should be responsible for the control of the quality and output of their own work. Writers on professionalism have often observed that while professionals usually have control over the content and the decisions associated with their work they do not have control over the conditions under which work is undertaken nor the resources available to them in doing their work (Freidson 1973).

LEVELS OF CONTROL

Control is exercised at different levels and it is easiest to conceive of control at the operational level of services. In response to the question who is in control during a surgical operation the answer would normally be a named individual, the senior surgeon. If something happens which is unexpected the control process implies that the unexpected event will be monitored, measured, its importance would be interpreted, and appropriate action would be taken. Similarly the anaesthetist on duty would be expected to check his/her equipment before the session and to monitor the condition of the patient taking action, and perhaps informing her colleagues, when she judges it to be necessary. Such action is commonplace and might not be thought of immediately as a control system.

If we consider control of the use of the four operating theatres in a local hospital things are not quite so simple. In general terms, the purpose of the theatres can be described without too much difficulty. The theatres will be used by a variety of clinical specialties who will have expectations derived from their own needs and those of their patients. There will be a need for the theatres to be cleaned and maintained on a regular basis and the theatres will have to be available for a combination of emergency and routine work. Thus, while we agree that the theatres have a clear purpose, the activity which goes on within them is complex and subject to potentially conflicting demands. The day-to-day activities of the theatre will be managed by a theatre manager but there will be occasions when policies and patterns of theatre use have to be discussed by a group or committee which represents the interests of its users.

If we move to a higher level of complexity we can examine the issue of control within the surgical directorate of a hospital Trust. Typically, such a directorate would include general surgery, orthopaedic, traumatic, cardiothoracic, urology and other special-ties and would work to contracts negotiated with appropriate purchasers, and to internal contracts or service agreements with specialist services such as diagnostic and imaging departments. The clinical director has formal responsibility for the work of the department but serious questions arise in connection with his/her ability, time and resources to control the work of the department. Likewise the business manager may have the responsibility for monitoring the work done by the department making sure that funds are received for the work done but it is not clear that the business manager has the authority or the all round competence to control the work of the directorate initiating corrective action where appropriate. This is not a criticism of the ability or commit-ment of clinical director or business manager but rather a question about the structure and systems which enable such a complex entity to be managed and controlled.

If we look to the hospital as our focus for analysis the same questions arise in more complex form. As an NHS Trust the hospital is a quasi independent organization which is obliged to balance its books by obtaining contracts for health services and thus achieving an income. It is also a very complex set of interdependent activities. It is expected to respond very quickly to a busy Accident and Emergency (A&E) department yet it is not expected to have empty beds waiting for such an eventuality. It is expected to deal with planned elective and with unplanned emergency work in which the precise combination of services required is uncertain since their needs are only predictable in aggregate. It follows that the control systems of the car factory, while undoubtedly complicated, will not meet the complex demands of the hospital or large directorate.

The last decade has seen the development of a wide range of mechanisms set up by the state to assess and evaluate the performance of its public services and one only has to glance at a list of titles published by the Audit Commission or the National Audit Office to see that the control of public services has been a key concern. One author has gone so far as to write about the New 'Evaluative State' which emphasizes the importance of empirical data and the conclusions which can be drawn from its collection and interpretation (Henkel 1991). Others have identified a new 'managerialism' in which the dominance of professional cultures and professional staff has given way to a new breed of managers with the authority and power to control the pattern and quality of services but, arguably, without the professional experience or understanding necessary to understand those services nor the real needs of the beneficiaries (Harrison 1988). In each of these settings we are faced with the problem that different individuals have only a subset of the information, understanding, and expertise with which to interpret it. In some sense, therefore, control must be a collective exercise in which individuals collaborate to ensure the

Figure 7.1
A simple control
system

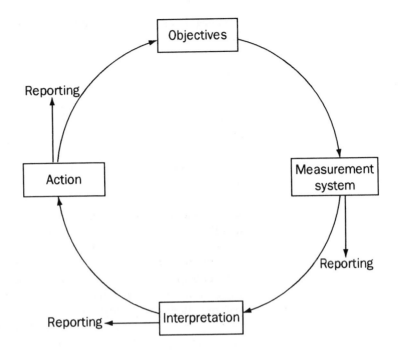

best possible service within the resources and to make adjustments where necessary. I will return to these concerns later. It is important to be clear at this stage what is meant by control.

BASIC ASSUMPTIONS UNDERPINNING A CONTROL SYSTEM   Any system of control, whether explicit or assumed within the practice of a professional role, assumes that a number of activities will take place. Firstly, it assumes that there will be a clear set of *objectives* for a particular activity which are underpinned by indicators or standards that define the objectives or allow them to be operationalized. These objectives may be explicit, such as the objectives of a service to screen for cervical cancer among a defined population, or harder to define, such as the objectives of a health promotion service providing advice to teenagers on healthy lifestyles. Indeed the objectives of some services may be clear to the practitioners who provide those services but unclear to interested others. This is not unusual within the private sector where a sole practitioner may only begin to set out clear objectives when seeking a business loan from the bank who require a detailed business plan. Indeed these objectives may not be a true guide to the purpose or direction of the organization. There may be disagreement about objectives or about the balance and ranking of objectives. We all start from the position that our particular area of work should be unmolested.

A control system assumes that there will be a *measurement system* in which the activity or outcomes of a service will be compared with the detailed objectives, indicators or standards providing a raw measure of whether those standards are being achieved. I describe the measure as 'raw' since the measurements alone may have very little meaning. How are we to assess whether a particular measure is good or bad, whether it constitutes a creditable improvement or a disappointing level of performance? As the system we are attempting to control becomes more complex we may have difficulty in finding appropriate comparators. For instance, the Audit Commission observed that some NHS Trusts appear to spend twice as much as seemingly comparable Trusts on their senior management. As a measure of expenditure the Audit Commission could not say whether the high or low cost Trusts were achieving value for money but only that the difference was significant and worth investigating.

To translate the raw data from a measurement system into useful information requires a process of *interpretation* in which the data is placed in an appropriate context and various informed value-judgements are made about the performance in question. For instance, does the performance of an ophthalmic unit in clearing a waiting list represent an exceptionally good level of performance by the members of the team, or were the team and its facilities augmented by additional manpower and facilities such that the level of performance represents the minimum acceptable in the circumstances? Such interpretation often requires local knowledge and implies examining a variety of indicators rather than assuming that a single indicator tells the whole story. This is sometimes referred to as the balance scorecard approach (Chakravarthy (1986), Carter (1991)). For instance, Chakravarthy points to the inadequacy of the formal accounts of an organization to act alone as an indicator of the strategic performance of that company. Questions need to be asked about whether the company is well positioned to compete in its markets, whether it has competitive advantage and low cost structure, whether it is able to demonstrate new applications of its technologies which are likely to result in new and profitable markets. Rosabeth Moss Kanter writes about the multiple-constituency approach which recognizes the full range of stakeholders in voluntary and public organizations and the wide variety of expectations which they hold of the organization. For instance a teaching hospital will have to meet expectations for service delivery, research, and education and training. These activities will have different timescales and will frequently cause conflicts of interest for professionals and managers (Moss Kanter 1990).

While the primary purpose of a control system must be to operate and adjust the particular service or activity involved, a secondary purpose is often some form of external *reporting* or accountability system. This may be designed to compare performance with other similar services or to provide information to interested parties – hence the popularity with government of hospital league tables. It should be noted that the accountability and reporting objectives may subvert the primary purpose of the control system.

All of these processes are central to the discussion of performance assessment and evaluation and the critical difference lies in the final component of the control process, namely *action*. A control process requires that there is a link between the interpreted data or information and action to influence or adjust the activity in question. Failure to take appropriate action, or to leave well alone where control information indicates so, implies that there is no effective control process and may have serious negative effects on attempts to manage or develop services in the future.

This picture of control works well when we are talking about a consistent and predictable system with a limited number of variables with relationships which are clearly understood. The classic example is the mechanical or electronic thermostat which is used to control the temperature in a room. The difficulties arise when we attempt to use this analogy to address the complex systems and subsystems which comprise a community health centre, general practice, secondary or tertiary hospital. The thermostat is concerned with one variable, temperature, which can be measured without ambiguity and which can be reduced or increased by the use of simple mechanisms. If our health centre is keen to ensure a welcoming and comfortable atmosphere for its staff and patients then the thermostat is only one subsystem of a much more complex process which is intended to achieve that objective.

ORIGINS OF CONTROL SYSTEMS

Control systems may be imposed by some level of management or government or designed by the individuals and groups providing a service. Frequently they will have to meet the needs of both groups. For instance, the Royal Colleges may insist that there are a series of control systems in those departments accredited for the postgraduate training of doctors. If such procedures are not in place then accreditation for training is sometimes withdrawn.

The control systems with which we are all familiar can be accounted for in a number of ways. They may result from a clear choice by an individual or group to pursue an objective and to put in place controls to increase the probability that the objective will be achieved. Alternatively, they may be seen as a contingent response to an objective imposed elsewhere or to some other influence within the environment. At the time of writing, the government has demanded that health authorities should demonstrate adequate procedures and controls to ensure that community services for mentally ill people in the UK are adequate to the needs of those people. It may be argued that the August 1995 announcement from the Minister of Health is a response to growing public disquiet following the closure of the hospitals for the mentally ill and a growing number of violent attacks on members of the public which have been attributed in the press to mentally ill people. It is thought by the government that the community services which have been set up to replace the institutions have not been sufficiently well planned, developed, and managed to meet the needs of this group of patients. Health authorities have been given three months to demonstrate that they have appropriate services in place for their patients and the Regional Directors of Health Authorities are expected to check at the end of this period that these plans are in place.

Thus, this example may be seen as a contingent response to public pressure and humanitarian concern by the government which has resulted in the decision to set objectives for health authorities and social service departments. These authorities have to show the development of joint plans, services, and control systems to ensure that the mentally ill being treated in the community receive the service they require. Thus the indicator is an indirect sign of the service available to this particular patient group. Another similar example which could be quoted is the case of children thought to be at risk of abuse and the setting up of a registration system with controls to ensure that such children are visited and their situation monitored and that they are not simply forgotten by the community and its agencies.

It is clear that the provision of an effective community service for the mentally ill is a complex process requiring the cooperation of a range of disciplines, state and voluntary agencies. It follows that to ensure that such a service meets its objectives is going to require the simultaneous coordination of a range of activities and an integrated set of control systems monitoring the component services. If we return to the systems model which was discussed in the introduction we shall see that control systems can operate at a number of levels. We can operate controls to ensure that there are appropriate resources for the services which are required and that the funds are used in the ways in which they were intended. This can be seen as control systems at the level of inputs. It might be argued that all that is being controlled is the allocation of funds and the resources which those funds are used to purchase. More interestingly but at a higher level of complexity, we could devise control systems to ensure that the planned activities take place as anticipated, looking at questions of volume and quality of those activities. Indeed various protocols are set up in an attempt to ensure that particular conditions are treated in what is thought to be the most efficacious manner. Neither control of inputs or activity necessarily ensures that the patient benefits in the desired fashion from the service and so we, in principle, need to think about control systems designed to ensure that particular outcomes (individual) or impacts (social) are achieved.

One common experience of the process of contracting has been that when purchaser and provider examine activity across a range of services at year end, the planned activities for particular services/conditions are at significant variance with actual levels for reasons which might not be immediately apparent due to changes in demand or need. Frequently, positive and negative variances for different services contracted with one purchaser will be reconciled since uncertainty of demand places limits on the accuracy of projected service levels and the cost of unscrambling the variances may outweigh the benefits to the parties.

CONTROL SYSTEMS AND COMPLEXITY

If control systems in health care are to be of any value they have to deal with complexity; stakeholder requirements including those of purchasers, providers, beneficiaries; the complex interactions and interdependencies between healthcare systems and subsystems; the balance of routine service and more clearly defined projects; and the pervasive influence of uncertainty.

Control systems need to be of sufficient sophistication to match the complexity of services. The complexity is caused by a number of factors:

♦ The various stakeholders in health care have different sets of objectives which overlap yet contain different priorities and latent if not manifest conflicts. The purchaser's objectives will be set out in the contract and may include a requirement to provide the same levels of service for 3% less money than last year. The provider Trust's objective will be to meet the contracted level of service at a cost which is less than, or at least equal to, the contract price. The patient's objective will be to receive a painless, convenient, comfortable service which effectively solves their problems. All this is expected to take place within the constraints of the Patient's Charter and to help achieve the objectives set out in the Health of the Nation.

♦ Healthcare activities are provided by a series of services which operate singly and together in order to provide an appropriate service. Thus a patient may require the services of imaging, pathology, surgery, medicine and rehabilitation services in the treatment of a particular episode. The effect of a delay in any of these services might have an impact on the whole pattern of treatment and indeed possibly on the outcome experienced by the patient.

Thus we have a series of treatment subsystems which operate independently yet disturbance in one subsystem can have a serious impact on other related systems. Everyone knows that if a hospital portering system is not working then many related systems operate less efficiently.

♦ Health services are characterized by uncertainty. A treatment which works well for one patient may be unsuccessful for another and it may take weeks or months for the outcome to be apparent. Many health service procedures will require short- and long-term measurement.

♦ Health services include routine services which are characterized by stable demands and subject to a variety of controls both explicit and intuitive. They will also include projects and programmes of limited duration, with clear objectives, and which can be planned since the resource requirements are straightforward to predict.

So far we have pointed to the complexity of the systems of health care which we might wish to control without explicitly addressing the key factors of that complexity. In the literature these factors are sometimes referred to as contingency factors (Dent and Ezzamel 1987). It is argued that to be effective control systems must take account of a series of such factors which form the subject of the next section.

In the light of this complexity a common response is to measure what is easily measurable and to measure the activity of clearly defined subsystems rather than of complex combinations of services. It has been suggested that what gets measured gets done. Thus quantifiable inputs such as the use of money are measured and there are methods to identify and investigate significant variance from budgetary targets. The use of capital and equipment is recorded in capital asset registers. The numbers of beds and the numbers of staff have been measured for many years as if these are acceptable indicators of the level and quality of services. As argued above, these measures are only of use if they are part of control systems which involve interpretation of data and action in the light of existing or new targets.

If control systems are to contribute to the search for value for money they have to examine both sides of the equation and to date they have paid more attention to money than to value.

SYSTEMS AND SUBSYSTEMS The easiest way to examine the interaction of systems and subsystems within the control process is to look at two examples from general practice and institutional settings.

The fundholding general practice If we consider the GP fundholding practice as a system within the wider healthcare system we can describe the activities within the practice in terms of a number of important subsystems (Figure 7.2). The precise definitions of subsystems are a matter for debate and would depend upon the analysis of a particular practice yet a

Figure 7.2
The fundholding
practice system

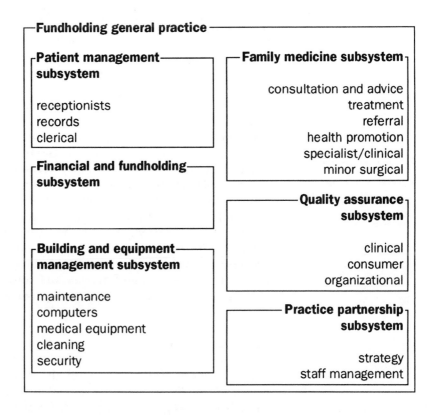

cursory approach would suggest that the following subsystems can be identified:

- patient management subsystem;
- family medicine subsystem;
- financial and fundholding management subsystem;
- building and equipment management subsystem;
- quality assurance subsystem;
- practice partnership subsystem.

Each of these systems have objectives and will be the subject of a variety of control systems. The patient management systems will be designed to ensure that patients receive appointments and attend at times which are appropriate to their own particular need whether defined in terms of medical urgency or the particular consultation and treatment regime required. The family medicine system will ensure that consultations are properly recorded and that where necessary appropriate action is taken such as referral or the follow-up of a patient at an appropriate time. The patient management system will have to take account of variations in the family medicine system such as the annual leave or sickness leave of a doctor requiring the rearrangement of appointments and perhaps clinics. The financial and fundholding system will be designed to ensure an accurate record of the commitment and use of funds and appropriate action in claiming capitation and other fees where appropriate.

The practice partnership system will be concerned with some strategic objectives such as the maintenance of the quality of services provided by the practice, the financial viability of the practice and its development. While it will want to be aware of key indicators to ensure that the practice is viable and working towards its objectives, it will also make decisions to adjust and vary its activities on an intuitive basis. It may occasionally decide to undertake feasibility studies to see if a particular activity such as a well-woman clinic would be financially viable and what impact it would have on the existing patterns of work of the practice.

While the partners will want to be aware of important information and issues within the practice it will usually appoint a practice manager to manage the non-medical subsystems, taking action where necessary to adjust activity and bringing significant variances to the attention of a managing partner or the partners' meeting.

The partners' meeting may have a standing agenda which will cover a series of indicators emanating from the various subsystems and their control systems. For instance they may want to know the state of patient registrations with the practice, the costs of a month's prescribing and perhaps more important the trends in the cost of prescribing. They will want to know the trends and costs of extracontractual referrals (ECRs) against the budgeted levels of activities and they may want to know the projected financial out turns for the end of the financial year.

It should be noted from this example that all subsystems will relate with each other although in some cases the relationship is closer than in others. Also the subsystems relate to other parts of the healthcare system through activities such as referral, pathology and imaging activities on which the medical subsystem is based.

The NHS Trust system   Similarly the NHS Trust system is a larger example of a set of interdependent subsystems, each with their own control systems feeding the needs of operational and strategic managers. Simple mathematics tells us that an organization which is large in size, split into numerous departments, using a variety of technologies to address complex and varied problems will require a similar variety of control systems.

Figure 7.3 points to some of the subsystems which require control and integration if value for money is to be achieved. Some of the subsystems are concerned chiefly with the value side of the equation while others are concerned with the resource side. It is not realistic to think of a fully integrated control system which will permit the equivalent of auto pilot on a jumbo jet it may never be so. Professionals and managers will be responsible for the manage-

Figure 7.3
The NHS Trust system

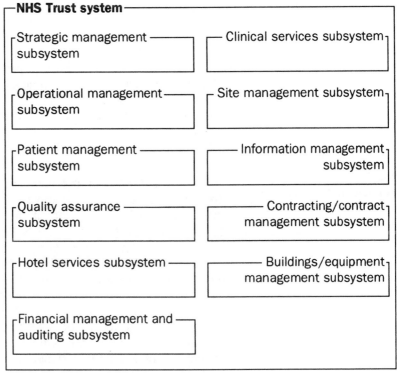

ment of the various subsystems which may well be the subject of contracts, service level agreements and protocols.

Changes in the pattern of services such as shifts towards outpatient and primary care services will have an impact across the whole system and will require a variety of responses requiring departmental action and central coordination.

CONTINGENCY
FACTORS
UNDERPINNING
CONTROL SYSTEMS

The identification of contingency factors was initially part of an academic attempt to identify the best organizational structures (themselves control systems) for particular organizations in their own businesses. While the factors may be thought to be common sense, they must be clearly defined if effective control systems are to be designed and activated. For instance, clinical control systems must take account of the varying patterns of demand due to seasonality, epidemics and infectious diseases.

Each of these contingency factors has a bearing on the control systems and their effectiveness in supporting the management of a particular activity. While they are isolated for the purposes of our discussion, they act together in complex patterns which have to be recognized before it is possible to develop effective control systems.

Technology   Technology includes knowledge and treatment processes as well as the pattern of social relationships and activities which allow it to be implemented. Medical and clinical professionals are amongst the most innovative of workers and are backed up with vast educational, research and commercial enterprises on an international scale. It is not surprising that developing technologies have such an important impact on the viability of control systems. The following examples show that technology can enhance control systems or reduce their effectiveness.

Box 7.1
Example from general practice

In the past the general practitioner had very little in the way of technological resources available to him/her. The stethoscope and a limited collection of drugs combined with a medical education, some medical textbooks and (hopefully) a good deal of practical experience might describe the available resources. Where a patient's symptoms went beyond the personal experience of the GP a referral would be made to a consultant at an appropriate hospital. Many patients would be advised how to deal with their symptoms, given a prescription to take to the local pharmacist, and advised to return in a given period if the symptoms were not alleviated. Payment was on a capitation basis with limited fee from service items paid from an open budget administered by the Local Executive Council. How different this sounds from the new total budget fundholding GPs who purchase the full range of services from a range of providers on behalf of the patients on their list, working with perhaps 50 staff, engaging in minor surgery, training new GPs and perhaps addressing their own research and publication agenda.

While it might be fairly simple to diagram the healthcare subsystem managed by the GP of yesterday the requirements of the fundholding GP are highly complex and in some contexts controversial. At its simplest the development of medical technologies such as imaging and diagnosis, pharmacology, and new treatment options have increased the range of activities undertaken by GPs and also the range of other staff with whom GPs communicate and interact through the exchange of information and various forms of collaborative working. Each of these activities involves the GP in a series of subsystems which have their own objectives, measurement and control systems. In short the need for coordination has increased significantly due in part to the new opportunities offered by a range of technologies. It is difficult even to describe the healthcare systems in which the GP is involved, let alone devise consistent objectives and control mechanisms (Whitehouse 1995).

Box 7.2
Example from mental
health services

The technological developments in the field of drug treatment are in part responsible for the move from institutional treatment regimes to community care for many seriously ill patients. The provision of community care in part implies the abandonment of a strictly medical model of care to a model which attempts to integrate medical and social elements among others. This requires the joint working of different professions and developments such as multidisciplinary case conferences, designated care workers, personal care plans which are all examples of attempts to integrate services made up of contributions from disparate sources.

Where such systems fail and no action is taken we are all too aware of the personal tragedies which occur. Since these failures are of importance they reach the national news and reinforce the belief that there should be no failures. Health and social services aspire to excellence in the treatment of patients and therefore tragedies lead to inquiries, the publication of results and recommendations which all providers are expected to adhere to. Indeed many of the developments in services are a result of public and internal Inquiries and their recommendations for development (e.g. Normansfield 1978).

Box 7.3
Example from hospital
services

The development of minimally invasive therapies has had a significant effect on patterns of healthcare delivery yet it has been argued that an absence of some controls has led to poor quality services for some patients and to avoidable damage to others who in effect have been used as guinea pigs. From a professional practice perspective the traditional powers enjoyed by consultant surgeons meant that there was nothing to prevent an interested surgeon from adopting the new methods when they became available. The new methods of diagnosis and treatment implied reduced need for inpatient stays and increased requirements for operating theatres than were previously needed in more conventional forms of surgery.

Age and size of organization　As organizations grow, whether measured in terms of employees, activity, income, scope or range of activities, the problems of control become more complex. The smallest organizations consisting of one person, such as a single-handed GP, often operate an intuitive form of control as far as the environment in which they operate will permit. As organizations grow the requirements to communicate and coordinate activity with a wider range of people inevitably demand the development of more explicit methods of control. This may imply a regular meeting to discuss workload or problems with workload and to assign responsibilities on an ad hoc basis. As organizations mature they develop patterns and operating routines which add consistency and predictability to the activity of the organization. Sometimes it is necessary to set up departments whose sole purpose is the planning and coordination of the work of separate subsystems.

Organizations of a certain age develop their own traditions as has been shown in the attempts to reorder the pattern of health services in London where the future of long established institutions has been threatened. These traditions are vitally important in the development of expectations, standards of excellence, and patterns of professional performance by which individuals consciously or unconsciously control their own performance. This organizational culture has been described as the 'organizational glue' which holds organizations together and provides consistency in activities in which there are no explicit or adequate control systems (Morgan 1986).

Organization structure and process
The organizational structure is a control process in itself and is also a contingency factor which influences the pattern and possibilities for control. There are a number of principles of structure including the grouping of staff with similar skills or from similar backgrounds, the grouping of staff servicing patients with similar problems or other shared characteristics, the grouping of staff according to the geographical site of their activities, and the grouping of staff pursuing a management activity, e.g. the planning or the quality assurance group. A structure will be made up of a variety of these characteristics and the precise structure will influence the possibilities for effective control processes. For instance, a clinical directorate system may include seven or more directorates pointing to the diversity of clinical work or expertise. Alternatively, there may be only two or three directorates pointing to the need for central coordination.

In a functional system it may be assumed that the work of accountants will be controlled by accountants and the work of nurses by senior nurses. A general management system will assume that a general manager is responsible for services and the incumbent is appointed regardless of professional discipline but rather on the basis of suitability for the managerial task. A decentralized system will attempt to ensure that those with the appropriate knowledge are those who are responsible for the management and delivery of services, that they have the authority they require to make decisions, and that they are able to run their own control systems. A locality based system will give priority to the coordination of services for a defined residential population, perhaps a small town or district of a larger city.

When a constituent part of the NHS is criticized for overspending three kinds of action may be contemplated: replace key managers, restructure the organization, introduce new control systems. It is instructive that within the NHS the critical indicator is the control of expenditure which follows from the funding base in taxation and the annual parliamentary vote of funds for the NHS as for other state services.

Environment   Fahey and Narayanan (1986) have described the environment of an organization in terms of sociological, technological, economic and political factors (which usually includes regulatory factors). This framework can be expanded for our purposes.

Epidemiological environment
In its broadest sense the epidemiological environment including factors such as the age/sex profile and disease characteristics of a population impact on the pattern of needs which are translated into demands through attendance and referral but also through the plans and strategies adopted within health services. Clearly health services have to respond to an epidemiological environment which in some cases they attempt to shape through programmes of health promotion and treatment.

Sociological environment
In the past health services have been provided in an environment which has been willing to trust doctors and medical staff to provide a good and efficient service making decisions about resource allocation. Now in the 'evaluative state' it is necessary to report widely on aspects of healthcare delivery. The development of consumerism has resulted in new patterns of doctor–patient relationship as well as Charters throughout the public sector.

Economic environment
Pettigrew (1983) has described what happens when organizations move from rich to poor environments as might be seen when an economy moves into recession and public services face a new level of resource constraints. The impacts of such a shift include the obvious issues of contraction rather than expansion, more attention to control of activity, shifts in the importance and sometimes prestige of particular roles. There are also psychological impacts including changes in morale and other soft but important factors. The economic environment will have a considerable impact on healthcare services through the labour market, the level of wage pressure, as well as more directly through the public resources available to the purchasers. Its impact will also be felt throughout

the health of related systems such as the private healthcare industry.

Political environment

No-one would doubt that there are strong ideological views about the nature of the NHS held within the political context. These place different importance on issues such as equity, efficiency, democracy, and local responsiveness. The NHS is too large a service for governments to ignore representing a significant component of total public expenditure.

Regulatory environment

The regulatory environment goes beyond the UK and ties in the European Union which is increasingly important in its attempts through regulation to create an open employment market across the community which has had a significant impact on the training of hospital doctors and through that on the nature and numbers of staff available at different grades.

Nature and distribution of power

The distribution of power can be considered in terms of the formal NHS structure and also in terms of questions of professional power. The introduction of general management in 1985 implied a particular form of power within the formal structure of the NHS and overturned assumptions previously held about the need for a consensus between key professions in the management of services. This did not overcome the systemic needs for integration of the activities of service and management subsystems but meant that a service delivery system had to work alongside a management system which was responsible for the achievement of hierarchically imposed targets and later for the introduction of the NHS market, the negotiation and fulfilment of contracts for service.

Like the wind, power is often only visible indirectly in its effects. There may be a shifting pattern of power within complex organizations and considerable patterns of uncertainty as to whether groups and individuals have the power to achieve their particular objectives.

TECHNICAL CONSIDERATIONS IN THE CONTROL SYSTEM

Rosabeth Moss Kanter (1990) suggests that performance measurement systems have to meet a series of requirements:

◆ Institutional requirements – the need to attract resources, maintain legitimacy, and develop the reputation of institution and its members.
◆ Managerial requirements – including the need for internal resource allocation and coordination of activities.
◆ Technical requirements – ensuring the effectiveness of technical procedures within the organization.

It follows that control systems have to meet a number of requirements and have to be designed with considerable skill if they are to be successful. In healthcare systems there are a number of technical considerations which need to be addressed.

Who is the control system oriented towards?

Is the control system designed for the customer, consumer, provider or is it expected to act for a variety of stakeholders? If there are separate control systems then there is likely to be a problem of incompatibility, while a single control system might not meet the needs of any stakeholders entirely. In the past a frequent complaint was expressed that data was provided for the needs of the Department of Health and Regional Health Authorities who were not involved in the operational delivery of health services. Thus the information was of little use to clinicians and managers in their everyday work.

How does the control system address the definition and agreement of objectives?

The definition of objectives in health services is no easy exercise and the articulation of paper objectives does not imply that individuals own or work to those objectives. As we move from inputs to activities and then to outcomes and impacts the precise agreement and definition of objectives becomes more difficult and is likely to be intuitive rather than explicit. Even where an outcome/impact objective is set, such as the reduction in the number of suicides as set out in the Health of the Nation, it is not clear what activities of health services and related agencies will necessarily ensure the achievement of the objective.

It activity defined and recorded in consistent fashion?

As has been discussed in chapter 2, the definition of objectives, activities and the underlying processes is a complex business. However a clinical procedure is defined the process of definition and coding is complex. Put another way, the variety of clinical practice does not easily lend itself to the more comfortable definitions of the manufacturing plant where every product, and associated component, has a clear specification. In some areas of work such as the treatment of childhood cancers a large proportion of the patients will be enrolled on one or more clinical trials with clear treatment protocols and explicit definition of actions and procedures. However, this remains the exception rather than the rule and in many areas of care consistent recording of activity is a problem.

Practical problems concern the coding and recording process. Is the coding process accurate? Relatively error free? What is the error rate for the coding process and how significant are errors in the data collection process? While zero-defects in data collection might be a laudable objective it might prove very expensive to attain and if errors in data are as easily recognized as some clinicians would suggest then perhaps new patterns of data review are needed rather than throwing the baby out with the bath water.

How does the control system work? Does the control system focus on exceptional incidents or does it continuously focus on all activity? Management by exception may be seen to be cost-effective since it focuses attention not on the activity which meets predetermined standards but on that which is thought to be unacceptable. It is, however, important that exceptions are identified quickly and dealt with. The identification of exceptions or variances implies that there is an appropriate comparator. This might be performance in a comparable practice or service or more frequently performance in a comparable time period. A GP practice might want to know how many patients aged over 65 take advantage of the offer of free vaccinations against influenza in winter 1995 compared with those who were vaccinated in 1994 while at the same time it might want to know why certain patients decided not be vaccinated in 1995 who took advantage of the service in 1994.

Comparators might be imposed by a central authority and so the league tables of NHS Trusts give star ratings according to a number of factors including Patient's Charter objectives such as the size of waiting lists and the times which patients have to wait to be seen by a doctor or other member of staff.

Who exercises control? In a complex organization where the variety of work is high and the technical knowledge of staff is complex and wide ranging, one would expect that control would be in the hands of the doctors and others who provide treatments and indeed this was very much the case in public healthcare systems until relatively recently. However, the demands of the public paymaster and the development of public purchasing agencies imply that there is an inevitable contest between professional priorities as exemplified by the concept of clinical autonomy and the value for money concerns of the public purse.

Routine activity or projects? Most of our consideration has related to control of routine activities which make up the day-to-day work both elective and emergency. Another key consideration is the control of projects and of changes which make up much of the investigative work of the Audit Commission and National Audit Office. Projects frequently have a clearly defined objective whether they relate to a capital development or to a service objective such as the reduction of particular waiting lists. They have a defined timescale and identified resources. This allows the use of conventional planning and control techniques such as critical path analysis, Gantt charts, milestone planning, and accountability charting. This permits the analysis of variance from plan and the identification of appropriate action which might include use of additional resources, rescheduling of the plan, etc.

Issues of timing   A key feature of control systems is the timing of different elements of the control loop. To some extent this follows from the nature of clinical and healthcare processes. The development of clear and agreed objectives may be a complex process as shown by the difficulties experienced in the early years of the NHS internal market contracting process.

   ♦ *Feedforward control* implies control takes place before the activity concerned. This might imply computer or other modelling of the process. For instance, the computer modelling of a course of radiotherapy treatment is intended to ensure that the real treatment which follows will achieve its objectives and there will be no errors. Computer modelling might be used to display the data regarding attendance at an A&E department showing the numbers of patients attending at different times of the week and their needs. This enables the appropriate staffing patterns to be adopted and a good use to be made of the physical facilities available to the department. It may also give some ideas of what inpatient beds might be required to meet the needs of patients admitted in a typical weekend in the winter in a London hospital. This could be particularly important in designing a new hospital or redesigning an existing department. For instance, 'what if' questions can be addressed such as what would happen if the neighbouring Accident Centre had to close for the weekend, or what would happen in the event of a serious accident or infectious disease.

   ♦ *Concurrent control* implies that the time gap between observation, interpretation and action is instantaneous or at least very short. This implies either that the activity being controlled is simple and an immediate adjustment is possible if, for instance, the anaesthetist thinks it is important to adjust the mix of gases being administered to an unconscious patient. The thermostatic type of control mentioned earlier might be understood as concurrent control.

   ♦ *Feedback control* implies a significant time gap between the observation and interpretation of activity and subsequent management action. This may be because the process of observation, collection and processing of data takes a significant time, it may be because the process of interpretation is complex or time consuming, or it may be because the management action requires detailed or complex planning. Feedback control might mean that management action has to be directed at new activity rather than the activities which were measured.

How effective is   Effective control systems depend upon the ability to process
information   complex data and to interpret its meaning. A management account-
processing?   ing system must be able to give information on spending patterns to the responsible managers quickly so that they can make

adjustments if necessary. It is of very little value if expenditure information is only available six months after the event or if the recipients find it comes in a form which they cannot easily understand. This may require investment in hard information systems as well as matching expenditure in training for users.

The introduction of fundholding was predicted upon the recognition that most eligible practices had neither the information processing nor the management capabilities to manage the fund and the associated volume of activity required in fundholding. Allowances were required. Special funds were made available for the purchase of computer equipment and the employment of required administrative staff. Significant start-up problems required resources for data entry and staff training to ensure that the funds could be appropriately managed.

Clinical data is generally more complex than financial and other administrative data. Clinicians have collected patient data for many years in the cause of ongoing research programmes and in order to learn from their own experience. The outcomes and collective impacts of services often take many years to identify and it might be inappropriate and indeed dangerous to be too precipitous in coming to conclusions on the basis of short series of patients.

BEHAVIOURAL ISSUES IN CONTROL

Positive or perverse?

We know well that the use of control systems can have perverse effects. There is good evidence in the past that the introduction of control systems causes incentives to identify loopholes. For instance, a GP fundholder might advise a patient to attend the A&E department since that attendance may be accounted for in a different way to that of a conventional referral letter followed by the offer of an outpatient appointment to the patient and such an action might enable the patient to jump the queue and be seen more quickly.

There is evidence to suggest that what gets measured becomes the centre of attention perhaps to the exclusion of those things which are not measured despite their importance. The significance of the waiting list initiative and the research rating exercise has had considerable influence on hospitals and research institutions despite the fact that the indicators which they measure are only a small part of the overall activity.

Control processes are social and technical procedures in that they assume that the individuals and teams involved will accept and conduct the processes as they are designed. In practice there may be a number of reasons why control processes are ignored or not given appropriate priority. Staff may not believe that the measurement processes are valid or if they are valid that they are important. They may not have been appropriately trained to undertake the measurement or they may believe that alternative measures are more appropriate or valid. Staff may feel that the control process is not important or that it threatens professional judgement or intuition. It may be that a control system will only be regarded as legitimate if it is introduced after cooperation or even participation of the group concerned. There may be good reasons for setting up a control system after participation since the group concerned may have the necessary specialist knowledge needed to create a good control system yet the symbolic value of participation should not be underestimated.

If we examine the purchaser–provider split as a means of setting clear service level agreements and control systems it has been pointed out that the purchasers can enter into a contest with their providers or they can view the process as one of collaboration in which both are seeking the best value for money from the funds available for services. The competition analogy implies the behaviours associated with games in which cards are held secret and moves made with the intention of gaining an advantage over purchasers or other providers.

Effective operation of the quasi-market demands an effective series of operational controls, procedural controls, payment controls etc. Contracts include items which require that the provider will provide data for monitoring/control processes to the purchasing authorities.

Internal service agreements between departments which treat patients and those supplying services such as pathology and imaging which provide services or information for doctors will involve indicative levels of activity and may or may not be costed. While costing such services may cause careful reflection before costs are incurred the costs of monitoring and charging for transactions may outweigh any significant improvement in the levels of use of a service.

Control and learning At several points in the control process, there are opportunities for learning which may improve the possibilities of achieving greater value for money. At the objective setting, or contracting, stage close attention to the needs of beneficiaries, the clinical or service process may allow better objectives and measures or indicators to be identified. These may be better in technical and in behavioural terms.

The process of measurement also provides an opportunity for learning. Variances need to be identified and investigated providing an opportunity for learning more about the clinical and service processes involved. Since the clinical needs of patients vary it is important not to take particular care in the interpretation of measurement data which do not meet expectations.

If as a result of a control system the activities in question are adjusted there will often be a need for active experimentation to identify the best way of adjusting services, measures or objectives to bring activities back into control.

COSTS, BENEFITS AND PAYBACK OF CONTROL SYSTEMS

As the well documented case of Wessex Health Authority shows, an attempt to create information and control systems covering the activity of health services across a region was immensely complex and ultimately unsuccessful. However, most control systems are much simpler in technical and social/political terms. Clinicians will want information from a variety of systems and senior managers will want to be informed about serious variances from planned activity. While integrated systems may seem attractive, it is still the case that in sophisticated systems medical and financial information is recorded and managed using different control systems.

Control systems must themselves be subject to analysis to ensure that they provide value for money. There is considerable debate at present about the value provided by the UK breast screening service, which is thought to be very expensive in terms of the number of lives saved, and the possible alternative uses of the money involved. Additionally the technical failings of the system mean that significant numbers of women are alarmed without cause since they prove not to have malignant disease only after being sent an alarming letter and asked to attend for further examination.

SUMMARY

The discussion of control systems in itself should not be a cause of anxiety. The process of agreeing objectives, measuring and interpreting results, and taking appropriate clinical or managerial action is central to the normal working practices of clinicians and managers. The range of activity, interdependence of action, and uncertainty of both clinical and service outcomes suggest that we should develop control systems with care. It is better to build slowly and carefully, making sure that measurement is appropriate and considered action is taken, than to impose heroic control systems that count everything and measure nothing. Control systems must be 'made to measure' and must provide value for money.

FURTHER READING

♦ Moss Kanter, R. (1990), *When Giants Learn to Dance*, Unwin, London.

♦ Chakravarthy, B. (1986), Measuring strategic performance, *Strategic Management Journal*, 7: 437–458.

♦ Henkel, M. (1991), The new evaluative state, *Public Administration*, 69: 121–136.

REFERENCES

Carter, N. (1991), Learning to measure performance: the use of indicators in organisations. *Public Administration*, 69 (Spring): 85–102.

Chakravarthy, R. (1986), Measuring strategic performance. *Strategic Management Journal*, 7: 437–458.

Committee of Inquiry into Normansfield Hospital Report (1978), *Cmnd 7357*. London: HMSO.

Dent, J. and Ezzamel, M. (1987), Organisational control and management accounting. In Dent, J. and Ezzamel, M. *Advanced Management Accounting: An Organisational Emphasis*. London: Cassell Educational.

Fahey, L. and Narayanan, V.K. (1986), *Macro-Environmental Analysis for Strategic Management*. St Paul, Minnesota: West Publishing.

Freidson, E. (1973), *The Profession of Medicine*. New York: Harper and Row.

Harrison, S. (1988), The Workforce and the New Managerialism. In Maxwell, R.J. (ed.), *Reshaping the National Health Service*. Hermitage, Berks: Policy Journal.

Henkel, M. (1991), The new evaluative state. *Public Administration*, 69 (1): 121–136.

Morgan, G. (1986), *Images of Organisation*. London: Sage.

Moss Kanter, R. (1990), *When Giants Learn to Dance*. London: Unwin.

Pettigrew, A. (1983), Patterns of response as organisations move from rich to poor environments. *Educational Management Administration*, 2: 104–114.

Whitehouse, C. (1995), General practice and primary healthcare services. In Glynn, J.J. and Perkins, D.A. (Eds), *Managing Health Care: Challenges for the 90s*. London: Saunders.

SECTION III

AUDIT BASED APPROACHES

***SECTION
INTRODUCTION***

In introducing this section it is important to be clear what we mean by audit. In common parlance audit is understood as the independent scrutiny of accounts to see whether they provide a true and fair representation of the activity which they purport to describe. For the purposes of value for money audit whether clinical, managerial, or external we are concerned with the appraisal of systems and procedures to ascertain the effectiveness and efficiency of those systems and to identify potential areas for improvement. Thus audit aims to support a process of continuous improvement and is not primarily concerned with detecting isolated errors.

Audit needs to take place at a number of levels if it is to be effective and these different forms of audit need to inform each other so as to create a mutually reinforcing process and to allow the organization to learn and implement the findings of audit. Clinical audit has been given considerable national attention in recent years backed by increasing levels of national resources. It is recognized that the purpose of the NHS is to provide services to patients and communities and that if the clinical activity is of poor or inconsistent quality then there is no way in which services can be rescued by exceptional management. For instance, the outcomes of cancer services in the UK are thought to stand up poorly to comparison with some of our European neighbours. This issue is a problem to be addressed by clinical audit but it also becomes a problem for organizational or management audit. Are the resources allocated between primary and secondary care in the right way? Are the screening services using robust systems so that patients whose tests suggest possible malignancies are efficiently contacted and provided with appropriate advice and treatment? A well managed service will ensure that there are active systems for clinical and managerial audit and that the findings of one form of audit are fed in to the other.

It is also possible to learn from the experience of others and to identify what is thought to be best practice on a national or international basis. There are classically two approaches to external review, namely systems based and substantial review. The former focuses on the clinical and management systems in place within an organization and the latter concerns primarily the outcomes which are achieved by the service in question, making comparisons with comparable performance elsewhere. Whichever approach dominates it is the case in the UK that while the National Audit Office and the Audit Commission spend much time in data gathering and analysis, they recognize that clinical judgements and clinical effectiveness are the province of clinicians and while it is sometimes appropriate for external reviewers to ask challenging questions, it is the job of clinicians and not of auditors to provide the answers.

CLINICAL AUDIT: VALUE FOR MONEY?

CHAPTER 8

Fiona Moss and John Mitchell

OBJECTIVES

◆ To discuss the nature of clinical audit.

◆ To map out the processes by which medical audit has been introduced together with difficulties surrounding its implementation.

INTRODUCTION

Background

Medical audit was introduced into professional practice throughout the National Health Service as one of seven key changes outlined in the 1989 government health reforms *Working for Patients*. Its stated aim was to 'help to ensure that the best quality of medical care is given to patients' (Department of Health 1989a).

The inclusion of medical audit within this package of radical reforms can be seen as a response to a longstanding and increasing concern about the standards of care within the NHS. But by incorporating medical audit, a programme that aimed to improve the quality of care, within the 1989 NHS reforms those championing the changes within the NHS were able to justify a commitment to the quality of care that balanced the otherwise financial and managerial focus of the reforms. This commitment was made tangible by substantial funding of £48 million per annum of new, ring fenced, monies for the implementation of audit.

Why was a quality improvement initiative needed?

The argument for an effective programme to improve the quality of care within the NHS was gathering pace before the 1989 health service reforms. Some of the pressures came from an increasing general concern about the quality of service in the public sector. Other influences such as the call for accountability and for the evaluation of clinical practice in the 1983 Griffiths report on NHS management structures have come from within the NHS.

The need for a mechanism for quality improvement is supported both by anecdotal account and, crucially, by published studies that provide details of some of the problems that underlie the concerns about the quality of care in the NHS. These include the first confidential enquiry into perioperative deaths (CEPOD) (Buck *et al*. 1988), which showed that non-routine surgery was often performed out of hours by undersupervised, undersupported junior surgeons; statistics that demonstrated variations in rates of operations that could not be explained by population differences (McPherson *et al*. 1982); studies that indicated that some people were not receiving effective and appropriate care or that others were subjected to inappropriate interventions, for example the underuse of steroids in acute asthma (Bucknall *et al*. 1988), and the inappropriate use of coronary arteriograms and coronary bypass surgery (Gray *et al*. 1990); and audits such as the Lothian audit which showed that mortality for patients with ruptured aortic aneurysm treated by non-specialist surgeons was twice that for those treated by surgeons with an interest in vascular surgery (Gruer *et al*. 1986, Jenkins *et al*. 1986). Thus a body of objective evidence had been accumulating that suggested that an *effective* quality improvement programme could have substantial benefit on patient care and healthcare outcome.

What was in place before the introduction of audit?

An essential characteristic of audit is that it includes *systematic* evaluation of the quality of care. Before the introduction of audit few clinicians approached quality assessment or improvement systematically and most hospitals did not provide the infrastructure needed to support audit or any other systematic approach to quality improvement. Thus although some clinicians attended regular local morbidity and mortality meetings few collected aggregated information about specific aspects of medical care – such as the proportion of patients admitted with asthma treated with parenteral steroids or the proportion of those admitted with myocardial infarction treated with thrombolytic therapy on admission – for the purpose of quality assessment or improvement. Of course, this is not to say that before the introduction of audit that doctors and other healthcare practitioners were not concerned about the quality of care. They were. But responsibility for the quality of care was largely a matter of professional performance regulated by each profession. For many people within the NHS medical audit represented a new way of looking at care.

Audit and other systematic approaches to quality improvement   Audit is one of several strategies for quality improvement that involves a systematic evaluation of the quality of care. Others include quality assurance, continuous quality improvement or total quality management (TQM). The terminology that is used to describe each of these lacks clear definition. There are both areas of overlap and important distinctions to be made between them. And there are reservations about the validity of any distinction between clinical and managerial approaches to quality improvement.

What is audit?

Box 8.1
Definition of clinical
audit

> Clinical audit is the systematic critical analysis of the quality of clinical care, by all those who contribute to care. It includes the procedures used for diagnosis and treatment, the use of resources, and the resulting outcome and quality of life for patients – for this, patients' views must be sought.

The terms clinical or medical audit describe a systematic approach to quality improvement that centres on the evaluation of the quality of care by the healthcare professionals who provide that care (Box 8.1). Audit involves setting standards for a particular aspect of care, observing and measuring current practice, assessing how far, if at all, current practice varies from those standards, and if indicated, working out why it varies and making changes so that future practice will meet the standards set at the beginning of the exercise. These stages of audit are often described together as the 'audit cycle' which is repeated to assess whether change has produced benefit (Russell and Wilson 1992). An example of audit is the assessment of the use of thrombolytic therapy for people admitted to hospital with acute myocardial infarction – an intervention of proven benefit. Through the process of audit, various aspects of this intervention can be assessed; for example the time it takes for those with myocardial infarction to receive this treatment. If the time from admission to intervention is longer than the accepted maximum, and thus not all patients gain maximally from this intervention, the next stage of the audit is to determine the cause of the delay and then to change practice (Nee *et al.* 1994, Crombie and Davies 1993).

The difference between medical and clinical audit is that medical audit refers to audit by doctors of medical care whereas clinical audit has a wider remit and includes audit of the care delivered by the whole clinical team. Medical audit was the subject of the 1989 White Paper but from 1991 the focus moved to clinical audit. The difference may appear to be small but the move from the uniprofessional medical audit to the broader inclusive process of clinical audit has been difficult and probably properly managed in only a few areas.

Quality assurance

Quality assurance is often used as a general term to describe all quality improvement programmes and initiatives. But it is also used to describe monitoring of performance against predetermined standards often by inspection by an organization external to the provider of care. Quality assurance programmes that are essentially inspectorial in approach have been a feature of health care in the USA (Wareham 1994). Criticisms of such strategies to quality improvement are that quality is assured only to the level of predetermined standards and that external inspection tends to promote a reflex defensiveness and thus limit the potential for improvement (Berwick 1989, Laffel and Blumenthal 1989).

Continuous quality improvement or total quality assurance
These mechanisms – which are largely indistinguishable – originated from work in manufacturing and industry and are based on a philosophy that considers quality a matter of importance for the whole organization; that includes recognition of the importance of measurement; that defines quality as meeting the needs of customers – including internal ones; and that encourages the workforce to look at the processes of production and not people for the cause of mistakes or faults. These approaches to quality improvement rely on internal assessment of quality and not inspection by outside groups or agencies. These techniques are associated with quality improvement in industry.

What was unique about the audit programme?
The near mandatory introduction of a mechanism that aims to improve the quality of care through a process of internal assessment of the quality of care independent of external assessment of performance has no precedent. Medical audit, as it is practised in the UK, is essentially a process that is carried out *within an organization*. Whilst motivation was external as the audit programme was initiated by a central directive and developed and facilitated by regional health authorities, the work required for the process of audit had to be driven by doctors and others working *within provider units*. This mix of incentive and directives and local action has allowed audit to develop. In contrast, in France where quality assurance initiatives are voluntary such activities are not widespread (Giraud *et al.* 1993).

Assessing the value of audit
Martin Buxton (1994) has described the medical audit programme as an 'emergent technology' and as such should be subject to rigorous evaluation. But although some case studies and other evaluations have demonstrated that, in specific circumstances, the process of audit can result in improvement in the quality of care the evidence is limited. Medical audit was introduced 'as an act of faith'. There was little research to support its *efficacy* and none that had tested or quantified the *effectiveness* of a whole programme (Walshe and Coles 1993). Furthermore, this untested programme was set up without a mechanism for its evaluation.

Improving the quality of the technical aspects of medical care by, for example, increasing the use of effective and appropriate interventions is a process likely to require both organizational and behavioural change. But the working papers on medical audit and many of the early descriptions of audit focused on the mechanics of audit and the audit cycle and the need for audit to be professionally led, and did not allude to the need for organizational development and the particular individual skills needed for any quality improvement to be an effective mechanism for change.

The audit programme is of immense complexity. And the theory of audit that has been presented underestimates this. Whilst the audit cycle presents a neat, theoretical picture of ways in which change in clinical practice might occur, in reality to get to the objective of improving patient care the process of audit challenges many barriers – organizational, managerial, behavioural, psychological as well as technical and professional. The omission of a step in the audit cycle that reflects on the reasons for poor quality care may partly explain the limited success of local audits (Crombie and Davies 1993).

Assessment of the audit programme cannot be just about direct benefit to patients as organizations and individual groups within hospitals have needed to grapple with the barriers to change. Some of the benefits of the audit programme may reflect these challenges. We have put together a brief overview that looks at the question of the value of the audit programme by first describing the investment in audit and the structures set up for audit (inputs) and then reflects on just some of the changes possibly attributable to the audit programme (outputs). We have considered the outputs in terms of benefits to patient and also in terms of overcoming organizational barriers.

Even recognizing inputs to and outputs from the audit programme may not be straightforward. If, for example, audit enables a group to develop, say, relevant team working skills then that might be considered an output. But these skills will become an input for further development of audit. We base this partly on observations from a three year programme of workshops for consultants leading audit in their Trusts that were run by the authors between 1990 and 1993. We focus on audit in the hospital services and mainly discuss the introduction of medical audit.

THE INVESTMENT IN AUDIT

Introduction

The funding for audit is the outstanding investment and the one that has to be justified. This investment needs to be understood in terms of what it was used to buy. Inputs to the audit programme other than money have been critical to its progress. For example, the directive that conferred on audit a 'mandatory status' while also acknowledging audit as a professional activity that should be professionally led and locally driven was a crucial catalyst for its implementation.

The financial investment

This amounts to about £50 million yearly; a total investment of over £200 million. At first central monies were ringfenced for medical audit and administered by the then 14 regional health authorities (RHAs). Each RHA transferred most of the monies to hospitals whilst retaining some to help with the implementation of audit. Funds were allocated to each hospital according to size. (Audit monies were at first allocated to district health authorities. But as Trusts emerged and DHAs evolved into purchasing authorities audit monies were allocated to individual hospitals.) An average district general hospital received about £60 000 revenue and a tranche of money for capital investment. The revenue recurred annually but the capital sums were gradually reduced. This process continued until (1995) when the money for audit was transferred into general funds. Clinical audit is now considered an expected activity supported financially through the purchasing authorities.

What was procured?

The funding for audit represented a serious obligation. The fact that money was being invested in a programme that aimed to improve the quality of care signalled that audit was considered an important activity and gave it attention and publicity. Broadly only two items were purchased with audit funds: people to work as facilitators or coordinators and equipment, largely computers, that were used to aggregate data. The people involved in audit were not isolated but were linked together and formed the 'organizational framework' that was one of the objectives outlined in the working papers.

The structure

Implementing the audit programme was dependent on robust organization. Structures to enable effective communication from the DOH through the Regional Health Authorities to individual Trusts and to provide an effective framework for the development of audit were set up. An audit coordinator was appointed in each RHA whose tasks included managing the allocation of audit monies; responsibility for assuring that structures for audit in hospitals – such as the appointment of a lead audit clinician and hospital audit committees – were in place; and for facilitating the development of audit. Most RHAs had regional audit committees and many specialty groups also organized themselves in regional groups to promote audit.

Each hospital was obliged to write an annual report for the RHA outlining audit activities and giving account of how the money for audit had been spent. Regional audit coordinators also had to consider the development of specific aspects of audit such as audit in small specialties (Collins 1990); interhospital audit and the development of audit at the primary–secondary care interface. Each year with each tranche of money the DOH outlined new priorities for audit that were implemented by the regional audit coordinators who themselves had to prepare a report on audit throughout their region for the DOH.

Support for audit also came from other sources including the medical Royal Colleges and some had a significant role in the development of audit. Some had been involved in audit and in projects that evaluated the quality of particular aspects of care before the introduction of the NHS-wide audit programme. The Colleges fostered development of audit research relevant to audit and supported national audits and the development of audit in specialties (Amess *et al*. 1995). Other influential groups that emerged as a result of the audit programme are the Clinical Outcomes Group, co-chaired by the Chief Medical Officer and the Chief Nursing Officer and the recently configured National Audit Office, which brings together organizations representing many of the healthcare professions and healthcare managers.

People

Most of the audit money was invested in staff. Audit facilitators were key individuals in the setting up of audit locally. Their influence was dependent on appointment of a consultant who acted as a lead audit clinician and chair of the hospital audit committee whose role was to coordinate, supervise and lead introduction of audit. (The original audit committees were organised on a District basis. But as Trusts emerged and DHAs evolved into purchasing authorities the District audit committees were no longer relevant and soon each hospital had its own committee.) The seniority of the lead clinician varied between hospitals. Some hospitals gave this role to junior consultants but in others a senior consultant such as the medical director included leading audit within their own brief.

The posts of audit facilitator or coordinator or audit officer were new to the NHS (Firth *et al*. 1991) and most appointees at first knew little about audit. Training programmes and audit workshops for audit facilitators and for doctors and other participants, funded by audit monies, were an important part of the initial development of audit. Many hospitals now employ two or more staff and have created audit units or departments that act as sources of information about audit; set up audit programmes; help prepare data for audit meetings and generally support the audit process. Most are now permanent members of staff, a situation that contrasts with the limited contracts that were offered to many audit staff at the beginning of the programme.

Computers

The capital invested in audit was relatively small. These monies were mostly used to buy hardware and software to support the information needs of the audit programme. The money available to invest in computers for audit was much too little to be able to make up for the clear deficits in access to information throughout the NHS. Thus whilst investment in personal computers to help analyse audit data was necessary there was not enough capital investment to provide systems that could overcome the practical difficulties of accessing data to audit routinely.

Commitment

As we have discussed, audit – or any quality improvement programme – involves organizational and attitudinal changes. Opinion leaders have an important role in any process of change and the commitment to audit by individuals was a significant input that enabled the implementation of the audit programme. And whilst such commitment may not have cost money it may have been catalysed by the support for audit implicit in the significant financial investment. Many others continue to give time to development of audit. All these opportunity costs of the time are probably unquantifiable.

Was the right amount invested?

In absolute terms £50 million annually is a large investment. But in relative terms this investment amounts to about 0.1% of the NHS budget and, compared with investments in quality made by companies in the commercial sector, this might be considered a small investment in quality.

In a report of a study that compared the implementation of TQM in the NHS and in the commercial sector, it was found that NHS invested up to one-third of that of the commercial sector in the TQM programme. The main differences were the amounts spent on training and internal and external surveys (Joss and Kogan 1995). The amount invested in medical audit was much greater than the investments in TQM in the NHS and it was clear from some of our discussions with audit lead clinicians that some hospitals found it difficult to spend all the money allocated for audit. This disparity between these two observations perhaps reflects the almost total lack of investment of audit monies in organizational development.

THE BENEFITS AND ACHIEVEMENTS OF AUDIT

Introduction

Audit has affected the way in which doctors in particular consider the quality of care and has resulted in the introduction of new organizational structures. But it is difficult, for a programme that was set up without an evaluation, to predict the range of benefits that are likely to accrue; the extent of such benefits; or when to expect any tangible, measurable change.

The audit programme has not been static. New areas for particular effort are outlined by the DOH each year. For example, the focus of audit has been moved from medical to clinical audit and audit at the primary/secondary care interface has been emphasized. And as the audit process develops and people and organizations continue to learn from it the benefits may be accruing like those of a long-term investment.

Improvement in patient care Quantifying achievement of the audit programme in terms of benefit to patients must be its ultimate test, but may not be the only test of success at this stage of development. However, some patients have certainly benefited from some of the audit activity and there are many published examples of successful audits that have resulted in improvements in care (Nee *et al.* 1994). Many more certainly exist in the 'grey' literature of regional reports (Stern and Brennan 1994) and more still that remain the property of hospitals. But these represent only a small proportion of all the work that has been invested in audit. There are probably a great number of unfinished audits; some will have resulted in change as the process of asking about quality may have provided insight into problems; others will not progress beyond observing practice and others will have failed to get started at all. The value of audit in terms of benefit to patients will be made up of small improvements to the care of many and overall it may not be possible to measure the total improvements in patient care and still less can a pound sign be put on any of these.

A change that might eventually be considered an important step towards an effective quality improvement programme is that hospitals now collect information on aspects of care such as the treatment of patients admitted with myocardial infarction. Whilst it may be argued that collection of such information per se does not indicate improvement in patient care, such data was not routinely collected before the introduction of audit and it does represent a change in attitude to assessing the quality of care and to the evaluation of care.

One difficulty of using direct benefits to patients as a measure of the value or output of audit is that it is difficult to put a price on the *benefit of maintaining good care*. Thus once care has been improved and repeat audits show that care remains very good without room for further improvement, then the process of further audit will merely demonstrate no need for action. And so the benefit of the audit will not be improvement but simply the knowledge that care is good.

Overcoming barriers to audit Several key problems have restricted the practical application of audit. Some are organizational and others attitudinal. Many remain but some that presented great difficulties at the introduction of audit have been resolved or at least no longer seem to present barriers. This suggests that although little attention was given to the organizational development implicit in a programme such as medical audit, an effect of introducing audit programme may have been to induce important changes.

Openness and confidentiality

The DOH papers on audit stated that the medical profession should lead audit and that audit should become part of routine professional practice. But some aspects of audit, for example openly discussing problems and mistakes, contrasted with the often closed shop of medical discussions. Considering the quality of care openly and transparently was new for many and for some very difficult, particularly where results of audit demonstrated that some aspects of practice were not 'up to standard'.

There was also a perceived need to maintain tight confidentiality and to limit access to the information and opinions expressed at audit meetings. Some felt that discussion about the quality of medical care should not extend beyond groups of doctors. This view was perhaps not surprising as this sort of information had not previously been collected systematically and aggregated. The concern about confidentiality prompted the publication of guidelines (Walshe and Bennett 1991).

Doctors have become less diffident about discussing the results of audit and concern about confidentiality has diminished considerably as audit has become part of routine practice. The role of consumers in the audit process is now being debated. In parallel with a more open approach to the discussion of quality, managers and other healthcare professionals are now more likely to be involved in the audit process than in 1989. Whilst the development of clinical audit has been slow, in our view multidisciplinary audit would not have been possible at all at the beginning of the programme.

Developing the organizational framework

Setting up the structures for audit in all hospitals was an early objective for the audit programme that has been achieved. But there are important organizational issues that go beyond the structure. Audit was set up as a process to be professionally led. But although individual professions need to have a view on the aspects of the quality of care pertinent to that profession, improvement in the quality of care delivered to patients is dependent on changes in the work of more than one group within health care. It may be argued that introducing medical audit before clinical audit was necessary in order to engage the medical profession in a process of systematic quality improvement. In a recent analysis of the implementation of TQM in 17 sites within the NHS it was noted that securing the cooperation of key clinicians at an early stage was important for implementation of TQM (Joss and Kogan 1995).

Now that the structures for audit are in place and audit is part of routine practice, it is possible to assess the characteristics of hospitals where audit works well. The authors of a recent evaluation of 29 audit programmes in provider units were able to define the characteristics associated with effective audit programmes. These included the quality of the audit staff; the availability of training; the level of strategic planning for audit within the Trust; and leadership and direction. Another feature was that the most effective audit programmes were those that had 'largely resisted demands for heavy investment of audit resources in information technology. Rather they had invested most of their audit resources in audit staff' (Buttery *et al.* 1995).

In retrospect audit can be seen as part of a broader organizational approach to quality improvement with medical audit as a crucial step towards developing that culture within the NHS necessary to bring doctors into the process. Although the participation of all doctors in audit was one of the original objectives of the audit programme, audit was not set out to be part of a wider approach to quality improvement.

Information for audit

Reliable and relevant information is a crucial prerequisite for audit for otherwise it is difficult to assess objectively the quality of care. Most information about patient care is within patient notes and thus medical records are crucial tools for audit. Many early audits looked solely at the standards of medical records and thus assessed the state of recording of information rather than the actual care given to patients. Two possible limitations of audit as a tool for quality improvement emerged from these early studies. First, these audits demonstrated incompleteness of medical notes (Gabbay *et al.* 1990). Thus the most important source of information for audit, medical notes, were likely to be unsuitable as a base for criterion based audits that looked at specific aspects of care. Secondly, although it was possible to demonstrate through the process of audit an improvement in the standard of medical notes these improvements were difficult to sustain (Gabbay and Layton 1992).

Despite the problems with notes audit has continued. It is probable that most audits now are topic or criterion based and are not about the quality of notes but focus on the quality of care. Information may be derived using specifically designed questionnaires. And audit facilitators have gained expertise gathering information. Two approaches to improving the quality of information in notes have been reported (Williams *et al.* 1993, Goodyear and Lloyd 1995) – the move towards integrated patient notes and preprinted assessment sheets. The impact that audit has had on such developments is difficult to assess.

Learning about audit

Before the introduction of audit few doctors knew about systematic approaches to quality improvement and although the notion of audit as a process for assessing the quality of care and promoting improvement may have been theoretically sound to the enthusiasts, many were uncertain about the need for audit, about what it meant and what it involved. Furthermore some doctors were not conversant with dimensions of quality or ways in which the complex tasks involved in health care can be categorized to help the process of quality improvement.

Many doctors were sceptical about audit as its effectiveness had not been tested through robust research and doubted whether audit could meet its theoretical outcomes. Other questions raised about audit included the relationship between research and audit; the relationship between data collection and audit; the need for information technology to support the audit process; how to implement changes once a problem in care had been identified through audit. Tough arguments against audit were voiced loudly – some of them were legitimate.

Support was available and much relevant, accessible information was published that disseminated and increased the understanding of audit – for example the report of a working party of the Royal College of Physicians (1989); a booklet on the quality of care by the Standing Medical Advisory Committee (1990); and a monthly section on audit included in the *British Medical Journal*. And in the past six years many other articles on audit and on quality improvement have been published. Working with colleagues to improve the quality of care and taking part in regular and systematic *clinical audit* is now considered a duty of a doctor outlined in guidance published by the General Medical Council (1995).

Audit and training

Incorporating audit into the training of doctors was an early objective of the audit programme. But doctors in training often find it difficult to engage in the audit process (Firth Cozens and Storer 1992, Packwood *et al.* 1992). Audit is an educational process and as such could be a useful approach to learning for doctors in training. One of the difficulties is that audit is, in our view, essentially an organizational approach to quality improvement, but as doctors in training may only spend six months in one hospital they are not in a position within the organization to gain much from the process of audit. Finding ways of involving these doctors properly in audit remains a challenge.

Changes in the audit programme

The focus of the audit programme has moved from medical to clinical audit. In theory at least audit should involve all healthcare professionals and encompass all aspects of care. Secondly, although audit continues as a provider function it is now to some extent linked with the purchasers through the funding arrangements – as funding to provider units comes via the purchasing authorities – and also, as the purchasers need to assure quality, through quality clauses in contracts between purchasers and providers.

One of the difficulties in assessing the impact of the audit programme is not only that the targets change year on year but also, that there has been a significant shift in what is understood by audit. The definition of medical audit given in the 1989 White Paper is similar to the definition of clinical audit in Box 8.1. This contrasts with the way the Alment Committee some years ago described audit as 'the sharing by a group of peers of information gained from personal experience and/or medical records in order to assess the care provided to their patients, to improve their own learning and to contribute to medical knowledge'. A definition of audit based on the experience of the last five years might include an emphasis on the relationship between improvement in clinical care and the organization of care and on the importance of acknowledging the work of other professions.

SUMMARY

The aim of an *effective clinical audit programme* as described in the working paper on audit that accompanied the White Paper was 'helping to provide the necessary reassurance to doctors, patients and managers that best possible quality of service is being achieved within the resources available' (Department of Health 1989b). That audit has not achieved these objectives is, in our view, not surprising. The notion of audit as a cycle of change is an appealing one but it gives a limited and perhaps naive view of the complexity of interpersonal interactions and organizational sensitivity needed for a hospital to develop an effective organization wide system responsive to the quality of care.

The main achievements of audit may have been to start the process of organizational change needed for the introduction of an effective quality improvement programme. But the many other initiatives introduced in the last five years will make it difficult to be able to attribute change to the audit programme with any certainty. Some of the problems uncovered in the CEPOD report (Buck *et al.* 1988) have been addressed and there are now clear guidelines for patterns of working and supervision of surgeons in training. The interest in evidence based practice; concern about the implementation of research finds; the NHS Research and Development initiative; the quality clause in place in contracts between purchasers and providers are all likely to influence the quality of care and work synergistically with audit programmes.

The introduction of audit was an extraordinary exercise. The fact that audit was taken up into routine practice was probably a combination of its juxtaposition to the rest of the reforms – audit was the least contentious of the seven key changes; the generous funding; an increasing perception of a need to 'do something' about the quality of care and the alarming simplicity with which audit was presented. These circumstances may have influenced organizational and attitudinal changes that have enabled the development of audit. The increasing tendency for more openness and inclusiveness suggests that audit could evolve into a process with more characteristics of continuous quality improvement.

There is a clear need for a research programme to analyse the benefits of audit (Barton *et al.* 1995). But the activities associated with audit are not static and its meaning and its relevance to routine care are also changing. In general practice audit is seen to contribute significantly to both professional and service development (Humphreys and Hughes 1993). In hospitals the organizational structures are more complex and it may be difficult to see the potential of audit. But it may just be that by chance of circumstances audit has created the opportunity for the sort of organizational changes that are needed for effective quality improvement.

In considering the cost benefits attention must be paid to the costs and implications of disinvesting in audit. It seems to us that it would be very difficult to stop investing in audit because it was now considered not to provide value for money, as in the NHS audit is the main organizational focus for systematic assessment of the quality of care.

The problems with quality of care that contributed to the stimulus to implement audit have not disappeared. Audit was clearly not a 'quick fix'. It may take another five years before the benefits of audit can be seen with any clarity. Meanwhile, there is a need to continue to develop robust systems for quality improvement and the introduction of audit 'UK style' may have provided a good basis for doing this. But from now on quality improvement programmes must be evaluated prospectively.

FURTHER READING

The first three books listed are in a series entitled 'Evaluating Audit', published by CASPE Research, London.

♦ Walshe, K. and Coles, J. (1993), *Developing a Framework*.

♦ Walshe, K. and Coles, J. (1993), *A Review of Initiatives*.

♦ Buttery, Y., Walshe, K., Rumsey, M., Amess, M., Bennett, J. and Coles, J. (1995), *Provider Audit in England. A Review of Twenty-nine Programmes*.

♦ Joss, R. and Kogan, M. (1995), *Advancing Quality. Total Quality Management in the National Health Service*, Buckingham, Open University Press.

♦ Cogan, M. and Redfern, S. (1995), *Making Use of Clinical Audit. A Guide to Practice in the Health Professions*, Buckingham, Open University Press.

REFERENCES   Amess, M., Walshe, K., Shaw, C. and Coles, J. (1995), *The Audit Activities of the Medical Royal Colleges and their Faculties in England*. CASPE Research.

Barton, A., Thompson, R. and Bhopal, R. (1995), Clinical audit: more research is required. *Journal of Epidemiology and Community Health*, 49: 445-447.

Berwick, D.M. (1989), Continuous quality improvement as an ideal in health care. *New England Journal of Medicine*, 320: 53-56.

Buck, N., Devlin, H. and Lunn, J. (1988), *The Report of a Confidential Enquiry into Perioperative Deaths*. London: Nuffield Provincial Hospital Trust.

Bucknall, C.E., Robertson, C., Moran, F. and Stevenson, R.D. (1988), Differences in hospital asthma management. *Lancet*, i: 748-750.

Buttery, Y., Walshe, K., Rumney, M., Amess, M., Bennett, J. and Coles, J. (1995), *Evaluating Audit. Provider Audit in England. A Review of 29 Programmes*. CASPE Research.

Buxton, M.J. (1994), Achievements of audit in the NHS. *Quality in Health Care*, 3: S31-S34.

Collins, C.D. (1990), Contribution of regional specialty subcommittees to organising audit. *British Medical Journal*, 300: 94-95.

Crombie, I.K. and Davies, H.T. (1993), Missing link in the audit cycle. *Quality in Health Care*, 2: 47-48.

Department of Health (1989a), *Working for Patients*. London: HMSO.

Department of Health (1989b), *Working for Patients: Medical Audit Working Paper 6*. London: HMSO.

Firth Cozens, J. and Storer, D. (1992), Registrars' and senior registrars' perceptions of audit. *Quality in Health Care*, 1: 161-164.

Firth Cozens, J. and Venning, P. (1991), Audit officers: what are they up to? *British Medical Journal*, 303: 631-633.

Gabbay, J. and Layton, A.J. (1992), Evaluation of audit of medical inpatient records in a district hospital. *Quality in Health Care*, 1: 43-47.

Gabbay, J., McNicol, M., Spiby, J., Davies, S.C. and Layton, A.J. (1990), What did audit achieve? Lessons from a preliminary evaluation of a year's audit. *British Medical Journal*, 301: 526-529.

General Medical Council (1995), Duties of a Doctor. Good Medical Practice.

Giraud, A., Amouretti, M., Derenne, Y. and Marrel, P. (1993), View from France. *Quality in Health Care*, 2: 189-190.

Goodyear, H.M. and Lloyd, H.W. (1995), Can admission notes be improved by using preprinted sheets? *Quality in Health Care*, 4: 190-193.

Gray, D., Hampton, J., Bernstein, S., Kosecoff, J. and Brook, R. (1990), Audit of coronary angiography and bypass surgery. *Lancet*, 335: 1317-1320.

Griffiths, R. (1983), *NHS Management Inquiry*. London: DHSS.

Gruer, R., Gordon, D.S., Gunn, A.A. and Ruckley, C.V. (1986), Audit of surgical audit. *Lancet*, i: 23-26.

Humphreys, C. and Hughes, J. (1993), *Audit and Development in Primary Care*. London: King's Fund Centre.

Jenkins, A.M., Ruckley, C.V. and Nolan, B. (1986), Ruptured abdominal aortic aneurysm. *British Journal of Surgery*, 73: 395-398.

Joss, R. and Kogan, M. (1995), *Advancing Quality. Total Quality Management in the National Health Service*. Open University Press.

Laffel, G. and Blumenthal, D. (1989), The case for using industrial quality management science in health care organisations. *Journal of the American Medical Association*, 262: 2869-2873.

McPherson, K., Wennberg, J., Hovind, O. and Clifford, P. (1982), Small area variations in the use of common surgical procedures: an international comparison of New England, England and Norway. *New England Journal of Medicine*, 307: 1310-1314.

Nee, P.A., Gray, A.J. and Martin, M.A. (1994), Audit of thrombolysis initiated in an accident and emergency department. *Quality in Health Care*, **3**: 29-33.

Packwood, T., Kerrison, S. and Buxton, M. (1992), The audit process and medical organisation. *Quality in Health Care*, 1: 192-196.

Royal College of Physicians. (1989), *Medical Audit. A First Report. What, Why and How*. London: RCP.

Russell, I.T. and Wilson, B.J. (1992), Audit: the third clinical science? *Quality in Health Care*, 1: 51-55.

Standing Medical Advisory Committee (1990), *The Quality of Medical Care*. London: HMSO.

Stern, M. and Brennan, S. (1994), *Report on the Medical, Primary Care and Royal College Audit Programmes 1989 to 1993/4. Medical Audit in the Hospital and Community Health Service (HCHS)*. NHSME.

Walshe, K. and Bennett, J. (1991), *Guidelines on Medical Audit and Confidentiality*. South East Thames Regional Health Authority.

Walshe, K. and Coles, J. (1993), Medical audit: in need of evaluation. *Quality in Health Care*, 2: 189-190.

Wareham, N. (1994), External monitoring of the quality of health in the United States. *Quality in Health Care*, 3: 97-101.

Williams, J.G., Roberts, R. and Rigby, M.J. (1993), Integrated patient records: another move towards quality for patients? *Quality in Health Care*, 2: 73-74.

MANAGEMENT AUDIT

Michael Murphy

OBJECTIVES

- ◆ To describe the key objectives of management audit.
- ◆ To highlight the importance of internal audit.
- ◆ To distinguish management audit from management consultancy.

INTRODUCTION

There are two very different views of management audit, although both agree about its core focus – the efficiency and effectiveness of management. One view holds that management audit is an audit of management performance intended to inform external stakeholders about the worth of this performance. As such it is viewed as forming an important adjunct to the corporate accountability process, helping stakeholders to form assessments of the comparative achievements of different organizations and to identify some of the factors leading to differential achievement. It adds a dimension of independent, and expert, appraisal of systems, procedures and judgements to the accountability process. Much of the work of the Audit Commission falls into this category. For management audit of this type to be credible much depends on the willingness of the auditors to arrive at unambiguous conclusions based on widely accepted criteria and their being regarded as having the expertise and resources to do this reliably. This is a major challenge, the realism of which is often questioned. The other view holds that management audit is a process intended principally for the benefit of management, normally conducted as part of an ongoing and integrated process of managerial self-assessment and improvement, i.e. it exists to help management improve their performance by providing formative rather than simply summative assessments of their activities. The two views of management audit recognize a common core – an informed appraisal of management capabilities, processes and performance. In practical terms, they will also frequently have a common technical base. However, the resulting audit reports have different purposes and are intended for different audiences and the audits themselves will involve different operational and planning considerations reflecting their different objectives. This chapter is concerned with management audits as audits for management. (Audits for external stakeholders are considered in Chapter 10.) It commences with a discussion of the nature of management audit and proceeds to a review of the elements of a successful management audit programme.

Box 9.1
Key concepts

Management audit:
A process via which management systems and procedures are appraised with a view to identifying potential improvements and evaluating the efficiency and effectiveness of current performance. It involves both formative and summative evaluations.

Internal control:
The totality of policies, procedures, systems and controls implemented by management to achieve organizational objectives and to ensure the proper use of resources, including achieving value for money.

Internal audit:
A process of monitoring the implementation of internal control and evaluating its effectiveness. Originally concerned with regularity issues but now also involved in broader auditing processes including value for money investigations.

THE OBJECTIVES OF MANAGEMENT AUDIT

It is the view of the author that the prime role of management audit is that of helping management to do their job better by providing them with informed evaluations of their policies and practices. This view accords with that of Santocki (1976) who defined management audit in the following terms:

> Management audit is an objective, independent, informed and constructive appraisal of the effectiveness of managers/teams of managers in their achievement of company objectives and policies in order to identify existing and potential weaknesses and strengths in all functions and operations within an organisation and to recommend ways to rectify these weaknesses and potential weaknesses. It must be seen as a managerial function, and as such must assist management, and in doing so strengths and not only weaknesses must be reported on.

This view of management audit has gained wide acceptance, being adopted by organizations such as the, then, British Institute of Management. Unfortunately, its wording, and all too often the implementation of management audit, overemphasizes the negative – detecting and correcting weaknesses. The positive and the constructive aspects of management audit, i.e. identifying organizational and management strengths so that they can be built on, need to be given at least equal emphasis. Management audit should always be formative rather than simply ex-post evaluative in its approach, i.e. it should look for ways of achieving improvement in a constructive rather than simply a critical way.

Since Santocki's work there has been an explosion in the range and scope of what are called audits, including of course value for money audits. There are clinical audits, quality audits, operational audits, human resource audits, knowledge audits, technology audits, performance audits, consumer audits and many others as well as the long established tradition of financially orientated internal audits. This is apart from audits carried out by regulatory agencies and the annual external audits of financial statements. Such a plethora of audits can easily lead to confusion on the part of observers, if not participants. For example, there has been considerable semantic confusion over the distinction between operational audits and management audits. Hammill (1982) described operational auditing in the following terms:

> In essence therefore the following questions are posed: what is management trying to achieve; how is the company going about it; and is performance up to management expectation in all areas of activity.

In the same vein, Chambers (1992) quotes Koontz and O'Donnell writing about operational audits in 1976:

> Operational auditors ... also appraise policies, procedures, use of authority, quality of management, effectiveness of methods, special problems and other phases of operations.

As Boys (1985) summarized the position (following Lewis Carroll) 'When I use a word it means just what I choose it to mean – neither more or less'. Distinctions have been created without differences. The view of this author accords with that of Vintnen (1991):

> Management audit is a comprehensive term which contains operational auditing. It includes the audit of management decisions themselves in relation to the organisational objectives and the quality of management – the resultant report both identifies problems and recommends solutions.

The distinction outlined in the introduction to this chapter provides a basis for analysing all the different types of audit referred to above. If an audit is primarily for the benefit of management it is a management audit. Otherwise it is not, even though management might well benefit indirectly from the conduct of the audit and its outcomes. Thus, externally required independent appraisals such as those of the Audit Commission and the National Audit Office are not management audits, although they may well be audits of management and their findings helpful to management. A useful analogy is that of the traditional external audit of the annual financial statements of an enterprise intended to assure readers of the credibility ('truth and fairness') of those statements. Such an audit is not primarily intended to benefit management. It is intended to comment on the reliability of their statements of accountability to stakeholders in the enterprise. However, during the conduct of their audit, the auditors will often come across issues likely to be of concern to management, e.g. matters relating to internal control and other systems. It is customary, indeed expected, that the auditors report to management on these issues so that necessary action can be taken and there are professional guidelines in this respect.

Insights into whether a particular audit is a management audit, as defined above, can be obtained by examining issues such as: to whom is the audit report addressed; who is the auditor; who appoints the auditor; who can control the auditor and the audit process; and who identifies what is to be audited. If the answer to such questions is management, then it is strong prima facie evidence that the audit in question is a management audit. In fact, with the exception of external and regulatory audits, most audits could satisfy these criteria and be regarded as management audits. A value for money audit would satisfy these criteria if it was an internally inspired and controlled investigation. An externally imposed value for money investigation would not.

Thus, management audits may appear in many different guises and involve many different groups of people within an organization. However, they all share, or should share, a common objective – helping management, at all levels and across all functions, to do a better job. The challenge is one of ensuring that this potentially diverse auditing effort forms a coherent and purposeful whole. It is possible to go so far as to say that management audit is a philosophy rather than a specific set of processes. Good managers should be constantly auditing what they and their teams are doing. Formal management audits of whatever type are, or should be, simply particular manifestations of this philosophy. In practice it is likely that the organization will have more to gain from formal management audits, including value for money investigations, if they are planned and carried out in a coordinated way reflecting organizational concerns and priorities rather than simply being carried out on an ad hoc basis. It is this coordination and planning which characterizes successful management audit systems. However, there are powerful forces at work which militate against such an integrated approach to audit effort. Not least of these is the fact that audits are not simple value free appraisals – they are potentially powerful devices for the imposition of particular sets of values. As Power (1994) comments:

> Audits do not passively monitor auditee performance but shape the standards of this performance in crucial ways . . . (Power 1994, p. 8)

and again:

> Audits do as much to construct definitions of quality and performance as to monitor them (Power 1994, p. 33)

There are important reasons why professional groups who have developed their own auditing concepts, procedures and values, e.g. medical audit, are unlikely to be easily persuaded that these should be subsumed into broader concepts of management audits. There are issues of professional and other 'ownerships' which need to be addressed and done so sensitively. To achieve this will require demonstration of the benefits, to all parties, of a more integrated approach to management audit. Fortunately, current work in the area is starting to do this. For example, Morris *et al.* (1995) provide a powerful demonstration of the potential benefits of an integrated audit approach in a clinical setting, that of hip replacement surgery. The thrust here is away from the 'uni-professional' audit towards a wider patient-centred audit. This has implications for the organizational locus of staff who support or facilitate the audit process as demonstrated by a recent reorganization of clinical audit support staff at the Hammersmith Hospitals NHS Trust. Here a common base has been established for the audit facilitators on the Hammersmith site to help them to work together on projects. However, the 'ownership' of the patient-centred audit remains ambiguous – is it purely medical audit or is it a part of management audit? This is an issue which healthcare organizations need to resolve.

INTERNAL AUDIT – THE FIRST FORM OF MANAGEMENT AUDIT?

The NHS, in common with the rest of the public sector, has long required management to ensure that all activities are conducted in accordance with the highest standards of regularity and propriety and that laid down policies and procedures are implemented, e.g. the requirements in the *NHS Trusts Finance Manual* (NHS Executive 1995). To help achieve this managements are expected to design and install internal control systems (e.g. NHS Executive 1995, s1/2 et seq.). An internal control system has been defined in the following terms (Auditing Practices Committee 1980):

> The whole system of controls, financial and otherwise, established by the management in order to carry on the business of the enterprise in an orderly and efficient manner, ensure adherence to management policies, safeguard the assets and secure as far as possible the completeness and accuracy of the records.

The span of this definition is worth emphasizing – it refers to 'the whole system', 'financial and otherwise'. Internal control is not restricted, as is all too often thought, to financial matters such as authorizing payments and monitoring cash receipts. It covers a much wider range of systems and procedures, e.g. in areas such as quality assurance, employment and operating practices, budgetary systems, waste management systems and performance assessment systems. Management should have clearly defined, communicated and monitored policies and control systems in these and all other areas. One important aspect of management audit which we shall return to later is appraisal of the suitability and adequacy of these policies, controls and their supporting procedures. For the present, it is sufficient to note that they should be in place.

In the case of NHS Trusts, the Trust Boards are under a specific responsibility for the:

> establishment and maintenance of a system of internal control designed to give reasonable assurance that assets are safeguarded, waste and inefficiency avoided, reliable financial information produced, and that value for money is continuously sought. (NHS Executive 1995, s4.4(b))

However, having systems and controls in place implies rather more than simply formulating and communicating policies. It also implies, as the above quotations indicate, ensuring that these policies are in fact implemented in practice. The origins of internal audit lie in this requirement. Internal audit is as old as accounting itself. In fact it is a moot point whether internal audit is older than accounting, at least as we understand it today. What is not in doubt is that throughout time and across society, organizations have found it necessary to have an internal audit function, however rudimentary and whether or not conducted by specialist auditors. Internal audit has been defined (Institute of Internal Auditors 1988) in the following terms:

> Internal auditing is an independent appraisal function established within an organisation to examine and evaluate its activities as a service to the organisation. The objective of internal auditing is to assist members of the organisation in the effective discharge of their responsibilities. To this end, internal auditing furnishes them with analyses, appraisals, recommendations, counsel, and information concerning the activities reviewed.

A further definition is provided by the Chartered Institute of Public Finance and Accountancy (CIPFA 1987):

> ... an independent appraisal function within an organisation for the review of activities as a service to all levels of management. It is a control which measures, evaluates and reports the effectiveness of internal controls, financial and otherwise, as a contribution to the efficient use of resources within an organisation.

As can be seen from the above, historically, a prime function of internal audit has been seen as assuring management that its designated policies, systems and controls are in fact being implemented in practice. Looked at in this light, it can readily be seen how clinical audit, quality audit and procurement audit could all be viewed as part of a broadly defined internal audit framework, at least insofar as they are concerned with monitoring compliance with laid down procedures, protocols etc. Unfortunately, up until the 1970s and even to some extent today (see, for example, the relevant sections of NHS Executive, 1995), internal audit has been seen as being primarily concerned with financial systems and controls. In large part this is the result of internal audit normally being located within the organizational ambit of the finance department, with many internal auditors being accountants, or accountancy trainees. Conceptually this was, of course, a mis-understanding, the consequences of which are still with us. One such consequence is the 'demonization' of the internal auditor. As Chambers (1992) puts it:

> the traditional stereotype image of the auditor as an inspector of compliance and probity can make it well-nigh impossible for the auditor to be a friendly, constructive adviser of change.

This view of the internal auditor has undoubtedly been re-inforced in many organizations by a misuse of internal auditors. All too often rather than being used for audit, i.e. appraisal and evaluation purposes, internal auditors are used for control pur-poses. They are used as an internal control resource, which frequently will involve them saying 'no – you can't do that, it is against the rules' – rather than in examining the adequacy and suitability of control procedures designed and implemented by others. This is a waste of a potentially valuable organizational resource.

A further consequence is that the technical auditing skills (e.g. as regards the collection and evaluation of evidence) developed by internal auditors over the years may be ignored. Another is that other professionals have viewed internal auditors as being primar-ily accountants and have rebuffed them when they have tried to involve themselves in audits other than financially orientated ones. This is not to say that internal auditors have all, or anything like all, the skills and understanding needed to carry out effective audits throughout a healthcare organization, but rather that they have, or should have, technical auditing skills which can be melded with the skills of other professionals to form effective audit task teams. Unfortunately, the history of much of internal auditing and the growth of the many different 'auditings' that we have today, with the associated delineation of professional 'patches', make this far from an easy task.

MANAGEMENT AUDIT – A WAY FORWARD

If the maximum benefit is to be obtained from the undoubtedly great effort that is now going into the different forms of audit process within the NHS this process must be properly planned and monitored. At the very least, the extent of the effort must be recognized, priorities established, gaps identified, and overlaps eliminated. Every organization needs an audit strategy, backed up by the necessary structures and authority to ensure it is implemented. Fortunately, a suitable organizational focus for achieving this exists – at least in the case of NHS Trusts. This is the Audit Committee. Each NHS Trust is required to set up such a committee (NHS Executive 1995, s3/17(1)).

WHAT IS AN AUDIT COMMITTEE?

The concept of audit committees originated in the private sector, principally in relation to listed companies, to help reinforce the independence of auditors from executive management and to monitor auditing activity on behalf of the Board of Directors. In the UK all listed companies are required to have an audit committee following the recommendations of the Cadbury Committee. The responsibilities of private sector audit committees and those

Box 9.2
The responsibilities of audit committees

- ◆ Oversight of the external (financial) audit process, e.g. appointment of external auditor, determination of audit fees, reception of audit reports etc., and in the case of NHS Trusts, dealing with value for money reports produced by external auditors.

- ◆ Oversight of the system of internal controls (as outlined earlier).

- ◆ Oversight of the work of the internal audit function.

required for NHS Trusts are broadly similar. They are listed in Box 9.2.

Audit committees are intended to be primarily comprised of non-executive directors although, for purposes of operational efficiency, they may have a minority of executive directors, normally including the finance director. As their membership demonstrates, they are supposed to be independent (at least as far as practicable) from executive directors and this independence should enable them to provide the board as a whole with an objective appraisal of the organization's audit activities; ensure that all audit activities are properly planned and conducted; ensure that all audit reports are properly produced and that appropriate action is instituted following such reports. However, while the remit of the private sector audit committees is specified fairly widely (particularly as regards internal corporate governance issues), that for NHS Trusts has been defined fairly narrowly, e.g. the specific reference to external value for money reports. An opportunity appears to have been missed in that responsibility for the generality of management audit activity is not an explicit part of their remit, possibly because the requirement for their existence comes in financial rather than general management regulations, or possibly because of a semantic confusion, with management audit being thought to be subsumed within internal audit. It is the view of the author that this should be remedied, and that the audit committee should be the oversight body for *all* of the audit activity within a Trust, and that non-Trust healthcare organizations should have an equivalent committee. Only by having a body with the authority and oversight responsibilities of an audit committee will it be possible to ensure an independent, purposeful and integrated set of audit activities of real benefit to the organization.

In practical terms, an audit committee should be constituted as a sub-committee of the board with a clearly specified set of oversight responsibilities, preferably set out in a formal charter, or equivalent document. Such a charter should specify the responsibilities of the audit committee, its membership, its mode of operation (e.g. frequency of meetings) and its relationships with other parts of the organization. These are matters to be determined by individual boards in the light of the particular circumstances of their organizations. However, Figure 9.1 sets out in schematic form the principal accountabilities and organizational linkages that need to be considered.

As the membership of the audit committee comprises principally non-executive directors, giving it an oversight responsibility for

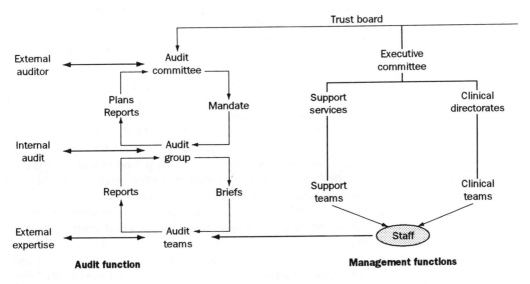

Figure 9.1
An integrated management audit structure

management audit, as well as external audit and traditional internal audit, would be a valuable mechanism not just for ensuring an integrated auditing effort, but also for ensuring that the non-executive directors are fully briefed on all aspects of the Trust's operations rather than focused on narrow financial issues. This should help them discharge their roles as directors more effectively. It should also ensure that the scale and the impact of the non-financial audit effort receives proper recognition at a board level within the Trust.

The role suggested for the audit committee is an oversight role – not an executive role. The responsibility for the detailed planning and implementation of the management audit effort would remain an executive management, including clinical management, responsibility. This will require the formation of an executive audit group, as discussed below, reporting to the audit committee. It is likely that the audit committee will need to meet three or four times a year to discharge its oversight responsibilities which, as regards management audit, should include:

1. *Planning*: the executive audit group should be required to submit to the audit committee, on an annual basis, a plan covering all aspects of the organization's internal and broader auditing activities, incorporating management audits, clinical audits and value for money investigations. This plan should incorporate both a strategic framework for these activities, covering a period of three to five years, and a more detailed short-term operational plan, identifying what areas of activity are to be audited in the coming year, why they have been chosen, how they fit in with the strategic framework and what the anticipated benefits are. The preparation of such a plan is discussed in more detail below. Once approved by the audit committee, this plan should become part of the mandate of the executive audit group.

2. *Resourcing*: together with the auditing plan, the executive audit should submit a resource budget for consideration by the audit committee. This resource budget should clearly identify the resources, staff and other, which will be needed to deliver the audit objectives specified in the audit plan and, equally importantly, how these resources are to be provided. Once approved by the audit committee this resource budget should also become part of the mandate of the executive audit group.

3. *Reporting*: the audit committee should be the ultimate addressee of all reports arising from audits conducted under the mandate of the executive audit group. These reports should not just comment on the audit findings but also include recommendations for action and an indication as to the steps being taken to implement these recommendations. It is important to emphasize the importance of this third aspect of the

audit committee's oversight role. It is no use investing in auditing if nothing is done about the resultant findings and reports. It is the experience of the author, and of other contributors to this book, that 'inconvenient' (to whomsoever) audit findings have all too often not been acted on because of the lack of a clear mechanism for dealing with them. The standing of the audit committee, being comprised of board members, should help prevent this happening.

MANAGEMENT AUDIT OR MANAGEMENT CONSULTANCY?

An important distinction that needs to be drawn is that between internal management consultancy and management audit. Both aim to help management. But there is a distinction and this is the evaluation element which is crucial to the audit role. While analysis of circumstances, processes and opportunities is common to both consultancy and purposive management audit, the audit function is at the end of the day an evaluative function – and one thing it evaluates is the availability and use of consultancy opportunities, both internal and external. Internal management consultancy and management audit have differing accountability relationships. The accountability of management audit(ors) should be via the executive audit group to the audit committee and the board. The accountability of management consultancy is to those who commissioned the consultancy assignment.

Satisfactory discharge of this evaluative role of management auditing means that all management audit activities must be criterion referenced, i.e. audit judgements must be grounded both in evidence and in reference criteria. The range both of evidential material and reference criteria is large. An important consideration for a successful audit, of whatever type, is the specification of, and agreement to, what will be accepted as evidence and what the reference criteria will be for the purposes of that audit assignment. These can be summarized in an audit brief, which is analogous to the engagement letters employed in the finalization of external financial audit assignments. In the case of management audits, the audit brief should be issued by the executive audit group and form the mandate of the team responsible for the conduct of the audit.

EXECUTIVE AUDIT GROUP

The executive audit group should be responsible to the audit committee for the management of all the internal audit activity, in the broadest sense including value for money investigations and ongoing management audits, of the organization. As such its membership needs to reflect the range of activities of the organization. In the case of a typical NHS Trust, it is likely that its membership will include: the Director of Finance, the Medical Director, the Director of Nursing and the Director of Operations, or more realistically their nominees. It should also include others who have specific auditing responsibilities, e.g. Chief Internal Auditor, Co-Ordinator of Medical Audit, Quality Assurance Manager and Patient's Charter Manager. The precise membership, constitution, frequency and format of meetings of the group will depend on the particular circumstances of a particular organization. However, they will need to reflect the fact that the group has executive responsibility for the success of audit activity. As such it will need to deal with:

◆ Audit planning – strategic and operational.
◆ Audit resourcing – strategic and operational.
◆ Agreement of audit briefs.
◆ Agreement of audit reports.
◆ Monitoring audit follow-up.
◆ Evaluating the contribution of the audit process.

This is a significant set of responsibilities. The cost, particularly the opportunity cost of the time of experienced and highly qualified members of staff, of auditing in the NHS is likely to be significant, although few organizations would in fact be able to quantify it. Management have a responsibility to ensure that benefits commensurate with this cost are being achieved. This can only be achieved if the audit effort is targeted as precisely as possible on those areas where it is likely to do the most good, is carried out to appropriate standards, and results in reports which are accepted by auditees and lead to better management and operational practices.

AUDIT PLANNING   There are two related but distinct areas of audit planning. These are strategic audit planning and operational audit planning. There is a strong analogy between these and business planning more generally, where the comparable concepts are strategic business planning and budgeting. The purpose of the strategic audit planning is to provide the longer-term framework for the management audit activity and to ensure a match between this activity and the broader business planning of the organization. Typically, such a plan might look forward for a three to five year period. The purpose of the operational planning is to ensure the shorter-term, typically one year, implementation of the objectives summarized in the strategic plan. Depending on the organization it might prove helpful to have a tactical auditing plan to act as a bridge between the strategic and operational plans. The analogy here might well be with business or service development programmes and Figure 9.2 illustrates this.

The three most important elements of the strategic management audit planning process will be:

1. Deciding on the overall approach that the organization wishes to adopt in its management auditing. Traditionally most 'inter-

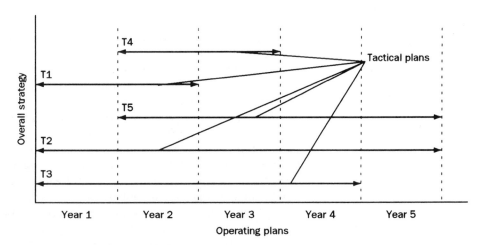

Figure 9.2
The audit planning process

nal' auditing has been function, task or control oriented, i.e. it has concentrated on auditing what are effectively assumed to be independent parts of the organization with relatively little regard to organizational interdependencies, except where information or resources have crossed unit boundaries. This approach, which is often characterized by a lack of central audit planning, has had a large part to play in the development of all the different 'audits' referred to earlier. If the integrated management audit, which this chapter argues for, is to be achieved then a different approach is needed – an approach based on processes rather than tasks or functions. The broader management analogy here is that of programmes, which will often involve many different parts of an organization. An example of such a programme might be coronary care involving a wide range of different clinical and non-clinical units, functions and staff. A corresponding process example in the auditing context is that of auditing the treatment of hip replacement patients already referred to (Morris *et al.* 1995). Thus, the implementation of integrated management audit requires the preparation of a strategic audit plan based on organizational processes. However, not all the processes so identified will be of equal importance to the organization. This is where the second main element of strategic management audit planning comes in.

2. Identifying the most important processes from an organizational perspective. There are a number of different bases which might be adopted for this purpose. These include: risk of process failure and the potential financial or healthcare consequences of such failure; trends in the development and introduction of new processes; and contractual arrangements. Both the identification

of the key organizational processes and their relative management audit importance will be closely linked to the organization's mission statement and corporate plans. Effectively what results from this analysis is a priority ranking of different processes for audit purposes. This priority ranking forms the basis for the third element of the strategic audit plan.

3. The specification of when, within the strategic audit planning time horizon, the different organizational processes, and perhaps sub-processes, will be subject to audit. The most crucial areas may need an annual audit to provide management with the assurances they require. This, for example, might apply to some key financial management control processes (e.g. payments); to key quality assurance processes (e.g. outcome monitoring); or to key clinical processes (e.g. emergency admissions). Other, less critical processes, might be subject to audit on a cycle basis where they are examined every two or three years.

Auditing, when properly conducted, is expensive. Accordingly an important objective of the strategic management audit planning process is to ensure that the organization is likely to derive maximum benefit from the audit process. This means that resource utilization must also be considered in the strategic planning process. It would be all too easy to plan to do lots and lots of auditing – if carried out to reasonable standards then there would undoubtedly be organizational benefits. However, without considering what the associated costs are, then there is no assurance that there will be an overall *net* benefit to the organization. In practical terms, many organizations are likely to look first at the costs (i.e. what they think they can afford to spend on auditing) and then at improving the benefit that they can obtain from this expenditure rather than carrying out some form of optimization analysis.

The end product of this strategic planning process should be an agreed medium to long-term management audit strategy summarizing:

♦ the objectives, and perceived benefits to the organization, of the management auditing strategy;
♦ the processes (and sub-processes) to be audited, or not, as the case might be;
♦ the timing of the planned auditing of these processes;
♦ the resources that are to be committed to implementing this management auditing strategy.

This strategy will, in practice, be prepared by the executive audit group – in consultation with the organization's management team – and approved by the audit committee. However, it is important that it is not seen as a purely senior management responsibility. Procedures should be in place to ensure that all tiers of management, clinical as well as non-clinical, are able to contribute to the determination of the strategy. Only by doing this will it be possible to ensure that the audit process is owned throughout the organization and perceived as having organization wide benefits. If it is merely imposed from the top then there is a danger of simply reinforcing perceptions of the auditor as a police-person or 'spy in the camp'.

Once the plan has been approved, it will form the executive audit group's mandate and it is then up to them to implement it. This will require them to prepare, and submit to the audit committee for approval, the operational audit plans on an annual basis. These plans, akin to annual audit budgets, will summarize the actual audit activities to be carried out in the planning period. Albeit in the context of internal audit, the Auditing Practices Board (1990) has summarized the main purposes of audit planning (see Box 9.3).

Box 9.3
Summary of the main purposes of audit planning (Auditing Practices Board 1990)

The main purposes ... are:

(a) To determine priorities and to establish the most cost-effective means of achieving audit objectives.

(b) To assist in the direction and control of audit work.

(c) To help ensure that attention is devoted to critical aspects of audit work, and

(d) To help ensure that work is completed in accordance with predetermined targets.

AUDIT RESOURCING As already indicated, an audit plan prepared without consideration of its resource implications is in reality little more than a 'wish list'. At the same time as the audit strategy is being prepared for the audit committee to consider an audit resourcing strategy needs to be prepared for similar consideration. This audit resourcing strategy should, like the audit plan, encompass both strategic considerations, i.e. what levels of resources of what types should/will need to be committed to the management audit process over a three to five year time horizon, and operational considerations, i.e. what resources will be required to achieve the audit plan over the coming 12 months. Obviously the latter will need to be much more specific than the strategic resourcing plan.

Audit resourcing plans involve what will be a new departure for many healthcare organizations – an explicit statement of the resources that will be expended on the management and related audit process. In its own right this is likely to lead to gains in improved management and organizational performance. As indicated earlier, there has in recent years been something of an explosion in the number and range of audits. A cynic might take the view that having an audit under your control, of whatever type, is almost a requirement for professional, or managerial, credibility. Unfortunately, the resource implications of this multiplicity of audits are often not stated explicitly, the organizational benefits they might lead to are assumed rather than considered, duplication of effort goes unnoticed and possibilities of synergistic gain are ignored. This in itself is poor management practice. An audit committee should not accept uncosted audit plans – it should insist on receiving audit plans, both strategic and operational, that make explicit the audit objectives, the resources that will be required and the likely gains to the organization.

It is probable that the key resource that will be involved in the management audit process is staff. These are likely to fall into two categories – staff who are primarily employed to carry out audit functions, many (but not all) of whom will be drawn from the internal audit and similar departments; and staff whose audit role is ancillary to, and perhaps a diversion from, their main function. Costing of the contribution of dedicated audit staff to the management audit process is relatively straightforward. It is more complex for non-dedicated staff. In the case of such staff their time has an opportunity cost, the contribution to organizational achievement that is sacrificed by their involvement in audit. This may be difficult to measure but an attempt to do so must be made, otherwise the true organizational cost of audit will be understated and any budgeted net gains overstated.

There are two other important issues relating to staff which must not be neglected. These are availability and competence. It is no use basing an audit strategy on the presumed availability of competent staff. This must be planned for and the implications of abstraction of non-dedicated audit staff allowed for in manpower and establishment planning. Similarly, consideration must also be given to the need for staff training to ensure that they are competent to discharge their audit responsibilities.

Other resources which must be allowed for in the audit planning process include: accommodation and related facilities, the buying-in of specialist expertise, computing and related services, and other support services.

AUDIT BRIEFS As indicated earlier, management audit is an evaluative process and therefore for every audit assignment there needs to a clear and agreed statement of what is being audited, the purpose of the audit, the timing of the audit, what will be regarded as being acceptable audit evidence and the criteria which will be employed in the evaluation. These should be summarized in an audit brief. There are a number of important factors that should be taken into account in preparing an audit brief. These include:

♦ Rationale for the audit: consideration needs to be given to exactly why the audit is being carried out. Is it, for example, to verify the operation of internal controls; to assess value for money performance; to review the quality of clinical or other decision taking; to examine cross-functional linkages; to assess the achievement of critical success factors; to identify organizational blockages; to investigate the outcome of investment decisions; to appraise the success of a programme. All too often audit rationale is assumed rather than made explicit.

♦ Audit methodology: different methodologies are appropriate for different types of audit investigation. Similarly different types of evidence are appropriate for different types of audit. Figure 9.3 summarizes the range of evidence that can be used in auditing. The audit brief needs to state which methodologies and types of evidence will be employed. If this is not done there is a danger that any audit conclusions may be rejected as not being properly founded.

♦ Audit team: auditors will be unable to complete their assignment satisfactorily unless they are recognized as having the authority, and expertise, to carry out their investigation. The audit brief should clearly identify the members of the team and the extent of their authority.

♦ Audit scope: the audit brief needs to contain an explicit statement of what is being audited. This has obvious links with the first point. Without such a statement the audit will be built on quicksand. Both auditees and auditors need to understand the extent of, and limits to, what is being audited and why.

♦ Interested parties: all members of the organization who might be affected by the audit findings should have a right to be consulted during the audit process and identifying who they are likely to be is an important part of audit planning.

Figure 9.3
Types of audit evidence

Type of evidence	Sources of evidence
Natural evidence	Physical inspection
Created evidence	Documents Contracts Records
Rational argumentation	Statistical sampling Analytic review Comparison Interviews

♦ Audit expectations: the different groups associated with an audit may have differing expectations about the audit process itself and the nature of potential audit findings. Such expectations need to be clarified, and systematized, such that there are common, and realistic, expectations for the audit.

AUDIT REPORTS The most visible outcome of any audit, including a management audit, is the resultant report. Accordingly, the credibility of the audit depends heavily on the quality of this report and it is worth investing resources in ensuring such quality. There are a number of steps that can be taken to achieve this. These include:

♦ Clearance of findings: auditors should be prepared to stand by their, justifiable, conclusions. However, they must ensure that the evidence on which they base these findings is reliable and factually accurate. Accordingly, prudent auditors will discuss their report at a draft stage with the auditees to provide them with an opportunity of resolving any misunderstandings. This is normal practice for the National Audit Office and the Audit Commission and is also followed by bodies as diverse as the Scott Committee investigating the 'arms for Iraq' affair and the Stock Exchange.
♦ Ensuring clarity of findings: there is a strong human tendency to avoid making clear and unambiguous statements in audit reports. This is not confined to public sector or management auditing. The Department of Trade Inspectors in relation to external audit reports on company accounts have commented on the use of 'hieratic' or coded language (Department of Trade Inspectors 1979) in audit reports.
♦ Conforming to a 'house-style': Hatherley and Skuse (1991) provide a framework for reporting, as does the Auditing Practices Board (1990). The core issues that a report must incorporate are:
  - Clarity of to whom the report is addressed.
  - Explanation of the purposes of the audit assignment.
  - Explanation of the scope of the audit assignment, including any significant limitations.
  - Summary of the audit work performed.
  - A clear and positive statement of the audit findings.
  - A clear statement of recommendations, including recognition of any management actions that have been taken since the audit was carried out.

Throughout the drafting, clearance and dissemination of the report it is important to remember that the purpose of the whole management audit process is to provide management with reports which are:

... clear, constructive and concise ... based on sufficient, relevant and reliable evidence, which should:

(a) state the scope, purpose, extent and conclusions of the ... assignment;
(b) make recommendations which are appropriate and relevant, and which flow from the conclusions; and
(c) acknowledge the action taken, or proposed, by management (Auditing Practices Board 1990).

AUDIT FOLLOW-UP Apart from any 'preventative' effects associated with the existence of an audit function (and this is more typically true of classic internal audit than of management audit) then the benefits of management audit come primarily *after* the audit because of management action in following up audit findings and recommendations. Such follow-up is crucial if investment in management auditing is to be worthwhile. Unfortunately, because it comes after the audit and, perhaps more importantly, because it will almost inevitably require change, this is where the management audit process frequently falls down. This is not to say that management must follow the recommendations of auditors. To require this would be an unwarranted constraint on management and medical freedom. But such recommendations must be given full and proper consideration at appropriate levels of management. This will be much easier to achieve if there is a formal process in place for such consideration. Important elements of such process are likely to be:

♦ Formal monitoring by the executive audit group, and by the audit committee, of the implementation of the audit plans, both strategic and operational. This should help ensure that all audit reports are considered by these bodies.
♦ Requiring responses to the audit report from interested departments in the organization. Such responses should state:
   - Whether the departments agree with the audit findings and recommendations, and, if not, why not.
   - What action has already been taken in relation to the audit report.
   - What future action is planned in relation to the audit report.
♦ Evaluation by the executive audit group of the findings of the audit in relation to the broader strategies of the organization.
♦ Requiring, where it is decided not to act on the recommendations of the audit team, a clear rationale for this, including an assessment of the risks involved in this decision.
♦ An analysis of the implications of the audit findings for the future audit strategy of the organization.

In practice, most of this work is likely to be delegated to the executive audit group by the audit committee. However, the audit committee will need to be assured that it is in fact being carried out.

EVALUATING THE CONTRIBUTION OF THE AUDIT PROCESS

An important aspect of the work of the audit committee should be that of evaluating the benefits the organization gains from the management audit process. To do this it will need to establish performance indicators for management audit. In doing so it will face the problem that while it will be relatively easy to identify the resource inputs, it will be more difficult to assess whether these resources are employed effectively and what the benefits from the process are. It is even more difficult to assess what the conse-quences of not having management audit process might be. However, the need for such assessments is inescapable. There is a wide range of performance indicators that an audit committee might use for this purpose, covering specific aspects of the efficiency with which audits are conducted and the effectiveness of the audit process. The danger is that of becoming unduly concerned with the minutiae of performance indicators. At least in the short term, a more useful approach might be to concentrate on some core questions about management and other non-external auditing:

♦ Does management audit have established goals emerging from the planning process?
♦ Will the achievement of these goals contribute to enhanced organizational performance?
♦ Is the resourcing of audits properly considered?
♦ Does the executive audit group plan and monitor audits in a way which is likely to ensure the achievement of established goals?
♦ Are the findings of audit teams properly considered and acted on?
♦ Are defined audit goals actually being achieved?

To help it answer these questions the audit committee might well choose to utilize a variety of performance indicators ranging from budget/actual resource inputs for particular audits to the proportion of audit assignments being completed on schedule and identified cost savings arising from audits.

SUMMARY

Management audits are a potentially very useful source for identify-ing possible improvements in managerial and organizational per-formance. However, if they are to realize this potential they must be properly planned, implemented, monitored and their findings given proper consideration. The difficulty that many healthcare organizations face is that for a variety of reasons in recent years many different types of audit have grown up serving the profes-sional and other interests of different parts of the organizations. There are many different audit agendas being implemented. There is a need for improved coordination, agreement on and clarity of audit objectives, recognition of the resource implications of the audit effort, and systems for implementing audit findings.

**FURTHER
READING**

- Auditing Practices Committee (1990), *Value for Money Audit*, ICAEW Publications, London.
  Originally published as an audit brief by the Auditing Practices Committee, this provides a useful summary of VFM auditing issues.

- Butt, H. and Palmer, R. (1985), *Value for Money in the Public Sector*, Blackwell, London.
  This is a very pragmatic book with many useful examples and case studies. Although published some time ago its approach is still relevant today.

- Buttery R., Hurford, C. and Simpson, R.K. (1993), *Audit in the Public Sector*, Institute of Chartered Secretaries and Administrators, London.
  This provides a useful overview of auditing activity throughout the public sector. The first section of the book concentrates on internal audit issues, the second on external audit issues. Both sections contain material directly relevant to healthcare management.

- Chartered Institute of Public Finance and Accountancy (CIPFA) – this organization publishes a number of useful publications which while oriented towards internal audit are directly relevant to broader concepts of management audit, including:
  CIPFA (1990), *The Client's View of Internal Audit*
  CIPFA (1991), *Audit Report Writing Made Simple*
  CIPFA (1992), *Measuring the Performance of Audit*
  CIPFA (1993), *Quality and the Internal Auditor*

- Sherer, M. and Turley, S. (1991), *Current Issues in Auditing*, Paul Chapman Publishing, London.
  While having a private sector orientation, this book is a good source of reference, particularly Part II relating to the forming of audit opinions and Part III which contains chapters on Modern Internal Auditing, The Audit Commission and The Audit of Central Government.

REFERENCES

Auditing Practices Board (1990), *Auditing Guideline: Guidance for Internal Auditors*. London: Auditing Practices Board.

Auditing Practices Committee (1980), *Auditing Guidelines 204: Internal Controls*. London: Auditing Practices Committee.

Boys, P. (1985), *Management Audits*. London: Touche Ross & Co. Technical Digest No. 17.

Chambers, A. (1992), *Effective Internal Audits*. London: Pitman.

Chartered Institute of Public Finance And Accountancy (1979), *Institute Statement – the Role and Objectives of Internal Audit in the Public Sector*. London: Chartered Institute of Public Finance and Accountancy.

Chartered Institute of Public Finance and Accountancy (1987), *Internal Audit Management*. London: Chartered Institute of Public Finance and Accountancy.

Department of Trade Inspectors (1979), *Inspectors' Report on Peachey Property Corporation*. London: HMSO.

Hammill, A. (1982), Choosing the right targets, *Accountancy Age*, 7 October.

Hatherley, D.J. and Skuse, P.C.B. (1991), Audit reports. In Sherer, M. and Turley, S. (Eds), *Current Issues in Auditing (2nd Edn)*. London: Paul Chapman Publishing.

Institute of Internal Auditors (1975), *An Evaluation of Selected Current Internal Auditing Terms*. Florida: Institute of Internal Auditors.

Institute of Internal Auditors (1988), *Standards for the Professional Practice of Internal Auditing*. London: Institute of Internal Auditors.

Koontz, H. and O'Donnell, C. (1976), *Management: A Systems and Contingency Analysis of Managerial Functions*. Tokyo: McGraw-Hill.

Morris, B., Bell, L. and Solieri, A. (1995), The use of Blueprinting in Auditing Healthcare Processes. *International Conference EUROMA*, University of Twente, Netherlands.

NHS Executive (1995), *NHS Trusts Finance Manual*. Leeds: NHS.

Power, M. (1994), *The Audit Explosion*. London: DEMOS.

Santocki, J. (1976), Meaning and scope of management audit. *Accounting and Business Research*, 6(25) Winter.

Vintnen, G. (1991), Modern internal auditing. In Sherer, M. and Turley, S. (Eds), *Current Issues in Auditing (2nd Edn)*. London: Paul Chapman Publishing.

EXTERNAL AUDIT AND VALUE FOR MONEY

CHAPTER 10

John J. Glynn

OBJECTIVES

♦ To explain the statutory basis for external audit embracing both financial and value for money audits.

♦ To discuss the nature of external value for money audit investigations.

♦ To discuss the nature of the auditor : auditee relationship.

INTRODUCTION

One clear way by which the NHS can demonstrate accountability for the services it provides is via the process of external audit. Typically in the NHS there are three divisions of such audits: One that relates to the direct quality of patient care - *medical audit*; one that relates to the economics of health care - *financial audit*; and, one that bridges both of the former - *value for money (VFM) audit*.

The term audit has traditionally been defined by the accountancy profession as:

> ... the independent examination of, and expression of opinion on, the financial statements of an enterprise by an appointed auditor in pursuance of that appointment and in compliance with any relevant statutory obligation. (Audit Practices Committee 1980).

External financial regulatory audit has been employed in the NHS since its inception. Up until October 1990 the various NHS Acts prescribed that the Secretaries of State should employ auditors to audit the accounts of all health authorities. For health authorities in England these auditors were civil servants of the staff of the Department of Health; for health authorities in Scotland, civil servants of the Scottish Office, and soon. With the passing of the National Health Service and Community Care Act 1990, the 1982 Act was amended to allow the Audit Commission to become responsible for the appointment of auditors to health service bodies in England and Wales. Those staff employed by the Department of Health were transferred to the district audit service of the

Audit Commission. Apart from its own staff, the Audit Commission also contracts with a number of private sector firms of auditors. Similar arrangements also came into force in Scotland.

The NHS as a whole remains subject to audit by the National Audit Office (NAO). Under the NHS Acts the Comptroller and Auditor General (C&AG), as head of the NAO, is required to examine, certify and report on the annual summarized accounts of NHS expenditure and he is permitted to examine the accounts, records and audit reports of individual health authorities. Rigden (1983, p. 173) likens the functions and responsibilities of the C&AG 'to those of a primary auditor of group accounts. He is entitled to take account of the work of the statutory auditors (now the Audit Commission) in deciding what further work he needs to undertake.' Pursuant to the provisions of the NHS Act 1977 and other enabling powers, the respective Secretary of State regulates on all aspects of financial control of health authorities.

Both the NAO and the Audit Commission undertake VFM audits in the NHS. This form of audit is relatively new; the powers of the NAO are prescribed in the National Audit Act 1983, which states in Part II (para. 7) that:

(1) If the Comptroller and Auditor General (C&AG) has *reasonable cause* to believe that an authority or body to which this section applies has received more than half of its income from public funds he may carry out an examination into the economy, efficiency and effectiveness into which it has in that year used its resources in discharging its functions.
(2) Subsection (1) shall not be construed as entitling the C&AG to question the merits of the policy objectives of any authority or body in respect of which an examination is carried out.

In summary the C&AG may examine the *economy, efficiency* and *effectiveness* of NHS expenditure and the use of NHS resources. The auditor must be apolitical and not concerned with health policy per se, rather with its effects and whether such effects correspond with the intentions of policy. The NAO's reports attract widespread interest in the media as the following commentary, from a national newspaper, illustrates:

Britain's £750 million-a-year maternity services need better planning and more resources to tackle unacceptably high levels of perinatal deaths amongst the babies of the poor and deprived, the National Audit Office, Parliament's financial watchdog, said in a report published yesterday. (*The Guardian*, March 1990)

The mandate of the Audit Commission is to be found in the Local Government Finance Act 1982, Section 15 of which states:

An auditor shall by examination of the accounts *and otherwise* satisfy himself ... that the body whose accounts are being audited has proper arrangements for securing economy, efficiency and effectiveness in the use of its resources.

The introduction of VFM auditing into the NHS has particular significance in today's environment of the internal market since the rationale of the market is to achieve both efficient and effective health care within the limits of the funding provided. VFM auditing has been seen as one of the more important mechanisms whereby the claimed success of the internal market can be assessed. It is the contention of this chapter that VFM auditing has, potentially, much to offer in providing insights into just how efficient and effective health care really is, but as a discipline much has yet to be learnt. Particular concerns centre on the nature of the investigations to be undertaken, what constitutes audit evidence and how practicable is it to audit the effectiveness of health care. In order to discuss these issues further this chapter is organized in the following six sections:

♦ The nature of the VFM audit
♦ Auditing efficiency
♦ Auditing effectiveness
♦ Managing the auditor : auditee relationship
♦ Implementation of VFM audit recommendations
♦ Is VFM auditing itself value for money?

The introduction of VFM auditing should advance four objectives:

1. Provision of a basis for the improved management of NHS resources.
2. Improvement in the quality of information on the results of NHS management that is available to policy-makers, legislators, and the general community.
3. Encouragement of NHS management to introduce and improve processes for reporting on performance.
4. Provision for more adequate accountability.

Although auditing has now been carried out for over a decade there is still much work to be done to develop relevant audit methodologies and techniques. At the end of this chapter we discuss some of the aspects that currently inhibit the development of VFM auditing.

THE NATURE OF THE VFM AUDIT   As indicated in the introduction, VFM auditing has developed in recent years as a way of expanding the more traditional role of the auditor away from the more straightforward examination of the fairness of the financial statements of a public sector organization. The introduction of VFM auditing is not unique to the UK. Similar legislation applies in such other countries as Australia, Canada,

Holland, New Zealand, Sweden and the USA though the exact terminology and extent of audit mandate may vary slightly. For example, the term *performance auditing* is used in the USA. It was originally promulgated by the United States Government Accounting Office (GAO) in the early 1970s. In its 1972 publication *Standards for Audit of Government Organizations, Programs, Activities and Functions* the objectives of government auditing were stated by the GAO as reviewing:

◆ financial operations and compliance with applicable laws and regulations;
◆ economy and efficiency in management's use of resources; and
◆ the effectiveness of programs in achieving a desired level of results.

In Australia, by contrast, the 1979 mandate of the Australian National Audit Office is more restrictive, being extended to undertake only *efficiency audits* in addition to fiscal regularity audits. The topic of audit mandates can require a chapter in their own right (see Glynn 1985); suffice to say for our purposes, differences aside, there is a good deal of collaboration between the different national audit agencies so that developments can be learned and problems shared. Much of this collaborative work is facilitated by the International Organisation of Supreme Audit Institutions (INTOSAI).

In adapting to this expanded mandate the auditor faces many difficulties. There is a need to train and recruit specialist staff who will have to work with NHS management to determine whether or not they and their staff have been successful in producing the level and quantity of service required by those responsible for determining health policy. The issue of whether accountants are the best qualified to undertake this type of investigative work has created some debate in recent years. Whereas in the USA about 60% of the GAO's staff are non-accountants but specialists in a wide range of disciplines, in the UK relatively few non-accounting specialists are employed by the NAO or Audit Commission. The accounting profession in the UK would probably claim that as their audit approach is essentially *systems based* they do have many of the necessary skills which other specialists do not necessarily have. Their role, being essentially an apolitical one, is to comment on whether management have established systems to monitor the efficiency and effectiveness of health care by which they manage. Certainly an auditor would not feel qualified to comment upon the relative effectiveness of, say, a particular treatment for cancer. Their view would be that clinicians should establish professional criteria for monitoring the effectiveness of this treatment and measure and appropriately report their findings.

As highlighted in other chapters, the term *value for money* has a wide and ambiguous meaning. Many government programmes, including those concerned with health care, reflect major attempts to improve the social and economic conditions in an increasingly complex society. As government expenditures have grown, the objectives and results of such programmes have come under increased public scrutiny. Holtham and Stewart (1981, p. 3) state:

> We see the concern as arising in an era of constraint, but see that the case for value for money stands apart from the political stance taken – whether it is for or against cuts in local government expenditure. Value for money is justified whatever level of expenditure is aimed at. Questions of value for money are about political judgement – the judgement of what is value for money. Value for money does not remove political judgement – it may well increase the emphasis on it. We argue, however, that the process for value for money *is* politically neutral, even though what is decided in that process will not be.

The last sentence of this quotation draws an important distinction (Glynn *et al.* 1994, p. 116). The auditor is not concerned with policy, which is the responsibility of elected politicians and public servants who administer their directions. The auditor is concerned with investigating the outcomes of healthcare policy and whether such effects correspond with the intentions of the policy. This is a monitoring function. To say that a particular department or programme provides value for money means that those who strive to provide the service do the best they can, given the resources that are available and the environment within which they operate. The auditor must examine whether resources could be put to alternative uses, whether objectives could be achieved by an alternative strategy and (if practicable) compare the operations of one particular department or service with another.

The role of the auditor should essentially be supportive to management by assisting in pointing out deficiencies and advising on possible courses of action. Ultimately though the auditor has the power to publicly sanction NHS management if he/she believes that they are not sufficiently monitoring the efficiency and effectiveness of the services they provide. Some commentators have likened VFM audit to management consultancy. Such an analogy is not correct. So how is VFM auditing different from traditional audit or management consultancy? A conventional (financial compliance) audit of financial statements is designed to provide independent, objective opinion that financial information has been presented fairly. As part of the process the auditor may include an examination of accounting and related information systems, and may make recommendations to management to improve these systems. Generally, such audit reports are predictable and short because the auditor is guided by generally accepted accounting and audit principles and standards. Management consulting assignments generally require solutions to perceived problems and experience at implementing solutions. They may frequently involve advice on specialized management decisions or implementing specialized management systems. The range of situations, solutions and systems is very diverse. There is no predictable form of reporting, and there are *no generally accepted* standards for decision-making or systems to guide the consultant. VFM auditing is a blend of both conventional auditing and management consulting. It benefits from the independence, objectivity and reporting skills of auditors, complemented by the specialized analytical systems and implementation skills that may be available from management consultants. VFM reports tend to be long-form and attention directing rather than providing detailed solutions. The auditor is not concerned with policy, but with its effects and whether such effects correspond with the intentions of the policy. This is a monitoring function, a comparison of the situation that exists with that which might have been expected. For each part of the organization it is then necessary to identify activities undertaken, and their purpose. An examination should be made of those outputs that are measurable and the costs involved: this information is needed to assess efficiency and effectiveness. The VFM auditor is concerned to see that planned activities have been achieved, and should not be involved in the setting of targets.

Earlier in this text definitions of economy, efficiency and effectiveness were provided. For the auditor the notion of economy is relatively straightforward. He/she is concerned to verify that the unit under investigation acquires resources of appropriate quality for minimal cost and that diseconomies such as overstaffing or the use of overpriced facilities do not occur without good reason. The assessment of efficiency and, particularly, effectiveness causes the auditor greater concern. For ease of discussion we discuss the auditing of efficiency and effectiveness under separate headings. In practice, of course, aspects of efficiency can often merge into aspects of effectiveness and vice versa; especially in the field of health care. For example, if the attendance times of ambulances at major incidences were increased (an aspect of the efficiency of the ambulance service) there is a clear knock on effect as to the effectiveness of the treatment offered on site by the paramedic team. On the other hand inefficient theatre scheduling will not necessarily impact on the effectiveness of an individual patient's treatment but can well deprive or postpone treatment to others. As Hepworth (1980, p. 239) has noted:

> The conflict between efficiency and effectiveness, particularly in sensitive services . . . is extremely difficult to resolve, and is best left to individual judgements, which really means the judgement of those concerned with the development of the service.

AUDITING EFFICIENCY Efficiency refers to the productive use of resources and ought not to be thought of, narrowly, as productivity. The Office of the Auditor General of Canada (1981, p. 2) draws an important distinction between efficiency and productivity (Box 10.1).

Box 10.1
Distinction between efficiency and productivity

> *Productivity* is the arithmetical ratio between the amount of goods and services used in the course of production; the ratio between output and input.
>
> *Efficiency* is the relationship of actual output/input (productivity) to a performance standard. The relationship is usually expressed as a percentage.

Efficiency is the relationship of output (or productivity) to a standard or target. In order to produce efficiency measures it is necessary to measure both programme outputs and inputs. Efficiency measures as such are only possible when outputs can be separated from each other and possess uniform characteristics. Typically the auditor would expect that the vast majority of services offered by a department or clinic would have a small number of key efficiency measures, developed by management and healthcare professionals, which could be in terms of the rate of return to production, work content measured over time or unit cost of output. The auditor would wish to see that such measures are relevant and actually used by management as a means of monitoring service delivery. The development of efficiency measures, as with the development of all performance indicators, is regarded by the auditor as evolutionary. In the early stages of development such measures might be time related or established by measuring output against some benchmark target. As an understanding of performance measurement develops, such measures might be changed such that comparisons are made relative to a standard or protocol, or perhaps an inter-authority comparison. The auditor will gather evidence in order to decide whether efficiency measurement is possible and if so whether the indicators developed are appropriate. At this juncture it ought to be stated that the auditor may well agree that, in certain circumstance, the measurement of efficiency is either limited or not practicable.

Audit evidence as such can be based upon three basic types of evidence: *documentary, oral* and *observed*. The auditor will examine source documents from which efficiency measures are calculated and the basis by which they are published, frequency etc. In addition a cross-section of staff will often be interviewed to assess their opinion of the measures produced – whether they consider them relevant, whether they consider alternative measures could be developed and so forth. As appropriate the auditor may well wish to observe particular activities in order to better assess the practical relevance of the efficiency measures used by management.

The 1981 Canadian Audit Guide (p. 5), referred to earlier (Office of the Auditor General (1981)), has discussed the importance of management using efficiency measures in the following terms:

> Standards and performance data are used (by management) for different purposes in various information and control systems. These are to:
> - demonstrate achievement of results by comparing performance to standards, targets and goals;
> - plan operations and budget resource requirements by providing data for comparing present and proposed methods and procedures;
> - provide a rational basis for pricing goods and services (when charges are made);
> - make trade-off decisions between efficiency and the level of service; and
> - indicate to employees and supervisors what results are expected.

These points seem fairly obvious but can have serious consequences if a particular authority fails to take the issue of developing efficiency (and for that matter effectiveness) measurement seriously. To take one instance from the above list – the budgeting of resource requirements – the auditor would nowadays regard it as very unsatisfactory for a health authority to budget on an incremental resource input basis. Key efficiency performance criteria can assist in a more rational approach to budgeting, one linked to programmes of planned activity. Such performance measures can better assist in the claim for more resources or can be seen as at least relatively fair when resources are reduced because activity has decreased and/or efficiency has improved.

Figure 10.1 provides a schematic overview of an efficiency audit (adapted from Glynn 1985).

AUDITING EFFECTIVENESS

Whilst the development of efficiency measures can cause concern to both managers and auditors alike, it is probably fair to state that both groups have not fared too well with the development of effectiveness measures. For the auditor there are very particular problems in the area of health care. As such, what determines satisfactory criteria for the assessment of effectiveness has to be determined by clinicians. The external auditor has neither the technical expertise nor mandate to comment on the effectiveness of health care per se. The audit mandate is effectively systems based and as such the auditor can question whether effectiveness is assessed and if so whether such a process is deemed satisfactory. This is clearly a contentious issue not only in the field of health care

Figure 10.1
Schematic overview of
an efficiency audit,
from Glynn (1985,
p.19)

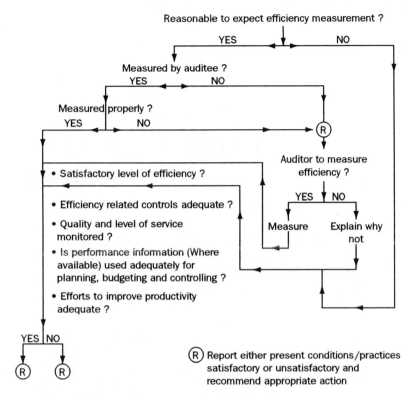

but also across the whole of the public sector. In the previous section some suggestions were offered as to the nature of possible efficiency measures. Effectiveness audit involves an examination of the measures used to monitor the relationship between the output and objectives of the department. However, this, the most important element of VFM, is the most difficult and challenging for management and auditor alike to conceptualize and operationalize.

As individuals, we may not have much difficulty in judging the effectiveness of our actions or those around us. This is probably because we use our own, individually based, criteria in evaluation. Assessing organizational effectiveness, however, is much more problematic with a seemingly endless variety of manifestations and criteria. Consider the two definitions in Box 10.2.

The Treasury definition is extremely vague whilst the NAO definition talks about outputs achieving 'intended effects'. The NAO terminology begs two questions – what exactly do we mean by *effect* and what if a policy actually produces an unintended effect which might be either desirable or undesirable? For the auditor to best assess effectiveness measurement he/she must have a clear understanding of what are the various degrees of effectiveness that may exist and what approaches might be adopted for their measurement. Glynn *et al.* (1992) have sought to clarify the issue

Box 10.2
Definitions of
effectiveness

> The extent to which the objectives of a policy are achieved. The most effective policy is one which achieves all its objectives. (Treasury 1988, p. 28)
>
> Effectiveness is concerned with the relationship between the intended results and the actual results of projects, programmes or other activities. How successfully do outputs of goods, services and other results achieve policy objectives, operational goals and other intended effects? (National Audit Office n.d., p. 5)

for the auditor by talking about *managerial effectiveness* and *policy effectiveness*. Managerial effectiveness is the extent to which the management of a service is effective to the extent that pre-specified outputs are achieved. These may be expressed as a quantity or quality. For example, the ability to treat a target number of patients (quantity), a drug dependency clinic to attract and satisfy addicts (quantity and quality), or a pharmacy to issue prescriptions within a stated time limit (quality). With respect to the last example, this could also be claimed as an efficiency measure. This is because managerial effectiveness subsumes the effective management of economy and efficiency.

Policy effectiveness is the extent to which outputs produce *outcomes* and *impacts* that are consistent with underlying policy. This is an area which VFM auditors throughout the world have been hesitant to enter for fear of being accused of dabbling in external political values. But it is legitimate for the auditor to make comments about (say) the functionality of the outcomes of a breast screening programme on its intended beneficiaries without making 'political' observation so long as the adjudication is restricted to the programme's effectiveness in promoting the goals and values defined for it. In other words it is not for the auditor to question the terms of reference of the programme by, for example, suggesting that the age range of women screened be widened or the frequency of screening be varied.

Policy effectiveness can be subdivided into *outcome effectiveness* and *impact effectiveness*. The first term reflects the contribution of the outputs of a treatment or service to the outcome of specified stakeholders – the stakeholders typically being the triumvirate of service provider (hospital clinician), the patient and the purchaser of the service (the GP or commissioner). There may also be a fourth stakeholder in some instances – the family unit. In theory it ought to be possible to identify the interests and objectives of these individual stakeholders but the difficulty is that often these may be in conflict. Typically conflict might arise between the service provider and the purchaser of that treatment or service.

From the foregoing it can be appreciated that the effectiveness audit can, pragmatically, operate at a number of levels depending upon the nature of the programme or service under review and the nature of the associated information systems. Figure 10.2 suggests that there are five potential approaches to or levels at which an effectiveness audit can be undertaken. The first two, evaluative audit and output audit, have a systems based approach. Evaluative audit examines the technical and organizational capabilities of programme or service managers. Here the auditor is concerned to see if there are appropriate databases available and whether there is expertise in quantitative and qualitative methodologies necessary for evaluation to be conducted and used, and the organizational capability to establish appropriate organizational structures and processes, such as authority and responsibility structures, reporting links, decision-making for the execution and utilization of evaluation. To the auditor these aspects would be seen as constituting the prerequisites for the effective conduct of evaluations. Measuring a programme's or service's evaluative effectiveness, therefore, requires identifying these elements and assessing their value. Output effectiveness, the next incremental stage, involves reviewing the extent to which pre-specified outputs are achieved. These may be expressed as a quantity or a quality measure and the auditor will wish to review their functionality in contributing to overall programme effectiveness. It is an extension of evaluative audit since it is the technical and organizational capabilities which lead to the determination of intended outputs. Such intended

Figure 10.2
Effectiveness audit.
Approaches adopted
and key issues
addressed

Effectiveness audit	Approach	Key issues addressed
1. Evaluative audit	Systems based	Technical capability/ Organized capability for evaluation
		Programme logic and structure
2. Output audit	Systems based	Functionality of outputs
3. Administrative audit (1+2)	Monitoring and control	Managerial accountability
4. Outcome audit	Function-orientated (internal emphasis)	Base objectives/effects Stakeholder objectives/effects
5. Impact audit	Function-orientated (external emphasis)	End objectives/effects

the management process. In this type of examination the auditor is concerned with whether outputs correspond with required need. To this end the auditor needs to know management targets: for example, a specified reduction in hospital waiting lists. Outputs can be reasonably detailed and relate to the way in which the programme or service is operationally structured. Valid effectiveness output measures show how well a goal or objective is being achieved. They are a different set of measures to those of efficiency which are designed to evaluate how well resources are utilized. Thus, key questions in such an audit include: are output measures available and, if not, why not? Are outputs functionally related to the programme or service under review? Are programme outputs achieved in line with planned targets? Clearly the auditor will be concerned not only with whether planned targets have been achieved but also, more importantly, with whether these outputs are functionally related to the programme structure under review.

The approach of outcome audit is principally function orientated, with an emphasis on the notion of the effectiveness of a particular programme or service on identified stakeholders. The auditor evaluates the extent to which programme objectives, as they affect identified stakeholders, have been attained. Outcome audit must link programme/service processes to programme/service outcomes. In a sense, therefore, outcome audit is the next level up from administrative audit, specifically from that of outputs. But outcome audit is possible without the latter, though requiring greater resources and involving a higher audit risk. In essence, therefore, outcome audit addresses a programme (or service) and stakeholder objectives and effects.

The approaches or techniques adopted in this type of investigation will be wide-ranging. For example, in some instances it may be possible to produce quantitative data to support audit conclusions and recommendations. In other instances, more qualitative sources have to be relied on. The role of the auditor is to use these sources in assessing both whether the approaches to effectiveness measurement adopted by management are appropriate in relation to the programme or service under review, and whether policy effectiveness has been achieved with respect to identified stakeholders. Thus the auditor has to bear in mind that, for some programmes, there will be no direct measures of output and that policy outcomes on identified stakeholders can only be measured by proxies. In areas such as social policy and health, it is particularly important to differentiate between a programme's or service's objectives, the outcomes to be monitored and the indicators of those outcomes. To this end, both the programme/service's base and stakeholder objectives need to be examined; the former link directly to immediate outputs, while the latter are concerned with the consequences of these outputs on identified stakeholders. Typically, the effectiveness of base objectives is demonstrated by the development of suitable performance indicators. However, performance indicators will not often indicate programme effectiveness with respect to stakeholder objectives. In such circumstances the auditor has to determine what alternative approaches to effectiveness measurement should be developed by management.

Impact audit, although identified as a separate element of effectiveness audit, can in fact be perceived as an extension of outcome audit. However, there is a distinction; impact audit goes beyond an examination of the outcomes of (narrow) programme or service outputs on stakeholders, and considers the broader impacts, not only on stakeholders but also in relation to externalities, including the way in which a particular programme or service affects the overall portfolio of government programmes and policies. The decision on whether to undertake this type of audit will depend in part on whether impacts are identifiable. Whilst end objectives or desired effects may be identified, they tend to be expressed in general terms. This means that often such objectives or effects are not directly capable of assessment by the auditor. Even if they are, their impact may still be concealed. The audit of impact effectiveness may also be limited by the time taken for programmes or services to take effect. Given the confines of most investigations, the auditor may thus only be able to provide limited comment on overall impact effectiveness. Yet even this can bring auditors close to the threshold of policy content, comment on which is outside their mandate.

Auditors may wish to examine the way management implement, control and evaluate programmes. Such an audit relies on both evaluative audit and output audit which, as they are systems based, provide the necessary background against which the auditor evaluates management's ability to manage the programme. This composite audit may be termed administrative because, ultimately, it tests a programme's or service's administrative capacity to monitor and review itself and translate resources into outputs. The aim of such an audit is to ensure that adequate systems are in place to enable managers to demonstrate that they have been effective. Thus, key questions in such an audit include: are programme objectives and intended outputs clearly stated? Have satisfactory means been established to monitor and report on the effectiveness of programmes and services? What use is made of the data? Is it collated, used for decision-making purposes and adequately reported upon? Such an audit does not comment on the nature and direct relevance of the effectiveness performance measures and indicators produced, but does consider the management and reporting activities.

This taxonomy implies not only that different approaches address different key issues (Figure 10.2) but also that auditors have choices to make in the planning and design of effectiveness auditing. Both when proposing and commencing an effectiveness audit, the auditor has to determine the scope of the proposed investigation. It can embrace both evaluative and substantive effectiveness, but a number of factors have to be considered. The nature of a particular programme or service, for example, might be such that neither its managers nor the auditors are able to determine policy effectiveness. However, this would not preclude the auditor from undertaking evaluative and output audits. Conversely, the auditor may well decide that scarce time and resources would best be concentrated on outcome audit. Part of this review might encompass a limited review of broader impact issues. Full impact audits appear at present to be only rarely practicable; much depends on the type of programme under review and the associated audit risk.

MANAGING THE AUDITOR: AUDITEE RELATIONSHIP

The first stage in any VFM audit is for both the auditor and auditee (client) to agree on the terms of the engagement. Whilst legislation can only direct that VFM investigations should take place and provide the auditor with the necessary powers to undertake such tasks, it is for the auditor to decide upon which areas he/she should investigate. In making such decisions the auditor will be influenced by a number of factors which can include:

◆ issues raised as a result of fiscal/regulatory audit (typically more related to issues of economy and efficiency than to effectiveness);
◆ responses to research and/or investigations undertaken elsewhere (the Audit Commission, for example, distributes reports on specialist investigations which it expects all of its appointed auditors to respond to); and
◆ topics suggested by the auditee.

With respect to this latter point, it is very much a sign of an open relationship if senior management feel able to raise issues with the external auditor whose objectivity can assist them in the improvement of service delivery. On an annual basis the auditor will advise management on the areas to be reviewed having determined the purposes of the forthcoming investigation (assessing performance, identifying opportunities for improvement, developing recommendations for improvement or further action, or some combination thereof). From the auditee's perspective it is important to have some idea of the approach and work plan to be followed by the auditor, including areas/activities to be included/excluded, databases to be reviewed, staff commitment and so on. The auditor will also advise the auditee as to the timetable of the investigation and the schedule of progress meetings proposed during this period.

Throughout the period of the investigation the auditor will be amassing data from which a draft report will be prepared. This data will be in four principal categories: physical, testimonial, documentary and analytical, which are summarized in Box 10.3.

Box 10.3
Principal categories of data

◆ *Physical* evidence is the type an auditor obtains by direct observation of what people are doing, the condition of property or similar matters. The auditor becomes, in essence, a witness to the problem he/she is researching when examining the physical evidence.

◆ *Testimonial* evidence is gathering data from those who have witnessed a situation or event which the auditor was unable to observe. The auditor should prepare a written record of the pertinent information obtained in such interviews which may include the use of questionnaires.

◆ *Documentary* evidence is what the auditor obtains by the examination of the documentation pertaining to the matter under audit.

◆ *Analytical* evidence is evidence which the auditor proposes by putting together data gathered to create new information or to use in a presentation to management of the organization.

Source: Glynn (1985, p. 101).

As the audit team formulate their findings they should be discussed with management. Audit conclusions will not just be based on whether greater economies can be obtained. It may be that changes could improve efficiency, redeploy expenditure to provide a more effective service, or lead to improved information to enable management to monitor the future development of a particular programme or service. Draft reports should also be discussed with management as their views might usefully be incorporated into the final report. For example, management might well agree that certain criticisms are justified but wish it stated, in their defence, that the prime cause is due to ambiguous legislation or lack of precise policy statements at a higher level. Alternatively, the auditor may wish to record the dissenting views of management when there is a lack of agreement on any of the recommendations being proposed. If the audit team have utilized the services of external specialists it may be useful to present their findings, in full or part, as a separate appendix. In the final analysis, having considered all available data, the auditor must exercise judgement on the final shape and focus of the final report; judgement as to the conclusions and recommendations made, supported by relevant information (in sufficient detail). VFM audit reports tend to follow a particular structure depending upon the sponsoring audit agency and readers would be well advised to consult relevant NAO and Audit Commission reports.

As with financial/regularity audits, the relationship between the external auditor and internal audit can be important. The duties of the internal auditor, which cover many aspects of internal financial control, should be seen as complementary to the work performed by the external auditor. The external auditor will want to review the work undertaken by internal audit staff to determine their effectiveness in assisting management to improve the quality of information that is necessary if they are satisfactorily to monitor financial, efficiency and effectiveness aspects of the programmes and services under their charge.

Internal audit is an integral part of an organization's internal control. The extent to which the external auditor can dispense with detailed work depends in no small part on the effectiveness of the system of internal control. The Chartered Institute of Public Finance and Accountancy (CIPFA) have produced statements on internal audit practice in the public sector. Based on these standards, it is possible to summarize the responsibility of internal audit as reviewing, appraising and reporting on the following matters:

1. The soundness, adequacy and application of internal controls. Internal control can be said to comprise the whole system of controls established by management in order to:
   - safeguard its assets;
   - ensure reliability of records;
   - promote operational efficiency; and
   - monitor adherence to policies and directives.

   The establishment of internal records is the responsibility of management, not of internal audit, but as a service to management it is part of the latter's role to review, appraise and report on the soundness and adequacy of these controls.
2. The extent to which the organization's assets and interests are accounted for and safeguarded from losses of all kinds. Proper arrangements for the control and custody of the organization's assets should be built into the organization structure. The role of internal audit is to ensure that these arrangements are implemented and that they remain satisfactory.
3. The suitability and reliability of financial and other management data within the organization.

For internal audit to carry out these responsibilities it is essential that it operates with adequate independence.

Unfortunately the standard of internal audit in the NHS has not generally been very good. It has often been regarded negatively as a 'necessary evil' for ensuring that the conduct of those responsible for operating an organization remains within prescribed rules, regulations and legislation. The Salmon Committee Report (DHSS 1983) recognized the shortcomings of internal audit in the NHS and recommended the pooling of scarce internal audit resources by the various health authorities. This report also laid great emphasis on internal audit to devote attention to the monitoring of value for money. This emphasis was, though, more directed at cost savings and efficiency issues rather than effectiveness. Particular support was given to the establishment of multidisciplinary value for money teams whose role would be to effect annual savings which could be used for improving services. Lapsley and Prowle (1978) carried out comprehensive surveys that lent considerable weight to these and other recommendations of the Salmon Committee.

IMPLEMENTATION OF VFM AUDIT RECOMMENDA- TIONS

As the external auditor has statutory powers of investigation and publication it is therefore an obligation of management to respond to any negative findings or recommendations for improvement. Increasingly commentary on the responses to such audit reports will be found in annual reports which already require an audit certificate with respect to fiscal compliance and sound financial management practices.

One obvious way in which recommendations of VFM audit reports can be discussed and responses disseminated is via the establishment of a VFM audit committee. Such a committee can also review those reports (if any) prepared by internal audit. A number of advantages can accrue from the establishment of such a committee; these include:

♦ helping management to explicitly undertake their statutory responsibilities in responding to such reports which are public documents;
♦ strengthening the objectivity and credibility of both financial and VFM reporting;
♦ improving the quality of accounting and management information systems;
♦ improving communication throughout the organization on VFM matters.

It is important that such committees are fully representational by including both professional grade staff and clinicians, as well as management. Clinicians in particular will wish to be concerned with aspects of clinical service/programme efficiency and effectiveness. It is important that, as appropriate, relevant elements of these VFM reports be reported to the relevant clinical committees. One such committee is that convened to consider medical audit. Another important aspect of a VFM audit committee is that it provides a forum for the external auditor to add commentary to his/her written report. Indeed it might also be that such a committee develops to embrace all aspects of value for money. A well motivated workforce could be encouraged to contribute suggestions for VFM reviews or to offer their opinions for improvements to service delivery. Finally this committee could be asked to screen and, if deemed appropriate, comment upon the VFM performance indicators produced by individual departments or units.

There is a sort of circular benefit that the external auditor also derives from the establishment of a VFM audit committee (particularly following on from the additional responsibilities suggested above) and that is that not only is he/she more fully able to gauge the overall corporate attitude and response to VFM issues, but is also able to consider more fully suggestions for future topics to investigate.

IS VFM AUDITING ITSELF VALUE FOR MONEY?

VFM auditing is, potentially, one independent means of ensuring that NHS organizations are called to account for their actions. The problem for the auditor is that those involved in the provision or receipt of services from the NHS do not necessarily have homogeneous expectations. This is particularly so in today's environment of short-term horizons. Not only do politicians look to re-election every few years but increasingly there is a culture within the NHS whereby key management positions are only filled on a short-term basis and human nature is such that those in such positions also look to the short-term. Payment and reward systems are also geared up to the short-to-medium term. Even members of the public are in the schizophrenic position of, on the one hand, demanding better provision and quality of healthcare services whilst, on the other hand, not necessarily wishing to make additional contributions through taxation or increased treatment charges (where applicable). As far as the Treasury is concerned, success is when health authorities keep within defined expenditure limits. This is, of course, a crude approach to emphasize aspects of economy and efficiency over aspects of the effectiveness of health care. Into this environment comes the external auditor whose mandate is not only to examine whether health authorities have utilized their resources economically and efficiently but also to ensure that they have also provided effective services.

It is certainly true that in the early years of VFM auditing most of the auditors' attention was focused on aspects of economy and efficiency. This was only natural as most health authorities generally had poor management information systems by which economy and efficiency were monitored. Equally, more attention was paid to hotel and other support aspects of health care. Why? Because this was easier for the auditor to investigate as there has certainly been much antagonism from the nursing and medical profession to the introduction of VFM style reviews, including VFM auditing. Auditors, by their training, have a natural affinity with assessing the robustness of management information systems. However, it has only been comparatively recently that the medical profession has started to formally regularize the assessment of the services they provide. This has to be seen as a source of regret and it is certainly true that many clinicians still feel that they ought not to be held to account in such a public way. The code of medical ethics has often, wrongly, been used as a cloak for secrecy and self-protectionism. Abbot (1988, p. 235), the noted North American sociologist who specializes in the study of professional groups, ends his book with a statement which places accounting at the centre of social and cultural life when he states:

> The jurisdiction of money requires the kind of attention long received by health. Perhaps sociologists and historians, as biological individuals, concern themselves more with the professions of life and death than with the profession of loss and profit, but *surely accounting is today more socially important than medicine*.

It is perhaps a sad fact, but true, that we live in a society where monetary values dominate. As a consequence we are all relatively familiar with terms such as 'time is money', 'my time is valuable' and, of course 'value for money'. It is into this environment that the auditor has had to extend his/her mandate. It is a negative environment in which management and professionals often feel that the balance of assessment errs too heavily on short-term efficiencies at the expense of longer-term issues of effectiveness. And who is to judge by what criteria the auditor is to assess overall value for money? The greatest challenge to the auditing profession, as VFM auditing becomes a regular exercise within the NHS, is concerned with the assessment of effectiveness. As yet, the development of performance indicators, whereby effectiveness can be gauged, is in a relative stage of infancy. It is also a politically sensitive subject littered with pitfalls. Lessons learned from the experience built up both in the UK and many other countries which now have similar audit legislation are a valuable but insufficient source of guidance. Much more by way of research needs to be undertaken. The auditor will continue to learn new skills and to seek the services of non-accounting specialists including clinicians. Indeed some of the larger international firms of accountants and management consultants do already employ small numbers of clinicians.

SUMMARY

It is the auditor's duty to press for the development of clear objectives, for the adoption of suitable performance measures and the implementation of timely and reliable management information systems. It is not only the auditor who needs education, the public too needs to be reminded that, whilst the auditor's role is to seek out areas that require attention, the ultimate responsibility for obtaining value for money rests with politicians, management and health professionals. Given this basic state of nature, it is clearly in the interests of clinicians to work closely with management and auditors in the pursuit of value for money. Why? Because the maintenance of, and arguments for increases in, the level of resources devoted to health care, both in general and with respect to particular areas of clinical concern, are increasingly being linked to performance indicators that can assist in demonstrating value for money. It is not possible for clinicians to absolve themselves from financial accountability. But there is also an advantage for the clinician in embracing this move to the development of VFM performance indicators. As these indicators become more and more refined the trade-offs between economy and the levels and ultimate success of health care become more explicit and more focused. The audit function can assist with both the development and reporting of all aspects of value for money. This should, over time, lead to a position whereby some of the accountability for the level and quality of health care in the UK rests squarely with those who sanction the level of overall funding available to the NHS – the politicians.

FURTHER READING

♦ External audit is carried out by the Audit Commission (Accounts Commission in Scotland) and the National Audit Office and their reports on the NHS provide particularly useful reading. These reports also provide important specialist bibliographies on specific topics.

REFERENCES

Abbot, A. (1988), *The System of Professions: An Essay on the Dimension of Expert Labor*. Chicago: University of Chicago Press.

Audit Practices Committee (1980), *Auditing Standards and Guidelines*. London.

Department of Health and Social Security (1988), *Report of the DHSS/NHS Audit Group* (Chairman P. Salmon). London: HMSO.

Glynn, J.J. (1985), *Value for Money Auditing in the Public Sector*. Hemel Hempstead, UK: Prentice-Hall International.

Glynn, J. J., Gray, A.G. and Jenkins, W.I. (1992), Auditing the three Es: The challenge of effectiveness, *Public Policy and Administration*, Winter.

Glynn, J.J., Perrin, J. and Murphy, M.P. (1994), *Accounting for Managers*. London: Chapman & Hall.

Hepworth, N.P. (1980), *The Finance of Local Government* (6th Edn). London: George Allen and Unwin.

Holtham, C. and Stewart, J. (1981), *Value for Money: A Framework for Action*. Institute of Local Government Studies, University of Birmingham.

Lapsley, I. and Prowle, M. (1978), *Audit of the National Health Service: A Conceptual Perspective*. Warwick University (CRIBA), Warwickshire.

National Audit Office (no date), *A Framework for Value for Money Audits*. London.

Office of the Auditor General of Canada (1981), *Audit Guide: Auditing of Efficiency*. Ottawa.

Rigden, M.S. (1983), *Health Service Finance and Accounting*. London: Heinemann.

Treasury HM (1988), *Policy Evaluation: A Guide for Managers*. London: HMSO.

US Government Accounting Office (1972), *Standards for Audit of Government Organizations, Programs, Activities and Functions* (The Yellow Book). Washington DC.

VALUE FOR MONEY AND SERVICE IMPACT

SECTION INTRODUCTION This final section widens the scope of the discussion to take in the questions of strategic management, purchasing and future developments and the equally difficult issue of the impact of these activities. A service perspective informs the links between clinicians and managers and between purchasers and providers. As will now be apparent there can be no universal blueprint for understanding and evaluating value for money. Equally there can be no universal blueprints for the most effective patterns of service provision in any particular locality. While government may set objectives such as those identified in The Health of the Nation, the design and delivery of services has to be a local responsibility. Services have to be provided to populations in particular environments who share diverse characteristics. Equally the distribution of resources, both capital and human, is little changed from that of the NHS established by Nye Bevan in 1948. The market will do little to equalize the provision of health care. The quality and impact of service delivery will depend upon the exploitation of good practice at a local level even if the distribution of resources remains patchy.

A key challenge facing the NHS is the need to balance local strategies with national priorities, recognizing the importance of local knowledge for service providers and the importance of the political process for the centre represented by the NHS Executive. Even at the periphery we find that clinicians have a broad perspective based on their professional and international affiliations as specialists while managers are more likely to focus on the needs of the purchasers and on career patterns which differ markedly from those of clinicians.

It is questionable whether it is possible for strategies to be made at the centre which go beyond the broad objectives we see at the present time. What the centre can do is to determine rules for the market through the processes of legislation and the development of accountability and resource allocation mechanisms. Despite these powers the local services will seek to identify loopholes wherever possible to meet local objectives and balance resource use with activity.

Neither policy-making nor strategic management are exact sciences as evidenced by the mixed experience of trying to provide high quality healthcare services within the complex political and social environment of the 1990s. It follows that while we pursue the study of value for money analysis and management, the volume ends in further questions which remain to be addressed.

Can Strategic Management Influence Value for Money?

CHAPTER 11

David A. Perkins

OBJECTIVES

- ◆ To define the concept of strategic management.
- ◆ To discuss the tensions that can arise between national objectives and their implementation at a local level.
- ◆ To assess the impact of strategic management on value for money.

INTRODUCTION

Strategic management is normally understood to mean the decisions and actions taken by senior managers and clinicians which determine the direction taken by the organization. The NHS is not an industrial or commercial organization and cannot decide overnight to change its services or to address different markets. It must respond to advances in technology, changes in funding, the needs of its patients, and the implications of the internal market. NHS managers are expected to develop a broad consensus among senior staff and to consult their populations about major changes. Many decisions will shape the practice of clinical care for years to come and may enhance or diminish the capability of local health services. This chapter reviews the practice of strategic management and asks how it might influence the achievement of better value for money.

WHAT IS STRATEGIC MANAGEMENT?

Theory and practice

It is perhaps easier to define the practice of operational management than that of strategic management. Operational managers usually work within clear constraints. This may take the form of a service level agreement or contract which defines the quantity and quality of work to be performed giving clear indications of the available resources. The plan may be clearly set out in one or more budgets which essentially translate the planned activity into a financial plan. The operational manager would be expected to deal with normal patterns of variance, obtaining higher authority if variances exceed this level. For instance, it might be assumed that a week in which the use of pharmaceutical prescriptions exceeded the budgeted level would be balanced by a week of lower use. If it appeared that a pattern of higher use was developing which threatened to exceed the sums budgeted for that department then the manager would be expected to take action by informing higher management and the direct users of the preparations. The operational manager would not normally be accountable for finding the resources with which to provide the services and would expect to call upon specialist skills to meet particular problems whether technical, human, or other.

Thus, operational managers operate within clear timescales, they have clearly defined limits to their authority, and the resources available to them are deemed, by someone else, to be sufficient for the task required. In contrast, strategic managers operate within conditions of uncertainty, addressing problems which are less easy to define and for which there may be no easy, programmed solutions. Strategic managers may set their own objectives which they 'sell' to higher authorities and these objectives may relate to extended timescales sometimes extending from 5 to 10 years into the future.

Robert Grant argues that strategic leaders require a clear and simple set of objectives, a profound understanding of the competitive environment, and a clear understanding of the full range of resources and capabilities available to the organization (Grant 1995). Yet who are the strategic leaders? Henry Mintzberg points out that in knowledge based organizations it is too simple to suppose that management determines what is to be done and gives orders to compliant workers who do what they are told (Mintzberg and Quinn 1991). Rather, much of the knowledge and skills on which the organization is based is held by staff within the core of the organization who work together in complex patterns to provide non-standard services to individuals, in this case patients. The decisions and actions of these staff determine, in large part, the overall direction of the organization. Service developments are dependent on bringing together staff with the correct range of skills and underpinning knowledge and providing them with the resources and facilities they require. It is often the case that important new developments stem from clinician entrepreneurs who are able to build up a research team using soft research monies and to obtain hard revenue funding to put new services in place.

In a related sense the direction of the organization is a function of small, incremental decisions and actions taken at the patient care level concerning treatment regimes, patterns of admission and discharge, the relationship between specialist and general medicine, and the overall needs of the population of patients served. The particular clinical interests of doctors will influence the development of the services they provide and ultimately the direction of the organization.

None of this is to deny the importance of GP partnerships or Trust Boards in setting the direction of an organization, but rather to point at the combination of interests in the strategy of the organization and the combination of decisions and actions which influence the course taken by the organization.

One of the key divisions in the NHS market is that between purchaser and provider strategy. The purchaser is charged with using NHS funds to provide a package of services for a defined population whether that be the patients registered with a GP, the population of a locality, or a particular patient or care group. The provider is an 'independent' organization charged with balancing income and expenditure and perhaps interested in achieving a 'profit' to reinvest in the services being provided. The purchaser's strategy will be concerned with the balance and availability of services for its population and with obtaining the best volume of quality services possible. As a secondary concern it will be keen to ensure the continued viability of the providers with whom it contracts. The provider will be primarily interested in the viability and development of the services which it provides. It will not be interested in the questions of equity and community need except in so far as it might persuade the purchaser to contract with it for further work.

In one sense both purchaser and provider will have implicit strategies whether or not they have a clear statement of their objectives and strategy and whether or not these statements are followed in practice. A Trust may adopt a very cautious strategy taking few risks and looking for evidence that others have tried particular options before doing so themselves. Alternatively, they may perceive themselves as leaders at the forefront of clinical and service development 'going boldly where no-one has gone before'. The *follower* strategy may not be explicitly acknowledged but it may be clear to the informed observer of a middle performing Trust or practice. The *leadership* strategy may be obvious to an observer from the speed of clinical and service innovation, the extent of exposure in press, journals and other media. The benefits to leaders include the possibility of being able to obtain resources available for innovation, research and development which are less easily available after the developmental stage. The followers may be able to learn from the successes and to avoid the mistakes and failures of the leader. It is sometimes the case that the leader develops a reputation for advanced thinking and practice which help them to obtain funds and attract high calibre, innovative staff.

Where purchasers and providers have explicit strategies, they cannot necessarily be understood at face value. Strategy documents are produced for particular purposes and with particular audiences in mind. They may be produced in a number of forms ranging from simple summaries for public consumption to detailed plans for managing the organization or for the consumption of purchasers or higher authorities. Capital developments may require clear evidence of strategic planning whether they are to be funded from public, private or charitable sources. There is considerable anecdotal evidence of private donors being concerned about the future of services in London which they have funded in part or in whole. In future potential donors are likely to require evidence from purchasers as well as providers about the future of services before making capital donations.

LANGUAGE AND PROCESSES

The language of strategic management is no more complex than any other area of management but nonetheless warrants some discussion.

A *mission statement* is an attempt to encapsulate the purpose and values of an organization in a few sentences providing a clear message to interested parties and providing a means to assess whether proposals or plans are consistent with the overall desired goal of the organization.

Box 11.1
Two examples of mission statements

◆ To achieve local respect and national renown as a user-focused, innovative, effective and efficient centre of excellence in metropolitan health care, teaching and research.

◆ To provide high quality, accessible and appropriate clinical services for all patients: to promote excellence in the research, development and teaching of psychiatry and its allied subjects and to apply and disseminate this knowledge through the development of treatments for the relief of suffering.

Objectives or goals define what it is the organization is trying to achieve and how it will know if it has achieved or is achieving them. Ideally such goals will be entirely consistent but in practice they often imply competing priorities which manifest themselves in conflicts or competition for resources and attention at lower levels of the organization.

Policies are usually used to refer to the way in which the organization chooses to operate. For instance policies on equal opportunities, patients rights, ethical and environmental practices are designed to send clear messages to the organization's members and other interested parties about how the organization operates and what are the values and practices which it intends to support.

There may be internal or external sanctions which will be applied if these policies are disregarded.

The term *strategy* implies a high level objective which is tied to a means of achieving that objective. For instance, to win new contracts by being the most efficient low cost provider is a clear strategy which implies an objective and means, even if that objective is undesirable for other reasons.

The term strategy may be prefixed by a time period to which that strategy refers or by a part of the organization or an activity undertaken within the organization. Thus we may have the 5- or 10-year strategy, the human resource strategy, or a research strategy. An organizational strategy may be created from a series of sub-strategies which together show the direction of the organization and the means by which it is attempting to achieve its objectives.

A *business plan* would follow from the mission and objectives of the organization and would show how the activity for a given time-period, usually 12 months, will help towards the long-term strategy. There would be a statement of the available resources and the patterns of accountability for achieving objectives within the business plan. There would normally be some milestones against which to assess progress and a budget to cover the period in question. A more sophisticated business plan might take account of variations in income or level of activity allowing some degree of variation in expenditure or costs to meet the actual as opposed to the predicted level of activity. A business plan is often required as a condition of funding in both private and public sector contexts.

WHAT 'LEVERS' ARE AVAILABLE TO STRATEGIC MANAGEMENT?

The term 'lever' refers to actions which are available to strategic managers to achieve their objectives, in this case to achieve improvements in the value for money equation in the services for which they are responsible. Some actions impact on the value side of the equation while others have their chief effect on the resources which are used to provide the service and create the additional value.

Impacts on value

In most organizations top management reserve various decisions to the board or its members since they are regarded as critical to the direction and success of the organization. These include decisions of the following types:

♦ Organizational focus – organizations which have no clear focus make life difficult for their members since it is hard to make intelligent decisions between competing objectives. Should a doctor be spending more time on research or service provision? Should he/she enter a clinical trial or is it a diversion of scarce clinical resources with little immediate and local outcome? Top management might make decisions like this easier if they make clear the focus of the organization in terms of clinical and research objectives.

◆ Key activities – from time to time an organization needs to re-examine its key activities and be clear that it has the resources to be successful in those areas and that they are likely to remain profitable. This will involve examining the activity itself, the impact of competitors in this area, and the particular resources which this activity consumes. The organization may decide that it has no particular expertise in an area of work which can be provided better elsewhere and the obvious course of action is to discontinue that activity. For instance, a Trust may for historical reasons have a tropical diseases unit for which demand is low and it may decide to close that department and cease that activity and redeploy the resources.

◆ Investment decisions – since funds for investment are always scarce and often have revenue implications they are usually made and approved at high levels within the organization. The decision to build a new phase of a hospital might require approval at ministerial level since it has political and perhaps electoral implications and will have revenue implications for many years to come.

◆ Key appointments – the decision to employ another consultant physician will have a significant impact on the pattern of services and may also require approval from authorities responsible for the postgraduate training of doctors if such an appointment will have an impact on the pool or accredited specialists in that field.

◆ Approval of plans, budgets and business plans – since top management are legally responsible for the performance of the organization they will inevitably announce the planning assumptions for a year, such as the requirement for 2% efficiency savings, and assess and approve the plans developed by units and departments.

◆ Agreement of contracts – top management will expect to be informed in advance of any agreements entered into by its members which have a significant impact on the resources available to the organization.

◆ Decisions about primary organizational structure and processes – the structure of an organization can have a considerable impact on the quality of services as can the key processes such as quality assurance, planning, budgetary management and information systems.

These decisions are not made without consultation and managers may feel that there is little real choice in the options they choose, which may be dictated by harsh economic realities, yet their decisions do have a considerable impact on the quality of services and the value side of the value for money equation.

Impacts on money   Since top management is responsible for the performance of the organization they will be concerned about its use of resources and will ensure that attention is paid to the uses of funds. This will include some of the following issues:

◆ Reviewing plans, budgets and budgetary management systems. They will be keen to ensure that effective systems are in place and that rapid action is taken to investigate the causes of variances to planned levels and costs of activities.

◆ Commissioning 'Efficiency Scrutinies' and ensuring their findings are implemented. Since the Rayner efficiency studies commenced, the use of ad hoc investigations to assess the efficiency of particular activities or departments has been growing. Particular emphasis is placed on the importance of widespread dissemination of results so that best practice can be widely understood and imitated.

◆ Ensuring that accurate costing (and contracting) systems are in place. The need to ensure 'a level playing field' has meant that government through the NHSE has had to try to devise consistent costing mechanisms to prevent unfair competition in which a provider might subsidize one service to win a contract at the expense of a contract where it faces little competition.

◆ Developing and reviewing input performance indicators (PIs) using internal and external comparators. Performance indicators supplement the economic values contained in contracts by establishing quantitative measures by which services can be assessed.

STRATEGIC CHOICES AND CONTINGENT RESPONSES   Organizations exist within environments both physically and socially. They have the opportunity to influence those environments but they must also respond to features within those environments. Writers vary in the extent to which they emphasize the active initiating elements of strategy and the passive reactive elements. In the pre-market NHS much of the active initiating elements of strategy took place at the health authority level where policies and decisions were made to be implemented in the units. The creation of Trusts has resulted in independent organizations who have every reason to pay attention to their own strategy since their status and success depends on obtaining and delivering contracts whether for research, training or service delivery.

The *strategic choice* approach emphasizes the role of organizations in choosing and attempting to influence the markets and environments in which they operate. Thus, a Trust may decide to compete for contracts for particular services and will attempt to show that they are well equipped and efficient providers of a particular type of service. Alternatively they may decide that they cannot expect to compete effectively for a particular specialty and may be happy for another Trust to secure contracts for that area of work. Some GPs show evidence of the wish to exercise strategic choice by going for GP fundholding and more particularly for total fundholding status.

The alternative *contingent response* approach emphasizes the impact of the environment upon an organization and its need to respond to external threats or events. Such a response would emphasize the importance of the purchaser's power to agree contracts, the role of the NHSE in the introduction and management of the *Patient's Charter*, and the role of neighbouring Trusts seen as competitors rather than potential collaborators.

In practice, strategic management will be a combination of strategic choice and contingent response, there will be opportunities to be exploited and threats to be averted and, like the children's game, the key is to climb the ladders and avoid the snakes.

NATIONAL OBJECTIVES AND LOCAL STRATEGY

National objectives

Given the cost of the NHS, the level of public interest and therefore the level of political interest the government will always have objectives for the NHS and will attempt to create mechanisms to ensure that those objectives are achieved through a combination of incentives and sanctions. Each level of the healthcare system has to take these objectives seriously since the NHSE is not constrained to act through the intervening levels of management but can bypass normal hierarchical channels. All other levels of the NHS have to plan in the light of national objectives and are called to account in terms of their impact on these objectives. This requirement has always been present but has become more stringent with the more explicit national objectives of the Health of the Nation and the Patient's Charter.

Local strategy

Purchaser strategy

The task of a purchaser is to identify and prioritize the needs of the population for which it is responsible and to secure appropriate services for them in the light of national policies, clinical effectiveness, ensuring that the resulting combination of services represents the best value for the available resources.

Life would be easier if there was a single purchaser for a given population with access to the total funds allocated to that community. In practice a given population will consume health and social care services from a number of providers which have been purchased by a variety of agencies. Thus a conurbation of three-quarters of a million people may consume health and social care services which have been funded by a district health authority (DHA), GP fundholders, a social services department, and a GP multifund. Additionally some citizens will be privately insured or will pay for services from their own pockets when they need them. In this section we will focus on the DHA/FHSA and the GP fundholder as purchasers. It follows that purchasers cannot act in isolation but need to take account of the other purchasers with responsibility for their population.

The key difference between these purchasers is the size of the fund available for purchasing health and social care. Thus a GP fundholder will have a relatively small fund while a total fundholder will have a larger sum at his/her disposal, while a combined DHA and FHSA will have a comparatively large fund and may have access to capital as well as revenue monies. When purchasers combine their activities their influence increases and this may be especially attractive to GP fundholders.

Purchasers also have to take account of the local provider system of primary and secondary services. Since NHS Trusts are largely dependent for their continued viability and existence on the contracts and the extracontractual referrals which they are able to secure, the actions of purchasers must take account of their impact on the provider system and its component services. A purchaser's decision to contract for children's services with a neighbouring Trust might mean the closure of a paediatric department in a particular hospital. While such a decision to switch provider may be taken as a last resort it illustrates the fact that Trusts will be unable to continue services in the medium term for which they are unable to secure contracts.

It follows that purchasers must consider the pattern of services over a longer timescale if providers are to be able to develop their services in line with population needs and the dictates of medical and service technology. Purchasers will also have to consider the breadth or balance of the services being provided, dealing with sensitive questions such as the balance between primary, secondary and social care and possible future shifts between care settings.

One of the first strategic decisions for a purchaser will be the extent to which they will collaborate in purchasing. A DHA may attempt to coopt GPs into the purchasing process through the introduction of some form of locality purchasing so that they can be sure that the purchasing plans incorporate the views of the primary care providers. It is also important that there be appropriate collaboration with providers so that services can be developed over an appropriate timescale.

DHA/Health commission purchasers
This group of purchasers have to produce strategies on the basis of local data about health needs and services which demonstrate how the resulting contracts will contribute to a range of national objectives such as those outlined in the Health of the Nation, the Patient's Charter, and the National Cancer Strategy (Expert Advisory Group, 1994). These strategies and the resulting patterns of contracts will be reviewed at the regional level to ensure that the operation of the market meets national priorities and does not

result in serious gaps in services or unacceptably poor access for groups of patients.

Purchaser strategies will aim to secure progress on both sides of the value for money equation. They will have to pay particular attention to the coordination of services from different providers and sectors and the pursuit of patient centred care.

♦ Increasing value
- Treatments of proven effectiveness - perhaps the most eloquent critique of medical practice is that of Cochrane in his volume entitled *Effectiveness and Efficiency* (Cochrane 1972). His argument, which has been followed by many others, was that medical care procures should be assessed for their effectiveness and that treatments of proven effectiveness should be provided. More recently the Cochrane Centre in Oxford has taken forward the task of promoting the use of controlled clinical trials and other methods of assessing the effectiveness of treatments. As can be seen elsewhere in this volume, purchasers are increasingly questioning the use of treatments which do not meet the requirements of clinically proven effectiveness.
- Insisting on medical audit and other analysis of benefits - the development of contracts for services within the NHS has included specific requirements for medical audit procedures.
- Agreeing, protocols - contracts and markets imply clear definition of activity, standardization, which is difficult given the diversity of medical practice and the variety of patient needs. While protocols make it clear what the purchaser requires there are some complaints that some patients are 'over-investigated' as a result.
- Quality as perceived by consumer - since the consumer does not pay directly for the services received in most cases the experience of the patient, such as waiting times etc, has often come low in the list of priorities for institutions. The advent of the Patient's Charter has placed certain measurable elements of the patient's experience on the agenda. Additionally some purchasers such as GP fundholders have sought other evidence about the patient's experience in the non-clinical aspects of their care.
- Monitoring/auditing contracts - purchasers have required providers to give evidence that the requirements of contracts are being met including monthly reporting on a variety of data items relating to the quality and quantity of activity.
♦ Reducing costs
- Ensuring treatment takes place in most appropriate context - purchasers have the choice about with whom to agree contracts and this implies the possibility of caring for similar conditions in different ways. For instance the care of some

patients might be entrusted to a community Trust or to a general practitioner.

- Promoting lower cost alternative treatments of equal value – the development of day care treatments as an alternative to inpatient services may represent a lower cost alternative treatment of equal quality or value. This may require investment by purchaser and provider to develop new facilities and new skills in areas such as keyhole surgery and imaging.
- Supporting capital investments where these will have an impact on cost or value of treatment – where provider facilities no longer meet the requirements of modern services or where there are bottlenecks which prevent the development of efficient practice, it may be necessary to spend money to save money.

♦ Organizational strategy
- Developing the capabilities of the purchaser organization - the use of contracts and the sanctioning of investments may permit the provider to develop new capabilities which influence both cost and quality/effectiveness of the service concerned.

Primary care purchasers

♦ Portfolio questions. Like any other entity within the healthcare system GPs will have to make decisions about the range and extent of the services they provide. These decisions will depend upon the willingness of the purchaser to pay for additional clinics or minor surgical work but the practice will have choices about what services they wish to provide and what capabilities they must develop and demonstrate.

♦ Independent contractor status. The particular status of GPs means that they have to balance their income and expenditures in much the same way as any similar sized business. The complexity of the GP contract aligned with the wide range of possible sorts of income has led GPs to adopt similar business planning and management process to those found in the private sector although there are still a few single-handed GPs practising in a traditional fashion.

♦ Financial strategy. The size and status of general practices is such that financial management is adopting a considerable importance and the need to adopt appropriate contingencies so that there are funds at year-end for referral to secondary care requires skilful management. Thus GPs are likely to need a purchasing plan and to adopt careful systems of budgetary management.

Provider strategies

NHS providers include NHS Trusts, private sector hospitals, GPs, and other private and voluntary enterprises. They share the characteristic that they are not directly managed by NHS purchasers, there is a separation between those who determine what services should be provided and those who provide the service. As separate entities with their own legal forms and status the strategic management of providers is meant to emulate that of similar private sector organizations and so the structure of NHS Trust Boards, including the membership of executive and non-executive members and the reporting mechanisms, is supposed to mirror that of similar enterprises in the private sector despite the public sector constraints which limit their freedoms. These constraints include the limitations on powers to borrow, the enforced balance and membership of their boards, and a variety of limitations which are designed to protect the interests of the NHS as a whole. These include requirements to take part in the training of professional staff, to provide services which are essential in a locality such as Accident and Emergency, and the requirement to participate in the pursuit of national objectives such as those outlined in the Health of the Nation, the National Cancer Strategy and the Patient's Charter.

NHS Trust strategies
The achievement of NHS Trust status was dependent upon satisfying government about a number of criteria including the financial viability of the Trust as demonstrated by the business plan, financial status and projections. Trusts had to show that they had the necessary management capability to take full responsibility for their affairs and that management had the support of senior doctors in their management of the Trust. The production of annual business plans is an ongoing requirement and many Trusts have thought it appropriate to produce strategic plans for the next five years in an attempt to persuade various authorities that service development matters are under control.

♦ Portfolio questions – perhaps the key question of top managers in a Trust is what activities are within the capabilities and resources of the Trust and therefore which contracts should be actively sought in developing those services. For instance, a mental health Trust was faced with the decision of whether to bid for services to prisons in its locality in response to tender documents circulated by the Home Office. This involved key questions about the trust's ability to offer good services in the shortage specialty of forensic psychiatry as well as the ability to manage services on a number of sites spread throughout a county.

In practice this will mean responding to bids for developments from innovative clinicians which have implications for the overall direction of the organization. Another example of the portfolio question relates to key activities of a Trust which include service delivery, education and training. Since these activities are interdependent, there will be conflicts which arise and there will be difficult questions about the apportionment of costs where a particular clinical activity may relate to all three objectives. Some institutions may aim to achieve as much as 40% of their income from research contracts. This will have significant influence on the style of the organization, the key appointments that are made and the resources available to staff. Other institutions will aspire to providing good quality service to their resident populations and will adopt structures and processes which meet this objective.

◆ Decisions to provide or buy in. A provider may choose to provide a service by directly employing and managing its own staff who provide that service. Alternatively, it may decide to purchase the service from another more experienced provider. While hotel services have been contracted out for many years, it is less common to contract out nursing or pathology services although they may represent a cost-effective alternative to providing them in house.

◆ Business plans. Business plans are common in public, private and voluntary sectors and usually relate annual objectives to longer-term strategic objectives showing the expected flow of funds into the organization and the contracts to which these funds relate. Since the business plan acts as a key document for review and accountability it demands good financial and information systems and it will also set objectives for individuals and departments which are stretching but not impossible, implying improvements in management and clinical practice.

A Trust business plan will often be developed from a series of directorate business plans recognizing that directorates are groupings of services which foster management clarity but that in clinical and service terms they are interdependent with linked services and service level agreements.

The business plan will be a key document in discussions with purchasers since it only makes sense to plan over a strategic period if there is some likelihood that the purchaser will agree with the general pattern and type of services and continue to contract for them over the strategic period.

Functional strategies:

◆ Human resources. While most Trusts will be structured towards the primary activities of the Trust such as clinical services and research they will require specialist departments to provide levels of expertise not available at the operational level and since manpower accounts for about 70% of Trust expenditure the human resource department will be concerned with issues such as recruitment, reward, training and productivity of staff. The operational management of these issues will usually be devolved to directorate level or below but issues such as the Trust employment and pay or reward policies will be of considerable concern especially given the present government's desire to shift from national to local bargaining as demonstrated by the difficulties over the nurses' cost of living pay increases experienced at national and local levels in 1995.

♦ Service strategies. Particular services will be required to develop strategies which reconcile the development of the services with the contracts for those services and the resources which will be consumed in providing them. While developments in the paediatric service may warrant only a paragraph in a Trust business plan, there will doubtless be a business plan for that service which will have been agreed with purchasers and perhaps also with GPs and neighbouring Trusts if there is the likelihood of overlap or gaps in services.

♦ Site/capital plans. It has been suggested that only half of the land 'owned' by the NHS is currently used for the provision of patient services. In some cases the land is valuable and that resource can be released for capital or other developments. In many cases the buildings and sites available to a Trust are not appropriate for its current requirements and so most Trusts would have a site plan which outlines its future needs and indicates ways in which those can be met and the necessary financial resources found. Since capital is no longer a free asset but is charged for, there are clear incentives to divest unwanted capital and to ensure that capital is acquired on the best terms whether donation, lease or purchase and that it is fully utilized.

♦ Research. As indicated above, research can be a major source of funds and can add to the reputation of an institution which may be valuable in attracting new contracts and extracontractual referrals (ECRs). Many Trusts will have a director of research responsible for promoting good quality research and obtaining new funds and grants whether from NHS sources, external funding agencies or the private sector. In some institutions the importance of the Higher Education Council Research Assessment Exercise and its ratings system means that Trusts are keen to attract highly rated researchers and to ensure that resources and facilities are made available to facilitate this process.

♦ Education. Much service provision in the area of nursing has been provided in the past by nurses in training who were paid lower wages than their qualified colleagues and acted as an artificial depressant on the largest area of NHS salary costs. Other trainees also provide an important service contribution and the management of the relationship with educational and professional authorities is an important part of Trust strategy. In some cases good relationships will be necessary to ensure an adequate supply of appropriately qualified staff while in others there will be new resources to those Trusts who can demonstrate that they are making a sufficient contribution to education or training.

♦ Income generation commercial activities. Trusts have moved a long way from the time when the only chance of getting a newspaper in a hospital was from the WRVS trolley. The development of shopping malls and the entry of high street retailers into hospitals has shown the possibilities for income generation as has the growth of aerial farms at those hospitals fortunate enough to have a tower building in a good location. More conventional forms of income generation include the revitalization of private wards and blocks providing services to private patients. Such developments frequently involve the combination of public and private finance and build on the reputatation of NHS staff for excellence.

♦ Marketing plans. The use of commercial language within the NHS has been discouraged but this does not hide the importance of the marketing function in identifying new opportunities for services development and purchasers willing to agree new contracts. Some Trusts have appointed marketing managers and departments while others have attempted to persuade the clinicians to engage in marketing since they alone have the clinical knowledge to be credible.

Strategic management of a Trust will be composed of formal planning and opportunistic reaction to new possibilities within the NHS market. The combination of service and functional strategies will come together in business planning and longer-term strategic planning to set directions for the Trust which fit its resources and the circumstances which it faces. In some cases that will mean the costs associated with an expensive London site, high wages, and highly specialized services while in others it will mean the difficulties in serving a dispersed population in the Highlands of Scotland. The strategy has to fit the circumstances faced by the Trust, enabling it to make the most of its opportunities and to manage the threats as well as it can. Thus, a London teaching hospital with high costs will not want to pursue a policy of low cost straightforward work which does not utilize its full capability while a provincial hospital will not want to engage in complex work for which it may not have the skills or facilities. All Trusts will need to ensure that their costs are as low as possible consistent with providing good quality services.

GP practices
All GP practices contract with FHSAs or Commissioners to provide services to an identified list of patients and are therefore providers, albeit in the form of partnerships which resemble small businesses. Around half of all GPs are members of practices which hold funds with which to pursue hospital and other services on behalf of their

patients. General practice is one of the few areas in the public service where it is permissible to be both a purchaser and a provider on behalf of the same group of patients. As with NHS Trusts GPs have had to demonstrate that they have the administrative capability and systems to manage a fund before being accorded the necessary status and resources. How then might the strategic management of a GP practice forward the objective of achieving value for money?

Again the portfolio question must be addressed implicitly or explicitly. A significant number of practices seem content to provide a basic service with the minimum of attached staff and a limited range of clinicians and other services despite the attempts of FHSAs and commissioners to develop services through the use of fees for service and other inducements. Partnerships have to decide whether they are to provide an extended range of services in which the possibilities include minor surgery services, the provision of therapy and perhaps even consultant outpatient services on their own premises. These decisions will have an impact upon the partnership income and expenditure but they may also have an impact on the lifestyle of the partners which in some practices may turn out to be an important factor.

GPs act as the gatekeepers to services and so decisions to refer, treat, or wait and monitor conditions will have an impact on the cost of the service and on the nature of benefits experienced by consumers. For instance, a GP practice which decides to offer minor surgery services will be able to cost those services and that cost can be compared against the price charged by local Trusts for those same services, the patient may be pleased with the aspects of convenience in being treated at the practice without the anxieties and inconvenience of attending the hospital, the hospital may be concerned about lost income, and local surgeons may be concerned about the quality of the surgical work and the arrangements in the case of a postoperative complication. It follows that a simple value for money judgement comparing minor surgery in the practice or hospital is not an easy question.

As small businesses GPs face similar difficulties to other business of comparable size when it comes to strategic planning. Many entrepreneurs are too busy with the demands of the service they are providing and the immediate administrative requirements to pay attention to anything more than the immediate presenting problems. While they have intuitive ideas about the future of their business these are often not developed in detail until they are demanded by some other authority such as the bank manager. The developing role of non-clinical practice managers has provided a new capacity for strategic planning in some practices, although practice managers are not full partners, and strategies which do not have partner backing are not likely to be of much value.

ASSESSING THE IMPACT OF STRATEGIC MANAGEMENT ON VALUE FOR MONEY

So, can strategic management influence value for money? Strategic managers cannot but recognize the importance of the variety of interests who have a stake in the pattern and quality of health services. The stakeholders include government, NHSE, purchasers, providers, consumers, managers and clinicians. From its inception the NHS shared the same broad goal, namely to provide a service largely free at the point of need on a national and comprehensive basis. In pursuit of this goal a system of roles and relationships developed which attempted through a variety of mechanisms to meet the varying needs of stakeholders for clinical autonomy, central control over resources, local responsiveness, and controlled service developments. The key to this process was the centrality of planning and the development of normative assumptions (bed norms) as the basic instrument of resource allocation and service development.

The introduction of the market and the development of national objectives has seen something of a shift from a concern about the distribution of resource inputs to the identification of service objectives in terms of outcomes and service impacts. This has been made possible by the growing redistribution of resources from south to north through the Resource Allocation Working Party mechanism and the subsequent switch to a capitation formula for revenue resource allocation to the new breed of NHS purchasers.

Another example of national strategies is the Patient's Charter, which has been concerned largely with activity and productivity measures such as waiting times and appointments. The clear identification of targets along with 'ringfenced' national funds has permitted the use of uncommitted resources as incentives to reduce waiting times. The political importance of reducing waiting times should not be underestimated but the success of this initiative is in large part due to the availability of new funds to address backlogs of work.

The NHS market empowers purchasers to determine the pattern of services through the contract mechanism and the requisite skills have taken some time to develop. Purchasers have the potential to influence value for money through the implementation of their strategies in the form of contracts. As discrete entities providers can develop strategies to meet their organizational aspirations with the policies and controls exercised nationally and locally through the purchasing system. The key strategic actions of purchasers and providers include the following.

Purchasers
♦ Purchasers are concerned with *effectiveness* and can make decisions how and with whom to contract for services. They are increasingly making use of information relating to the research basis of clinical practice and declining to purchase treatments thought to be ineffective although this is very much at the margin of medical practice. Important questions remain

unanswered about the capability of purchasers to make such technical judgements and there have been suggestions that some GPs seek investigations which experienced specialists think unnecessary.

♦ They are putting pressure on providers to increase their *efficiency* by producing the same volume of services at lower prices through the use of such techniques as market testing and through tough negotiating although it is not at all clear that increased volumes of work in contracts necessarily result in consistent quality of care.

♦ They have made decisions to purchase some treatments rather than others for the same condition, making judgements about particular providers (*effectiveness* and *efficiency*), the needs of particular communities (*equity*), and about technical aspects of treatment.

Providers ♦ Providers can, in theory, decide whether to provide particular services or not. Since there is considerable pressure on the budgets of both purchasers and providers, decisions to discontinue a service are the exception rather than the rule.

♦ Providers have shown the ability to reconfigure services in line with purchasers' requirements so as to reduce their costs or improve the quality of their services, thus contributing to efficiency.

♦ They can make decisions about the use of discretionary resources such as those for training, and other support activities, although these decisions may have long-term implications which go beyond the interests of a single Trust.

♦ GPs, whether they hold purchasing funds or not, can decide whether to refer, treat or wait. This has significant impacts on the ability of purchasers and providers to achieve their objectives and as the number of fundholders increases may turn out to be a critical issue.

SUMMARY

Any attempt to assess the impact of strategic management on value for money will require a 'balanced scorecard' approach. Since strategy is made and remade at different levels and by different authorities within the NHS, the impact of strategic management must be measured by reference to patients, communities, institutions, and the future resources of the service which are tied up in the outcomes of education and research. The currency of calculation will involve the tools of VFM analysis but must include qualitative as well as quantitative factors. It is critical that the timescale of analysis recognizes the need for immediate assessment as well as the importance of the long-term health of an organization which all parties agree is an appropriate vehicle for providing for the national health.

FURTHER READING

> ♦ The topic of strategic management in the NHS is not widely reported on. However, as will be clear from this chapter, much of the broader development of thinking on strategic management is equally applicable within the NHS. To keep up to date in this area readers should review journals such as *Long Range Planning* (Pergamon) and the more popular *Health Services Journal* (Macmillan) which is published weekly and widely available.
>
> ♦ Volume one in this series *Managing Health Care in the 90s* (1995) contains valuable articles by David Hunter, and Andrew Gray and Bill Jenkins, which address this area more generally.

REFERENCES

Cochrane, A. (1972), *Effectiveness and Efficiency: Random Reflections on Health Services*. London: Nuffield Provincial Hospitals Trust.

Department of Health (1991), *The Patient's Charter*. London: HMSO.

Expert Advisory Group to Chief Medical Officers of England and Wales (1994), *A policy framework for Commissioning Cancer Services*. London: Department of Health.

Grant, R. (1995), *Contemporary Strategy Analysis (2nd Edn)*. Oxford: Blackwell.

Mintzberg, H. and Quinn, J.B. (1991), *The Strategy Process*. Englewood Cliffs: Prentice Hall.

PURCHASING FOR IMPACT IN THE NHS

CHAPTER 12

Edward Colgan and Ian Carruthers

OBJECTIVES

- ♦ To consider the development of purchasing.
- ♦ To review the environment and current agenda facing healthcare purchasers.
- ♦ To show how health authorities and GP fundholders are purchasing for impact drawing on a number of examples of good practice.
- ♦ To examine the barriers and challenges to purchasing for impact that purchasers will need to address.
- ♦ To explore the future role of purchasing.

INTRODUCTION

Central to the internal market framework introduced to the NHS in 1992 was the purchaser/provider split. Whilst the provision of health services could be thought to be well understood, the concept of purchasing services was new. As the importance of the purchasing function becomes better understood so too does our understanding of what is meant by the value for money obtained from services. Purchasers now require providers to state clearly in their contracts much more information which can be used to assess the value for money to be achieved through the provision of services. Contracts typically address issues such as: agreed treatment protocols, timetabling of services, mechanisms for feedback to patients and GPs etc. Clinicians are explicitly required to undertake clinical audit. Given the impact of purchasing activity on the NHS the chapter sets out to consider the development of the function, to give examples of good practice and to examine the challenges facing purchasers in the future.

PURCHASING FOR IMPACT

What do we mean by purchasing for impact? We would suggest that there are three main goals for successful purchasing:

◆ improving health by targeting resources at effective ways of delivering care and promoting health;
◆ improving the quality of health care – making it more responsive to the needs and wishes of people;
◆ ensuring as many people as possible receive high quality care from available resources.

THE DEVELOPMENT OF PURCHASING

Working for Patients introduced the concept of the internal market with the separation of the roles of purchaser and provider (Department of Health 1989a). Purchasers, both health authorities and GP fundholders, are responsible for assessing the needs of their local population or individual patients and securing services to meet these needs. Providers, hospitals and community health services trusts, and increasingly primary care providers, are responsible for delivering those services.

At the outset of the NHS reforms attention focused on the establishment of NHS Trusts and GP fundholding. Concerns were expressed about the new autonomous status of Trusts and the possibility of a two tier service resulting from the development of fundholding. The achievement of Trust status became a key priority for hospitals and community services. There was, however, little discussion on the new purchasing function and the changed role of health authorities. As with other aspects of the reforms, the nature of purchasing only became clear in the process of implementation.

Over the last few years the ideas and practice of purchasing have developed significantly. The two principal forms of purchasing, by health authority and GP fundholders, have developed side by side. Most purchasing remains in the hands of DHAs, but fundholding has grown rapidly. Currently some 10 000 GPs are fundholders in 2600 practices covering 41% of the population nationally – in some parts of the country coverage is as high as 80–90%.

One of the most important developments in purchasing has been the concept of 'shared purchasing' where the strengthening of links between DHAs and fundholders through closer working has led to a number of benefits:

◆ the promotion of clinical effectiveness, social care and Health of the Nation objectives through shared information and shared purchasing plans;
◆ better planning – purchasing plans increasingly demonstrate that DHAs have developed effective links with GPs, and that their views have informed decision-making and planning;
◆ more effective direction of resources and investments;
◆ the sharing of information on patients' needs and wishes, leading to more responsive health care;
◆ more responsive contracts and better management of budgets.

It has become evident over the last four years that purchasing delivers more appropriate services when GPs are involved, and particularly where they are involved by taking on the direct control of the resources used by their patients.

The development of these stronger partnerships linked to the benefits of GP fundholding led to the issuing of EL(94)79 *Developing NHS Purchasing and GP Fundholding – Towards a Primary Care Led NHS* (NHSE 1994), which announced plans to extend options in GP fundholding (including total fundholding), a more clearly defined role for the health authorities, and an emphasis on partnership between DHAs and GPs. The principal role of the new health authority as outlined in EL(94)79 will be to facilitate the move to a primary care led NHS which we will discuss below.

THE ENVIRONMENT FACING PURCHASERS

While successive governments have made explicit commitment to the founding values of the NHS, the underlying values which influence the present NHS embrace:

◆ a clear focus on the delivery of high quality, value for money health services;
◆ greater commitment to deliver public services but not always from public sector organizations;
◆ rewarding of providers and individuals for excellent performance;
◆ promoting real choice for patients;
◆ increasing accountability of both organizations and individuals;
◆ the more efficient use of resources;
◆ a continuous search to secure continuous improvement in service access, technical competence, and the treatment of the patient as an individual;
◆ increasing accountability to the consumer for the services available and provided.

While many of these 1990s values do not appear to be revolutionary in their content it should be remembered that in the past it was possible for high performing services to be penalized for their contribution since the resources did not follow the patients, at least not quickly enough to compensate for justifiably increased costs.

THE AGENDA FACING HEALTHCARE PURCHASERS

In the last four years purchasers have had to develop new organizations and new capabilities. They are no longer responsible for the direct management of patient services and have had to restructure, learn new skills, and in many cases merge with neighbouring authorities. The agenda that purchasers have been addressing in recent years includes:

♦ maintaining and improving access times for inpatient and out-patient care, the re-shaping of acute hospital settings as increases in day surgery, shifts to primary care, changes in working practice and responding to advances in medical technology which take place at a rapid pace;

♦ changes in service pattern which flow from primary care being increasingly the principal focus for health;

♦ the development of primary care led purchasing through the extension of fundholding and development of general practitioners as providers of an increasing range of community care through joint working;

♦ the implementation of Care in the Community as set out in *Caring for People* (DOH 1989) and the successful development of community care through joint working;

♦ the introduction of new or alternative providers to supply services including the private sector, general practice, the voluntary and independent sector and other bodies;

♦ a focus on health, balanced with the need to secure high quality health services without increasing resource pressures;

♦ increased expectations of government for the National Health Service to deliver the agenda locally, i.e. The Health of the Nation;

♦ responding to diminishing growth in the level of resources with the necessity for innovation and creative solutions;

♦ ensuring continuous improvement in quality and standards – including The Patient's Charter targets;

♦ an increased focus on clinical effectiveness and clinical outcomes.

This is, without doubt, a challenging agenda for well-established organizations with a long timescale for implementation. It is more difficult for fledgling purchasers who had to create strong working alliances with a variety of partners who may have different priorities and different paymasters. The movement to primary care, the development of community care and the impact of changes in acute hospital provision mean that all purchasers must undertake the following essentials if they are to deliver the current and developing purchasing agenda.

THE ESSENTIALS FOR PURCHASING

If purchasers are to address the lengthy and challenging agenda described above it is essential that they recognize three critical factors:

♦ They must develop a strategic orientation despite the temptations to focus on the short-term negotiation and operation of contracts. This will include thinking and planning future patterns of delivery which will include a significant shift of activity and resources to primary care. The focus has to shift from a concern with inputs and activity to a concern with outcomes and the impact of services on the community. They will need to develop effective working relationships with providers which will include a long-term approach to contracts and frameworks to manage care with providers. Without such an approach providers will have no incentive to invest in the future of the services they provide.

♦ They need to adopt a collaborative working style in which they communicate with and respond to the views and needs of local people. Purchasing loses its legitimacy if it departs from the needs of the people who are served. Meeting those needs will require them to develop healthy alliances and collaborative working relationships with providers, general practitioners, voluntary organizations, local authorities and other health authorities – and in particular to work increasingly through general practitioners;

♦ Thirdly purchasers need to develop their own organizational capability if they are to meet the agenda set for them. This will require them to improve their skills in the managing of the contracting process ensuring sophisticated processes for securing value for money, quality, monitoring and the evaluation of contracts. They will need to develop a sound knowledge base for informed purchasing decisions, and to improve their organizational capacity to deliver such change. This will mean ensuring appropriate investment in the purchasing organization and the development of personnel within it.

REVIEWING PROGRESS IN PURCHASING While there were some important models of healthcare management drawn from international sources in the design of the NHS reforms, the concept of purchasing was an entirely new function at the outset of the reforms with no readily applicable models from which UK purchasers could draw lessons. Initially, the primary focus was placed on establishing NHS Trusts – strengthening and supporting the new provider role. In the last two years an increasing emphasis has been placed on the development of the purchasing role – both for health authorities and fundholders. It was the recognition that purchasers are the drivers of change, and that the success of the NHS reforms was dependent on the development of effective purchasing, that has driven it up the ministerial and managerial agenda.

Purchasers, both health authorities and fundholders, are increasingly delivering the purchasing agenda. Progress in developing purchasing will be considered further by drawing on examples of good practice from across the country with a particular focus on:

♦ assessing community need;
♦ contracting for VFM;

- effectiveness in purchasing;
- improving provider services;
- achieving health gain in purchasing;
- the use of information and intelligence.

Assessing and prioritizing community need

In developing local strategies purchasers need to integrate information about the demand for and use of acute, community and primary healthcare services, with information on the morbidity, demographic, social and economic characteristics of local populations and the environment in which they live and work.

Coupled to this, they also need to assemble information to evaluate the effectiveness of alternative clinical and therapeutic interventions, community support and health promotion programmes. To do this they rely on local and national sources of information some of which may have been collected for a very different purpose than that required by the particular purchaser.

Successful locality purchasing requires a detailed understanding of the health needs and priorities of local populations and effective and appropriate methods of meeting these needs – with the aim of better targeting of resources. General practitioners have a crucial role to play in developing this local database, and through its use as purchasers to purchase healthcare services which better reflect local priorities.

The NHS Executive's Purchaser Information Management and Technology Progress Review (October 1994) identified that most health authorities still had much work to do developing information and systems to support their work in identifying health needs and the development of purchasing strategies to achieve health gain.

There are, however, a number of examples of good practice, given in Box 12.1, where purchasers are assessing health needs to inform their health strategies and determine priorities.

Contracting for value for money

Contracting is the cornerstone of the management system of the new National Health Service. In some parts of the service contracts are, perhaps more accurately, referred to as service level agreements. It has become the means of doing business between purchasers (both health authorities and GP fundholders), providers, and the clinicians who supply their services to the patients. The contracting process has become the medium for achieving strategic and operational change within a planned framework and its development has been shaped by the context and environment of the NHS (see earlier).

Amongst the principal changes which have resulted where the contracting process has been implemented successfully are:

- improving the range and availability of services;
- raising quality standards;

Box 12.1
Examples of good
practice

♦ *Walsall Health Authority* recognized that its purchasing plans needed to address the needs of a significant Asian population within its boundaries. The Health Authority also knew that within the district as a whole there were high levels of mortality from coronary heart disease (CHD). It was believed that CHD was particularly high within the Asian population. Using locally obtained data and health event linkage software the district has developed health strategies that have enabled health gain strategies to be developed within the Asian community to reduce the incidence of CHD.

♦ In *Bradford*, electoral ward data and the analysis of hospitalization rates have been used to inform a district wide review of stroke services and to develop a more effective purchasing strategy to meet the needs of stroke victims with the introduction of a specialist stroke unit.

♦ In *Coventry*, a detailed analysis of 12 key variables, including deprivation, demography and access rates to a range of secondary, community and primary care services are being used to develop health strategies at ward level.

♦ In *Huntingdon*, geographically based community profiles have been developed to support the process of health needs assessment and contracting by drawing on a multi-agency information workstation which brings together information on social services, Office of Population Censuses and Survey (OPCS) data, voluntary sector services and local authority planning information including housing. The information has been initially used to produce area profiles of the incidence of hearing impairment, analyse the needs of the elderly, and the elderly mentally infirm.

♦ a greater focus on rationing;
♦ achieving value for money;
♦ improving efficiency;
♦ engendering managed competition;
♦ creating incentives for change in practice;
♦ securing the wishes of general practitioners and patients in terms of the care they require;
♦ developing more cooperative working styles within provider units as doctors, nurses and other professionals are engaged in the contracting process.

A number of purchasers have used the contracting process to purchase for impact – the examples of good practice in Box 12.2 show how purchasers have achieved value for money through their contracts:

Box 12.2
Examples of good practice

♦ In *Basildon* the setting of a contract for the development of a leg ulcer clinic has led to savings in time and cost for the community nursing service, linked to improved health education.

♦ In *Chesterfield* the development of contracting at directorate level has seen improvement in the nature and level of services. A maternity services contract has been developed between their main purchaser, which will see the contract adjusted over two years, to reflect the shift from inpatients to outpatient treatment.

♦ In *Wandsworth* negotiating contracts at specialty level has seen the provider reduce costs whilst maintaining activity, deliver service changes around inpatient and day-case treatment, tackle problems around waiting times, waiting lists and cancellations and redirect resources more effectively.

♦ In *Dorset* a focused contracting approach using regular monitoring reports, joint working and incentives and sanctions has seen waiting times drop to nine weeks for an outpatient appointment and six months for non-urgent inpatient treatment. Shorter waiting times are being pursued for non-urgent cardiac investigations, cataract and prostate surgery.

Effectiveness in purchasing   In the last two years it has become increasingly evident that purchasers are seeking to move away from contracts based on 'inputs' to contacts based on 'outcomes'. As part of this process a number of purchasers are using clinical effectiveness information to influence their purchasing decisions – in particular around the use of contract exclusions and the effective management of extracontractual referrals (ECRs).

It is evident that purchasers are making more use of a range of information and material including the Effective Healthcare Bulletins, the Cochrane Database and other sources such as Oxford's Bandolier. Purchasers are increasingly seeking to maximize investment in effective health care and minimize investment in less effective or unproven treatments. This does not eliminate the difficulties in defining what are, or may be, ineffective treatments. Linked to this, contracts are increasingly being driven by treatment or referral guidelines. Particular use has been made of referral protocols in the management of cochlear implants by a number of purchasers. In 1994–95 nearly 70% of all contracts negotiated included some form of treatment or referral guideline.

In *Dorset*, one of the priorities for the Commission has been to establish the necessary infrastructure to promote research and development and clinical effectiveness through the implementation of its research and development strategy, and ongoing work in clinical audit. The Commission has established a Clinical Effectiveness Forum including quality and clinical audit representation from the local Trusts and the Medical Audit Advisory Group. Initial tasks of the forum have included:

◆ the agreement of the clinical audit agenda, reflecting recent issues in clinical effectiveness literature;
◆ the development of clinical outcome indicators and assessment of areas for potential investment/disinvestment during the year.

The Clinical Effectiveness Forum provides an opportunity for ongoing debate with clinicians with their involvement in setting the quality criteria for contracts and hence the clinical audit agenda. The Forum is also tackling the issue of potential investment and disinvestment based on evidence of clinical effectiveness, with a target of one investment and one disinvestment per health gain area. This will be supported by pump-priming which is available initially on a non-recurring basis, with a target of at least this amount in total being recovered from within existing contracts on an individual provider basis.

Some of the effectiveness issues that have been addressed in the last year by the Dorset Health Commission are included below:

◆ Sub-fertility services where there has been a reduction in tubal investigations and surgery and reinvestment in IVF treatment.
◆ The use of antenatal corticosteroids for pregnant women where there is a risk of pre-term delivery.
◆ Watchful waiting for children with glue ear.
◆ A reduction in the use of dilatation and curettage in abnormal uterine bleeding.
◆ The use of thrombolytic therapy in myocardial infarction.
◆ The use of anticoagulants in patients with non-rheumatic atrial fibrillation.

Improved provider services   One of the key tasks facing purchasers has been to facilitate improvement in the services provided by hospital and community units with the purpose of improving the health and health services available to the local population. This has meant developing contracts and agreements which encourage local providers to meet a wide range of national policies.

Purchasers have been working with providers to achieve a wide range of objectives such as reduced waiting times and more localized services. Reductions in waiting times have been quite dramatic and represent a clear improvement in services to patients. Improving the productivity of services, measured by increased activity has meant changes in working practices and service patterns with the move to increased day care and outpatient work.

While the Trusts have been accorded new freedoms to accompany their changed status it has required the active involvement of purchasers to enable the removal of inefficiencies in services embedded in professional habits, organizational structure, bureaucratic or legal rules. These include the avoidance of unnecessary hospital admissions, excessive lengths of stay, blocked in or unused beds, medical procedures not proven to be cost-effective, accountability for clinical work, professional and managerial freedoms, underdevelopment of self-care, under- and over-funding of staff and facilities.

The achievement of strategies to achieve the objectives set out in the *Health of the Nation* (DOH 1992) and *Patient's Charter* (DOH 1991) require purchasers and providers to work together since there are not simple blueprints for achieving what are challenging targets. In each locality novel strategies and solutions are required due to the idiosyncracies of local services and the particular needs of populations. A particular instance involves the implementation of *Caring for People* (DOH 1989b) which requires well established jointly commissioned and funded strategies which reshape the continuing care service provision in hospitals and the nursing home sector.

Purchasers have been working to increase the influence of the consumer, both general practitioner and patient, over the quality and design of services attempting to create a performance culture in primary and secondary care designed to secure patient responsiveness, higher quality standards and value for money.

Perhaps the biggest challenge lies in engineering a shift in resources to achieve a balance between primary and secondary care so that primary care becomes the principal focus for health. This can be facilitated by involving general practice more centrally in management, especially as practices develop their provider role by directly managing district nurses, health visitors and other health professionals. Purchasers and providers are engaged in the developing and reshaping of general practices, hospitals and community health and service providers to meet the future needs of the population.

Purchasers have sought to develop a number of purchasing levers – principally through the development of contracts to ensure inefficiencies are tackled, quality is improved and new services delivered. One of the most effective levers available to purchasers is the use of comparative information to assess and influence the performance of providers.

The introduction of the Patient's Charter, the work of the National Steering Group on Costing, the use of health service indicators, the production of performance tables, alongside the routine monitoring information of their contracts mean that purchasers increasingly are in a position to compare the relative prices and quality of services being provided and to make 'value for money' decisions.

One of the levers that an increasing number of purchasers are looking to use is 'market-testing' or 'tendering' for services. Through circulating a service specification, asking for tenders, and then comparing the responses of one provider with another or with a number of other providers, it is possible to provide incentives to providers be to innovative in the provision and management of services for the benefit of patients and the wider community.

Through the use of market testing, purchasers have sought to secure services more cost-effectively or to improve the quality of service provision or local access to services. Box 12.3 contains some examples.

Box 12.3
Examples of successful market testing

> ◆ In *Darlington* radiotherapy and cancer services were market-tested leading to improved local access with a dedicated consultant providing improved outreach services.
>
> ◆ In *Walsall* urology services were market-tested to improve unacceptably long waiting times.
>
> ◆ In *West Sussex* the market-testing of the Joints Replacement Service led to a reduction in prices and waiting times. Another purchaser market-tested its urology services and obtained additional service levels at very competitive prices and also achieved some significant improvement in quality.
>
> ◆ In *Dorset* the market-testing of chiropody and speech therapy services has led to improved access, reduction in waiting times, improved skills-mix, more focused provision of service and better value for money.

Purchasing for *health gain*   The ultimate success of a purchaser can only be measured by the improvement or positive change in the health of an individual or local population that their purchasing decisions and actions have brought about. Purchasers are looking to move away from purchasing based on 'inputs' to purchasing becoming more 'outcome' focused – delivering discernible improvement for the individual patient or population. In attempting to achieve 'health gain' purchasers are increasingly focusing their attention on effectiveness issues, effective techniques and interventions, ineffective technologies and treatments, priorities for investment, new and imaginative approaches to contracting, value for money initiatives, collaboration with other purchasers, providers and other agencies (Box 12.4).

Box 12.4
Examples of successful purchasing for health gain

♦ In *Portsmouth* it was recognized that the largest health gains could be achieved by focusing on people with the greatest health and social care needs. The health authority using indicators of deprivation were able to identify and improve the targeting of existing resources to those in greatest need. One initiative has seen health visitor work focus on one particular part of the city with a higher incidence of single parent families.

♦ In *Stockport* a 'swimbus' has been financed to encourage children to take more regular exercise by taking children from isolated estates with poor transport to leisure centres; similarly 'exercise prescriptions' are being used in preference to 'pharmaceutical prescriptions' for people with raised blood pressure and obesity.

♦ In *Ealing* school nurses have undertaken health profiles in schools and in liaison with teachers have recognized the need to target specific areas. The outcome of this work has already led to modification in service delivery and changes to the children's service contract.

♦ In *Dorset*, the Commission has been working towards clear and demonstrable links between contracting and health gain. The Commission's Health Investment Plan is increasingly looking to improve health status by not only investing additional resources, but by reinvesting existing resources either based upon disinvestment on the basis of evidence about ineffectiveness or through reshaping existing patterns of service.

Information and intelligence Purchasing with impact can only be achieved by informed purchasers. Successful purchasing depends on the effective use of information and appropriate investment in systems support.

Information and intelligence are key assets which purchasers need to exploit and manage.

Purchasers in making purchasing decisions need to have information on demographic and social and economic characteristics of their local population. They need to have information on the demand for and use of acute, community and primary care services. They also need to be able to access information to evaluate the effectiveness of alternative clinical and therapeutic interventions and treatment, community support and health promotion programmes.

The move to primary care led purchasing will see health authorities increasingly:

♦ sharing information with general practices and using information from primary care to support strategy development;
♦ supporting 'total fundholding' and other initiatives to involve GPs in purchasing;
♦ integrating information from a wide range of organizations – both hard and soft data – to provide a shared information resource to support strategy development.

Box 12.5
Examples

♦ *Norfolk FHSA*, who in consultation with their local providers and GP fundholders, identified information needs for every conceivable eventuality that might occur between a fundholder's patient being referred and discharged from hospital, with the aim of improving information in support of the contracting process.

♦ *East London and the City Health Authority* have developed an integrated monitoring system – Quality Intelligence System – that informs purchasing through the provision of comparative data on user views, clinical opinion, documented evidence, observed practice and baseline data on their providers.

♦ *Hertfordshire Health Agency* has sought to develop its Developing Information Systems for Purchasers (DISP) workstation to facilitate the sharing of multi-agency information with the aim of improving/enhancing purchasing decisions.

♦ *Buckinghamshire Health Authority* has installed a district information system (DMIS) which enables the health authority to monitor contracts at an individual patient level through the contract MDS provided by the provider unit, leading to more robust information on activity than has been available in the past.

Box 12.5 contains examples of purchasers who are seeking to improve their information and intelligence capability to assist their purchasing decisions.

CHALLENGES TO PURCHASING WITH IMPACT

Much progress has been made in purchasing over the last four years. It is apparent that some purchasers are purchasing for impact and are delivering improved health and health care to their patients or local populations. There is, however, a recognition that much still needs to be done. Purchasers, both health authorities and GP fundholders, need to focus their efforts on:

◆ improving and investing in information to inform health needs assessment and comparative performance between providers;
◆ becoming more 'outcome' focused by increased use of clinical effectiveness information to inform purchasing decisions and promote good clinical practice;
◆ working effectively with other purchasers, health authorities and GP fundholders – and forging alliances with other agencies;
◆ becoming more consumer focused and involving local people in purchasing decisions at all levels;
◆ purchasing becoming more 'patient' focused.

THE DEVELOPING ROLE OF HEALTH AUTHORITIES

The implementation of EL(94)79 (NHSE 1994) and the move to a primary care led NHS will see the role of the health authority change significantly as it relinquishes its direct purchasing role. The key elements of its new role could include:

◆ leading the healthcare system and ensuring it works effectively at local level;
◆ establishing a local health and social care strategy to deliver national priorities in a local setting;
◆ allocating resources to purchasing and provider organizations to meet agreed health/social care priorities on an equitable basis;
◆ regulation of the market, determiner of the numbers, range, configuration and size of purchasers and providing organizations;
◆ licensing the purchasing and providing organizations in terms of their competence to supply services. This could also include the licensing of clinicians' fitness to practise through accreditation, and the publication of outcomes and performance data to users: all of this information would be in the public domain;
◆ managing the performance of the local health and social care system through the performance management of contracts for delivery with the constituent organizations, creation of funding policy to achieve equity, strategic change, management through regulation and maintenance of standards both professional and managerial via accreditation;
◆ acting as the public authority to oversee probity and governance appropriate to the use of public funds;

♦ purchasing of general medicine, dental, optometry and pharmaceutical services and determining their pattern of distribution;

♦ supporting the development of primary care businesses, public, private and independent sector organizations so that they acquire the capacity to fulfil the role expected of them in the local healthcare system;

♦ undertaking residual purchasing on behalf of primary care businesses as this may include high cost, low volume activities where more central arrangements might be appropriate but such activity would be undertaken as agents of the primary care business.

As with many features of the reforms the precise form these changes will take is not clear and depends on the success of purchasers and providers learning from their successes, and also from failures, and establishing long-term collaborative relationships and capabilities which ensure that long-term benefits are not sacrificed to short-term expedience.

SUMMARY

It is evident that purchasers – both health authorities and GP fundholders – are increasingly purchasing for impact. Progress has been made in delivering the new purchasing agenda – however much work still needs to be done as GP fundholders develop their extended direct purchasing role and health authorities develop their new strategic and support roles.

The changes in EL(94)79 call for a major change in the way things are done – a change in thinking – a change in attitudes.

It is evident that health authorities are already recognizing that their future role will be empowering, non-bureaucratic, encouraging innovation and excellence in purchasing and providing organizations. It is recognized that purchasing can only deliver through integrated working, shared purchasing with other purchasers – principally GPs, and alliances with other agencies and organizations who are crucial to the success of the health agenda.

Purchasers need to become more consumer focused whether by involving their patients on the practice list or the local population in playing a more proactive role in purchasing decisions. Finally they need to ensure that their purchasing decisions and service delivery become more patient centred.

It is recognized that the change of nature suggested will require a major shift in culture. This can be achieved over time. In many ways it goes with the grain and builds upon current development and the progress that has been made by many purchasers over the last four years. Purchasers – both types – will need to ensure that they develop a strategy for culture change which ensures that they will continue to purchase with impact and build on their successes to date.

FURTHER READING

- ◆ *Bandolier* (Monthly) ISSN: 1353–9906.) Newsletter of Anglia and Oxford Region. Available free within the NHS and for a subscription of £30 per year from Ann Southwell, R & D Manager (West), Anglia & Oxford Region. Tel: 01865 226743; Fax: 01865 226775.

- ◆ *Effective Health Care Bulletin*
  Available from Nuffield Institute for Health, 71–75 Clarendon Road, Leeds LS2 9PL.

- ◆ *CCEPP Newsletter: The Cochrane Collaboration on Effective Professional Practice*
  Available from Emma Harvey, Research Fellow/Administrator, Department of Health Sciences and Clinical Evaluation, University of York, Heslington, York YO1 5DD. Tel: 01904 434577.
  Also available via the Internet at: hHp://hiru.mcmaster.ca/cochrane/newsletter/

- ◆ *Cochrane Database of Systematic Reviews*
  A disk/CD-ROM database containing 51 reviews in pregnancy and childbirth, subfertility, stroke, schizophrenia and parasitic diseases, protocols and tiles for 134 further reviews, bibliographies of previously published reviews and methodological articles and information on the Cochrane Collaboration. Available for £100 per subscription.

- ◆ *Cochrane Pregnancy and Childbirth Database*
  A disk/CD-ROM database containing 500 systematic reviews of interventions in pregnancy and childbirth, over 30 new Cochrane reviews and the complete text of *A Guide to Effective Care in Pregnancy and Childbirth* (2nd edition). Available for £95 per subscription (2 issues) from BMJ Publishing Group, PO Box 295, London WC1H 9TE. Tel: 0171 383 6185.

  Many of the examples of good practice referred to in this chapter are drawn from:

- ◆ NHSE (1994), *Managing Contracts - Examples of Further Good Practice and Innovation in Contracting*, July.

- ◆ NHSE (1995), The DISP series of publications principally: *Information Support to Purchasing: Overview*, March.

- ◆ Ham, C., Carruthers, I., Fillingham, D., James, J. (Eds). *The Localities Project Shifting Investment for Health and Health Gain* (March 1993)

- ◆ Ham, C., Carruthers, I., Fillingham, D., James, J. (Eds). *Purchasing in the NHS: The Story So Far*. Discussion document No. 34. (1995), H.S.M.C.

REFERENCES

Department of Health (1989a), *Working for Patients*. Cm 555. London: HMSO.

Department of Health (1989b), *Caring for People*. Cm 849. London: HMSO.

Department of Health (1991), *The Patient's Charter*. London: HMSO.
Department of Health (1992), *Health of the Nation. A Strategy for Health in England*. Cm 1986. London: HMSO.
NHSE (1994), *Developing NHS Purchasing and GP Fundholding*. Leeds: NHSE.

THE FUTURE FOR VALUE FOR MONEY

John J. Glynn and David A. Perkins

OBJECTIVES

♦ To examine how recent developments in VFM measurement influence clinical decisions and management practice.

♦ To show how new patterns of management in the NHS influence equity and efficiency.

♦ To point to the importance of the clinician in the pursuit of procedures and services that provide value for money.

INTRODUCTION

In this last chapter we consider what the recent developments in measuring and monitoring value for money in the NHS mean for the future management and operation of health care in the United Kingdom. What will be clear from earlier chapters is that there are now a number of initiatives that are providing clinicians, managers and other interested parties with more information on the efficiency and effectiveness of health care. This information is leading to more informed debates on the cost and quality of health care. At the time of writing the media have just become aware of the identity of 'Child B', a cancer patient who, having been refused treatment on the NHS in Cambridge, was treated, thanks to an anonymous donation of £65 000. The Trust had refused treatment because they believed the child's chances of successful recovery were extremely limited and that, although funding was available, this money would be better directed to other patients. The NHS internal market has required that greater attention be paid to value for money and that this be required as an explicit element in the contracting process. Treatment was refused to Child B because of an analysis of the probability of the likely success of her treatment, i.e. the effectiveness of her treatment, and this decision by the Trust was upheld with some regret by the High Court. Performance indicators associated with the efficiency and effectiveness of health care have featured with increasing prominence in this and many other recent cases. Berkshire Health Commission introduced in October 1995 a consultative list of operations it would no longer pay for, such as varicose veins operations and the removal of wisdom teeth. Many researchers believe that Berkshire's initiative will become the norm over the next few years. The impact of the Child B affair has not concluded. A number of issues have arisen from the public discussion on this case, not least a confirmation that, at present, there is little funding for experimental treatment on the NHS. How does experimental treatment tie in with research? Who should take responsibility – the universities, charities, the private sector or the Higher Education Funding Council (HEFC)?

EQUITY AND PROBITY

A feature of the move towards demonstrated value for money in the NHS is an increasing awareness that in the future greater concern is going to centre on the key issues of equity and probity; that is, the 'fairness' and 'integrity' by which health care is distributed. Value for money issues will cause a high degree of debate which will increasingly end up in the courts and feature in the media focusing on such issues as why is patient 'X' treated rather than patient 'Y' (in part, the current Child B debate) but also focusing upon why is it that the standard of treatment offered to one patient by one Health Trust is different to that offered to another similar patient by another Health Trust. The issue also applies to care groups. Why should more money per capita be spent on children than on, for the sake of discussion, the mentally ill or drug addicts? Unfortunately, the issues important to care groups do not tend generally to capture the public imagination or come before the courts. They remain more opaque. These issues are by no means limited to health care and have also arisen with respect to the provision of education and social services. Purchasers and providers will increasingly have to address issues of equity and probity into the contracting process and this will, therefore, need to be reflected in terms stating performance standards that match the delivery of treatment to anticipated outcomes. It has long been accepted that the quality of healthcare provision is, across the UK, variable for a wide variety of reasons. The advent of a concern with value for money issues now has the potentiality to make this debate more open-minded in the future and highlight a key contribution in society as a whole – that is that as adult members of the public we are (on occasions) the recipients of health care, we are taxpayers and we vote. These three aspects overlap (Figure 13.1).

Let us, of course, not forget that some one million members of the public are also NHS employees involved in aspects of purchasing and providing health care.

Contract accountability in the internal market essentially focuses on resource accountability which is defined by Glynn (1993, p. 18)

Figure 13.1
Citizens' overlapping
functions

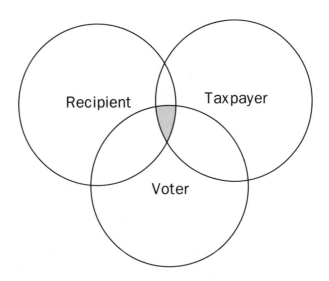

as 'adopting managerial practices that will promote the efficiency
and effectiveness of non-commercial entities'. However, the public
debate on and awareness of value for money issues will, in the
future, force increased attention to other aspects of accountability.
These can include (based on Glynn 1993, p. 18):

♦ *Professional accountability*. Defined as self-regulation (or peer
  regulation) by professional groups employed in the provision of
  public sector services. The Royal Colleges, the BMA and others
  clearly are much more aware of the need for their members to
  be more accountable for the efficiency and effectiveness of the
  services they provide. These bodies can assist in the promotion
  of standards of care if for no other reason than that they wish to
  protect their members from charges that they ignored issues of
  equity and probity. Being positive, responsible professional
  bodies they will also wish to influence the debate on what
  constitutes an acceptable level and quality of health care.
♦ *Judicial accountability*. Defined as a review of executive
  actions at the instigation of an aggrieved individual; decision
  should not be 'ultra vires' than those required by statute. The
  Child B case was, in effect, an instance of judicial accountability.
  In the UK the system of common law means that decisions taken
  in one case cannot necessarily be taken as a precedent in
  another, although it might be indicative of how future disputes
  might be settled.
♦ *Quasi-judicial accountability*. Defined as the control of administrative discretion, e.g. by review tribunals.

♦ *Procedural accountability.* Defined as a review of decisions by an external agency, usually an ombudsman.

Perhaps other divisions of accountability can be defined but these four classifications serve to illustrate that greater attention is being focused on value for money. Value for money embraces both efficiency and effectiveness and, as discussed in earlier chapters, the resolution of efficiency measurement is normally much more easily measurable than effectiveness. This is because efficiency tends to focus on process activities whilst effectiveness is focused more on the results obtained by various processes. We should also note that there is little point being efficient in doing something that is ineffective.

The contracting process has tended, in the past, to focus more on aspects of efficiency than effectiveness although the distinction between these two terms can, at times, become blurred. For example, efficiency measures relating to the time taken for a patient to see a specialist clearly often correlate to the potential worsening condition of the patient. In the future more attention will focus on the effectiveness of treatment, particularly with respect to the outcome derived by an individual patient from a particular course of treatment. Whilst this change in direction is to be welcomed the current structure of the internal market means that the broader impacts of healthcare provision are not systematically monitored. The reason that little or no attention is actually addressed to impact is that it is a far less tangible concept, related more to overall government policy. This arises because policy issues are often addressed by a number of programmes which are often managed by different parts of the public sector. For example, the government's wish to reduce the incidence of drug abuse is reflected in a variety of programmes run by the NHS, social services, the Department of Education and Employment and the police. Regrettably, there appears little hope in the future that impact will be seriously addressed.

SYSTEMATIC OR SUBSTANTIVE EXTERNAL REVIEWS (AND AUDITS)

The Audit Commission (or Accounts Commission in Scotland) and the National Audit Office both review aspects of the work carried out by the NHS. Often the approach to their work has been 'substantive'; that is, based upon an in-depth analysis of the operations of a particular activity or service; this is particularly so with the Audit Commission. To date this has been understandable given that clinicians and management have been on a steep learning course to adapt aspects of value for money, monitoring and review into the day-to-day provision of health care. These agencies will continue to identify local opportunities to improve various aspects of value for money, but as overall management control improves the emphasis ought to shift to a more systems orientated review. That is, a review that does not comment directly on the efficiency and effectiveness of healthcare delivery but rather reports upon the way in which management and clinicians measure, monitor and react to value for money based performance indicators. This is not unlike the approach adopted by quality assurance and British and international quality standards. This predicted drift in emphasis is essential if we are ultimately to reach a level of operation whereby all NHS purchasers and providers consider aspects of value for money as an integral part of the process of delivery and monitoring health care. It may well be that politicians believed that by providing such review bodies with a value for money mandate that they could somehow remove or reduce political judgement from the debate about the quality of the position of health care. Nothing, of course, could be further from the truth as Holtham and Stewart (1981, p. 3) state, 'questions of value for money are about political judgement – the judgement of what is value for money. Value for money does not remove political judgement – it may well increase the emphasis on it'. They argue that the process of search for value for money is politically neutral, even though what is decided in that process will not be.

Purchasers, too, are increasingly moving to social judgements as pioneered in the American state of Oregon, where the public and health professionals were asked to vote on what treatments they deemed important and which could be given lower funding priority. Oregon listed 688 possible categories of illness and their prescribed treatments, and ranked them in order of the seriousness of the condition and effectiveness of the treatment. After extensive debate, state officials decided to provide treatment only for the first 560 on the list. This approach is clearly controversial, deciding, for example, that babies weighing less than 1 lb 1 oz are not resuscitated. Agencies such as the Audit Commission and the National Audit Office have, by their statutes, to be apolitical. On occasions, in the past, because of their need to undertake substantive reviews they have been accused of commenting upon and influencing the future direction of policy. A shift to systematic reviews will require them to assure the government and public at large that management and clinicians do indeed manage and review the quality of health care that they provide. This systems based review approach will address the following key questions:

♦ *With respect to policy objectives*:
  - Are these clearly stated?
  - Are decisions made on sufficient and accurate data?
  - Have other options been considered?
  - Are the costs of alternative service levels considered?
♦ *With respect to contracts*:
  - Are these clearly understood by all parties?

- Are the nature of contracts appropriate and relevant for particular packages of care?
- Do contracts stress and require relevant and appropriate preference indications that address both the efficiency and effectiveness (with respect to outcomes) of healthcare provision?
- Do contracts recognize the normal range of variability which precludes absolutely precise contracts and therefore recognize some measure of sensible feasibility?

♦ *Do providers*:
- Provide a satisfactory level of efficiency?
- Operate efficiency related controls adequately?
- Monitor and review the quality and level of service provided?
- Use and review performance information (on efficiency and effectiveness) adequately for planning, budgeting and controlling?

THE PIVOTAL ROLE OF THE CLINICIAN

The ultimate responsibility for the effectiveness of healthcare delivery rests with the clinician. Traditionally clinicians have defensively hung on to notions of clinical autonomy as a means of avoiding the real world pressures on the funding of health care. Their role is now, in two respects, becoming an agency one:

♦ as an 'agent' for the patient, and
♦ as an 'agent' for the state and community.

The key issue is will clinicians accept this responsibility directly or are they likely to leave this to some quasi Oregon approach?

Clinical training continues to focus on the diagnosis/treatment/evaluation of individual patients whilst the NHS is charged with purchasing on behalf of the community the provision of health care. The range of 'purchases' vary from open-ended provision, such as 'Accident and Emergency', to fixed limits, such as 'X' heart bypass operations (notwithstanding the fact that clinicians have to deal with emergencies regardless of the nature of a particular contract).

The increasing utilization of inpatient facilities means that bed occupancy rates are increasing but this is usually because clinicians are having to share resources, notably beds. Clinicians are required to cooperate with one another as never before, managing across boundaries to achieve overall value for money. However, in the future, greater value for money will require a higher order of cooperation involving not only a greater integration of primary, secondary and tertiary care within the NHS but also the cooperation of the government agencies: social services, education, housing and the like.

Clinicians have to accept the external constraints that affect their internal environment. By accepting and recognizing these constraints they need to consider their pivotal role in attempting to reshape some of these externalities. They have to provide the data that informs the NHS on the effectiveness of alternative strategies. If this is currently difficult they have to enter the debate on how measurement might be more easily achieved. This will require changes directly associated with the provision of care, the assistance of agencies and suggestions as to how the NHS internal market could be improved to create the right environment and time-frame over which measurement needs to take place. For example, many clinicians believe that a move away from annual contracts to three year contracts would greatly assist by providing a more manageable time-frame to monitor effectiveness. If clinicians do not help shape and influence the debate on whether the NHS provides value for money, others will do so without them and this seems bound to produce some undesirable consequences. Rationing decisions are now having hidden effects on medical education and training, which means that the future of some specialist units are now under threat, even though the clinicians involved in these units may not necessarily realize this is the case.

SUMMARY

By 1997 two-thirds of patients will be covered by fundholding GPs. They and their hospital based colleagues must now discuss more openly the consequences of rationing so that guidelines and criteria can be laid down about why such steps have been taken. Health economists quickly point out that whilst Britain spends about 6% of gross domestic product on health care compared to around 12% by Germany, Sweden and the USA, all four countries share the same problems of supply and demand. The Netherlands, Canada and New Zealand have all recently announced curbs on health spending, with moves towards limiting care services and letting people who want other treatments buy them privately.

FURTHER READING

♦ For broader aspects of value for money readers should refer directly to the publications of the Audit Commission and the National Audit Office for issues of external audit.

♦ Specific clinical issues can be addressed from the references listed by Alison Frater in Chapter 3 and Fiona Moss and John Mitchell in Chapter 8 of this volume.

♦ A broader perspective is given in Jenkins, S. (1995), *Accountable to None*, Hamish Hamilton, London.

REFERENCES

Glynn, J. J. (1995), *Public Sector Financial Control and Accountability.* Oxford: Blackwell.

Holtham, C. and Stewart, J. (1981), *Value for Money: A Framework for Action*. Birmingham: Institute of Local Government Studies.

GLOSSARY

Accountability   Implies a relationship in which A is answerable to B for performance of a task and reports on that performance either in terms of the activity undertaken or the outcome achieved. Accountability might be *professional* in that it operates through a particular occupational group. It might be *legal* and require the exercise of legal process or perhaps the courts. It might be *quasi-legal* such as accountability through the NHS contracting systems in which contracts are not enforceable in the courts. It might be procedural in which an individual is held accountable for following the specified procedure.

Accountability Charting   A planning process in which clear accountability for tasks is explicitly given to named individuals and recorded on a chart.

Activities of Daily Living (ADL)   Those activities which all individuals need to perform to maintain personal independence e.g. washing, eating, moving about.

Audit   In its traditional form audit is the examination of accounts to see if they are in order. Nowadays the term refers to the examination of activities, processes, and practices either internally in an organization or by an external authority. Internal elements of audit include management, clinical, and medical audit. External authorities involved in audit include the Royal Colleges, the National Audit Office, and the Audit Commission.

Audit Brief   Clear written description of the parameters and processes to be followed within a particular audit.

Audit Commission   Independent public body charged with the audit of services provided by health services and local government.

Audit Cycle   A model of the audit process which includes the definition of objectives, the agreement of standards, the comparison of observation with standards and the interpretation of any deviation followed by appropriate action if deemed necessary.

Audit Facilitator   An individual who assists clinicians in the management of the audit process.

Balanced Scorecard Approach   An approach to organizational performance measurement which recognizes a wide range of stakeholder objectives and therefore measures performance on a wide range of indicators.

Barber–Johnson Diagram A diagrammatic representation of length of stay and turnover interval which helps in the calculation of required numbers of hospital beds for a particular specialty or service.

Block Contracts The payment of an annual fee for access to a defined range of services at a given indicative level of activity.

Budget A formal quantified statement (normally expressed in financial terms) of a plan of action.

Budget Variance The difference between the amount contained in a budget and the corresponding actual cost or revenue.

Business Plan A plan which sets objectives for an organizational entity, demonstrating the resources which will be used in the production of services. It usually refers to major developments which will affect the services and includes consideration of how the organization will respond to significant variations in demand for services.

Capital Funding The funding for buildings and equipment which have a significant life expectancy, usually more than a calendar year.

Cash Flow The actual cash receipts and payments of an enterprise for a particular accounting period.

Cash Limits The determination of a fixed cash sum from which services must be provided.

Cash Planning The planning of services within a fixed cash sum.

Clinical Audit The systematic critical analysis of the quality of clinical care by all those who contribute to care. It includes the procedures used for diagnosis and treatment, the use of resources, and the resulting outcome and quality of life for patients for which the patient's views must be sought.

Clinical Effectiveness The effectiveness of the clinical components of care as opposed to social and other aspects.

Clinical Trial An experiment to ascertain the effectiveness or otherwise of a procedure or treatment in which patients are carefully selected and their outcomes are usually compared with a matched control group who receive conventional or placebo treatment.

Community Care Plans Plans for providing care in the community which frequently involve the cooperation of statutory and voluntary agencies.

Community Health Council A community health watchdog which has statutory rights to be consulted and to comment on development in or problems with local services.

Compulsory Competitive Tendering (CCT) A government policy requiring public services to produce clear specifications of the services they provide and to seek tenders to provide these services from the private sector with the intention of ensuring high standards of efficiency and management practice.

Confidential Enquiry   An enquiry into an unexpected adverse health outcome, such as a maternal death during childbirth, conducted confidentially to ensure full cooperation and to prevent similar occurrences in future if possible.

Continuous Quality Improvement   Techniques that encourage innovation to achieve successive quality improvements.

Controllable Cost   A cost that can be directly controlled at a given level of management.

Cost and Volume Contracts   The payment of an annual fee for access to a service or a number of services at a defined level and mixture of activity.

Cost Effectiveness   The ratio of cost of services to the measured effectiveness of those services.

Critical Path Analysis   A planning technique which identifies the activities on which the whole project depends and shows how they relate in priority and timing. This allows project timescales to be calculated.

Dependency Models   Statistical models which attempt to calculate the needs, usually for nursing care, of patients with different types and severity of clinical conditions thus allowing a calculation of how many care staff of what grades and experience are required at a particular time.

Depreciation   The process of allocating the net cost (original acquisition cost minus estimated scrap value) of a long-lived asset over its estimated life.

Diagnostic Related Groups (DRG)   Groups containing similar diagnosis treatment categories designed to permit the calculation of average costs and prices for particular procedures. Originated from USA cost control developments.

Direct Cost   A cost which is specifically and measurably identified with a particular activity within an enterprise. Such costs are sometimes referred to as separable costs.

District Commissioning Agency   The organization which formerly purchased primary and secondary healthcare services on behalf of a local population (now the DHA).

District Health Authority (DHA)   An authority covering one or more local government areas which is responsible for assessing health needs and ensuring that they are provided. This is now achieved by purchasing care from Provider Units.

Economy   The utilization of resources of appropriate quality at the lowest price.

Effectiveness   The extent to which an activity or programme achieves its intended objectives. It will often be examined in terms of the nature and severity of unwanted side effects. See Outcome and Impact.

Efficacy   The theoretical effectiveness of a treatment as demonstrated in clinical trials or laboratory experimentation. It is seldom possible to achieve such levels of outcome in normal clinical practice due to a wide range of confounding variables.

Efficiency The relationship between goods and services provided and the resources used to provide them. An efficient activity produces the maximum output for any given set of resource inputs; or it has minimum inputs for any given quality and quantity of service provided.

Efficiency Index An Index used to compare the relative efficiency of services within the NHS and of the NHS itself in comparable time periods.

Efficiency Scrutinies Studies which are undertaken to assess the efficiency of clinical or support services which often give advice on best practice as a means of improving management.

Equity Fairness in the distribution of resources or services.

Executive Agencies New organization forms developed as a means of simplifying responsibilities for services which were frequently the responsibility of departments of the civil service or ministries of state.

External Audit Audit undertaken by an external agency.

External Financing Limits The limits imposed by central government on the annual use of external finance by public sector organizations.

Extra Contractual Referral (ECR) A referral of an individual for specialist treatment for which there is no pre-existing contract between purchaser and provider.

Family Health Services Authority (FHSA) The authority, formerly, responsible for managing the contracts of general practitioners, dentists, pharmacists and opticians. Now part of the DHA.

Financial Management Initiative A government initiative to improve the management of public funds in government departments with the objective of improving value for money and accountability.

Fixed Capital Items such as the premises or equipment.

Functional Accounting Accounting systems organized around the particular functions of an organization such as estate management, hotel services, clinical services.

Gantt Chart A linear time chart on which performance goals are marked allowing progress to be monitored.

General Practitioner A doctor of first contact. After qualification a general practitioner has to spend three years in further training before he or she can be admitted as a Principal in general practice. At least one year must be as a trainee in general practice. From 1996 there will be an assessment of this training, but many potential general practitioners currently take the Membership Examination of the Royal College of General Practitioners.

GP Fundholder A GP practice which holds a budget for services that can be purchased from hospitals and other providers of health and social care on behalf of patients.

Health of the Nation The UK government's long term health objectives for the NHS and others which are expressed in outcomes rather than activities.

Health Service Ombudsman The officer who is the final arbiter in the complaints procedure before the courts. Until recently excluded from complaints about clinical service and decision: the remit is to be extended to include this area as well.

Horizontal Target Efficiency The extent to which services go to everyone who needs them.

Incremental Scrutinies Examinations which relate to marginal changes or developments in a service or other activity as opposed to complete reviews of the whole activity.

Impact The results of a service on a broad population which might be seen as an improvement in the health of that particular population. This is particularly difficult to measure or to attribute directly to the service concerned. We might, for instance, be interested in the impact of a campaign to reduce the levels of smoking in the population.

Inputs The human, physical, and financial resources which are combined to undertake an activity or provide a service.

Internal Audit An independent activity or function within an organization which examines and evaluates its activities as a service to the organization.

Internal Market The NHS 'market' which resulted from the separation of those who plan and purchase local services and those who provide those services through the medium of a contract or service agreement.

Jarman Index An index which measures social deprivation and can be used for the assessment of relative needs between communities for social investment.

Joint Commissioning/Joint Purchasing Where services are purchased by more than one agency – frequently health authorities and social service departments.

Local Medical Committees (LMCs) A committee composed of local GPs and other independent practitioners through which they attempt to influence purchasers and defend their own interests.

Management Audit A process in which management systems and procedures are appraised with a view to evaluating the efficiency and effectiveness of services and identifying potential improvements which can be implemented. It involves both formative and summative evaluations.

Marginal Cost The increase in total costs associated with an increase in activity levels (usually of one unit).

Market Testing Initiative   See Compulsory competitive tendering. This is where a public service produces a specification of its services and seeks tenders from other organizations to see if those services could be provided more efficiently or effectively.

Medical Audit   A restrictive form of clinical audit in which the participants restrict themselves to the practice and efficacy of medicine.

Medical Audit Advisory Groups (MAAGs)   Committees set up to advise on the efficacy of medical audit procedures in provider settings.

Milestone Planning   Identification of key subsidiary targets or milestones within a more complex project or programme.

Mission Statement   A short paragraph which describes the purpose of an organization outlining its key aspirations and values.

NHS Executive   The 'management board' and its officers which are responsible to the Secretary of State for the NHS and its management.

National Audit Office   The body responsible to parliament for the audit of those services provided by government departments, executive agencies and some elements of health services.

National Cancer Strategy   In response to comparatively poor cancer outcomes alongside our European neighbours, the Chief Medical Officers developed a strategy to integrate specialist cancer centres and local cancer units in an attempt to improve patient outcomes.

National Steering Group on Costing   The group attempts to clarify the rules and procedures to be used in costing and pricing healthcare procedures and services.

New Public Management   A new approach to public management which builds heavily on private sector approaches to managing organizations.

Opportunity Cost   An economic concept which regards the costs of utilizing a resource as the benefit foregone by not using it in its best alternative use.

Oregon Programme   An American State programme which evaluated the clinical effectiveness and social value of disease-treatment pairs in order to allocate resources more fairly among low income citizens.

Outcome   The effect or result of a treatment on a patient measured in terms of functional improvement or improvement in quality of life as experienced by the patient. Of course some outcomes might be unintended such as a thrombosis following treatment.

Output   A unit of activity produced by an individual or service. The output of a hospital will include the measurement of medical consultations which come within the definition of consultant episodes.

Overhead Costs   The costs which are not directly associated with a particular activity. These are sometimes referred to as indirect costs.

Patient Participation Groups   Groups of patients who contribute their views to the running and development of services, often found in general practice settings.

Patient Satisfaction Surveys   Surveys to assess the level of patient satisfaction with health services.

Performance Indicator   Expressions, in measurable terms, of programme objectives, or the relative achievement of an objective.

Price Efficiency   When an enterprise uses its resources to achieve a specified volume of goods or services at minimum cost.

Probity   A term used by accountants referring to honesty.

Programme Budgeting   A system of budgeting that assesses resource input requirements by programme or activity. This is a top-down approach similar to Zero-based budgeting.

Programme Planning and Budgeting Systems   An attempt to plan and budget for public services from first principles and primary objectives which proved over-complex.

QALY   The term stands for Quality Adjusted Life Years and attempts to assess the outcome of a treatment in terms of the additional life years which might be experienced by the patient as a result of the intervention and the quality of that life.

Quality Assurance   Mechanisms to ensure that quality of services meets predetermined standards.

Standard Mortality Ratio (SMR)   The number of people dying per 100 000 members of the population per year adjusted for age and sex.

Tomlinson Report   The report of a committee set up to review the pattern of healthcare services in London and make recommendations.

Total Quality Management (TQM)   An approach to quality management originating in the private sector which claims to be comprehensive. It implies that quality must encapsulate every aspect of activity ranging from direct patient care to each aspect of the support services which impact on the experience of the patient and the outcome of their particular episode.

Vertical Target Efficiency   The extent to which services go to those who need them rather than to those who do not.

Zero-based Budgeting   A system of budgeting originally developed in the USA for non-trading organizations. Its approach is bottom-up and involves the ranking of the contribution that differing activities make to the achievement of organizational objectives in cost/benefit terms.

INDEX

Note: terms explained in the Glossary are indicated by **bold page numbers**; text in Boxes, Figures and Tables by *italic numbers*. Index entries are arranged in letter-by-letter order [ignoring spaces].